**THE JESUS LIBRARY**
*Michael Green, series editor*

# The Parables of Jesus

## David Wenham

INTERVARSITY PRESS
DOWNERS GROVE, ILLINOIS 60515

InterVarsity Press
P.O. Box 1400, Downers Grove, Illinois 60515, U.S.A.

InterVarsity Press is the book-publishing division of InterVarsity Christian Fellowship, a student
movement active on campus at hundreds of universities, colleges and schools of nursing. For information
about local and regional activities, write Public Relations Dept., InterVarsity Christian Fellowship, 6400
Schroeder Rd., P.O. Box 7895, Madison, WI 53707-7895.

Distributed in Canada through InterVarsity Press, 860 Denison St., Unit 3, Markham, Ontario L3R
4H1, Canada.

Cover illustration: Janice Skivington

ISBN 0-8308-1286-5

Printed in the United States of America

**Library of Congress Cataloging-in-Publication Data**

Wenham, David.
    The parables of Jesus/David Wenham.
      p.    cm.—(The Jesus Library)
    Bibliography: p.
    Includes indexes.
    ISBN 0-8308-1286-5
    1. Jesus Christ—Parables.   2. Bible. N.T. Gospels—Criticism,
interpretation, etc.  I. Title.  II. Series.
BT375.2.W46  1989
  226.806—dc20                  89-36270
                                     CIP

| 16 | 15 | 14 | 13 | 12 | 11 | 10 | 9 | 8 | 7 | 6 | 5 | 4 | 3 | 2 | 1 |
|----|----|----|----|----|----|----|---|---|---|---|---|---|---|---|---|
| 99 | 98 | 97 | 96 | 95 | 94 | 93 | 92 | 91 | 90 | 89 | | | | | |

# EDITOR'S PREFACE

David Wenham is one of the able, younger New Testament scholars who are beginning to make a significant mark today. He teaches in Wycliffe Hall, a theological college which prepares men and women for the ordained ministry, and also in the University of Oxford. He is an excellent technical scholar who has in this volume turned his talents towards expounding the parables of Jesus in a way which does justice both to the critical issues (largely discussed in the three appendices at the end of the volume) and to their meaning. He has in fact read widely in the subject, but he carries his learning lightly and has determined to make this a book which will help ordinary Christians as well as give fresh insights to those who have already done considerable study of the parables. I am delighted with the finished work, and am most grateful to him for this excellent contribution to the *Jesus Library* which sets out to bring before its readers the best in positive modern New Testament study in terms that are readily understood by those with little or no theological training. Dr Wenham has succeeded brilliantly in this task, which is always difficult, but particularly so in such a heavily worked area as the parables.

This book will be valuable for preachers and teachers at all levels. The material contained in the appendices, the select bibliography and the note on further reading gives a succinct and clear evaluation of difficult critical issues, but also contains a wealth of information on where further discussions of the relevant problems can be found.

Above all, something of the excitement and dynamism which must have accompanied the parables when they were originally given has rubbed off on this book, and will be sure to affect the open-minded reader.

Michael Green
Vancouver

# AUTHOR'S PREFACE

I am grateful to Michael Green for inviting me to contribute this volume to the *Jesus Library* series, I have long had a particular interest in Jesus' parables, but much of my work in the past has been of a rather technical nature, addressing academic issues. It has been a pleasure to have to write something rather more straightforward (and perhaps more useful!), seeking to explain the meaning of Jesus' 'pictures of revolution' in their present biblical context. The academic issues have not been ignored altogether, but they have been kept very much in the background. I hope the book will be thoroughly intelligible to the person without any theological training, but also stimulating to the student who is seeking to understand Jesus' teaching in its historical and religious setting.

I would like to thank all those who have helped me with the writing of the book: Angus and Sue MacLeay and David Stone read and commented on large parts of my manuscript, as did my father and my wife Clare who also prepared the indices. I am also much indebted to numerous authors who have written on the parables before me. The originality of my book lies mainly in the development of the theme of 'revolution', but in other respects I have been heavily dependent on the insights and observations of previous authors, including the renowned Joachim Jeremias, Kenneth Bailey and many others. Given the format of this volume, it would have been inappropriate to acknowledge my sources for every detailed point, but a select bibliography and a note on further reading are included at the end of the volume.

When quoting from the Bible I have usually used the New International Version, though sometimes I have given my own translation of the Greek.

David Wenham
Wycliffe Hall, Oxford

# 1 SETTING THE SCENE: JESUS' PARABLES

Have you heard the story of the manager of the electronics firm who had a big salary and was doing extremely well for himself when one day he was called in by the directors and given his notice – for supposed business malpractice? The once-powerful man was in a real spin: he had a big mortgage on the house to pay off, and all sorts of other things on credit; and he knew that his chances of landing another well-paid post were slim. The humiliating prospect of going on the dole loomed over him and his family: 'What shall I do?' he asked himself in desperation. Then it suddenly came to him: 'I have worked out what to do!' he said, and quickly rang round to several other large firms with which he had dealings . . .

For the continuation of the story look at Luke's gospel, chapter 16 verses 1–13! It is a remarkable fact that the parables of Jesus are (with a little updating and adaptation) as interesting and absorbing today as they were when Jesus first preached them in Palestine nearly two thousand years ago. As a teacher Jesus had at least two things that many modern preachers conspicuously lack: he had a clear and powerful message to proclaim, a message about God's love, his judgement and his call; he also had the ability to communicate that message in an interesting, intelligible and forceful way. Unfortunately many modern preachers, who claim to be followers of Jesus, have in the confusing fog of modern secular thought lost sight of the good news Jesus proclaimed; or, if they have retained an understanding of the good news, they often preach it in ways that are ineffective and boring.

As Christians today, we need to rediscover both the contents and the method of Jesus' teaching. When the crowds heard Jesus they 'were astonished at his teaching, for he taught them as one who had authority and not as their scribes' (Mt 7:28–29).

## What is a parable?

Christians tend to associate parables particularly with Jesus, and have the vague idea that parables were a rather special and out-of-the-ordinary way of teaching. In fact the Greek word for 'parable' (*parabole*), and particularly the Hebrew and Aramaic word (*mashal/mathla*), which Jesus probably used himself, are very broad terms, which can be used of pictorial sayings and stories of all sorts.

In this sense all of us use parables from time to time, for example, when we use similes or metaphors like 'He rushed out of the room like a scalded cat' or 'The garden was a jungle.' The modern preacher who illustrates his sermon with stories is using parables. Literature, ancient and modern, abounds in 'parables' in the broad sense. Indeed, one whole Old Testament book is entitled 'Parables': we know it as 'Proverbs', but the Hebrew word for proverb is the same word as is translated elsewhere in the Old Testament as 'parable'. The Jewish rabbis of Jesus' day used parables, some of them strikingly similar to Jesus' own parables. To say then that Jesus taught in 'parables' is not in itself to say that he did something mysterious or very innovative: any good speaker or writer uses 'parables' from time to time.

What made Jesus' teaching different from much other teaching then and now was the centrality for him of parabolic speech. Many preachers pop the occasional illustration or story into their sermons in order to add interest and to illuminate the idea that they have been trying to explain. Someone like Paul does this in his letters (*e.g.* Rom 11:16–24), but Jesus, especially when speaking to the crowds, spoke almost entirely pictorially, explaining his ideas in and through stories, and not just using stories as an aid to illustrate his points. Whereas much preaching is like a monochrome carpet with a little pattern round the edge to relieve the monotony, Jesus' teaching is like a carpet with bold and distinctive patterns woven throughout. Jesus taught profound theology, yet he did so not in long and complex discourses, but through down-to-earth, real-life stories.

Jesus' stories and sayings reflect vividly the world in which he lived: there are stories and sayings about family life, like the story of the rebel son who came back home, about agriculture and the natural world, like the story of the unproductive fig tree, about trade and commerce, about weddings, rich and poor people, politics and kings.

## Master-communicator

The fact that Jesus taught so graphically through stories and sayings which reflect first-century Palestinian life tells us much about the sort of person Jesus was. He was no ivory-tower theologian expounding abstract and abstruse theories; he was someone with his feet very much on the ground, able to talk to ordinary people in ordinary terms. The Christian doctrine of the incarnation is that in Jesus God became man; it is evident from Jesus' parabolic teaching that he was not simply human, but that he was a man who felt with, and identified with, the world and situation of his contemporaries in a way that is not always characteristic of religious leaders. This makes theological sense: the incarnation was not simply a matter of identification, but also of communication. Jesus' parables reveal him as a master-communicator.

It is, of course, not just the fact that Jesus used a large number of lifelike parables that justifies the claim that he was a master-communicator. It is also the appropriateness and force of the parables he used. Anyone can devise banal and/or inappropriate sermon illustrations. Jesus' parables are consistently appropriate and powerful, capturing the listeners' attention and then bringing them face to face with some aspect of his message which would be far less effectively communicated through non-pictorial language. Sometimes the power of the parable lies simply in the use of a thought-provoking analogy, such as that of the new wine in the old wineskins. Sometimes it is in the unusual twist and challenge that a story contains, as in the parable of the good Samaritan, which has particular biting force because it is a Samaritan, a religious and social outcast, who is the kind hero, or in the parable of the labourers in the vineyard, who work for different periods of time but all receive the same wage. Sometimes the story is one that stimulates thought and leaves people to make their own connections, as with the parable of the prodigal son, with its powerful portrayal of the runaway son, the loving father and the righteous elder brother.

It is not only Jesus' parables that show him to have been a master-communicator, but his whole life and ministry, because Jesus did not paint vivid, visual pictures of God's love only through his words, but also through his actions. His giving of the bread and wine to his disciples at the last supper was an acted parable, as was his carefully planned entry into Jerusalem on a donkey before the crucifixion. His eating with tax-collectors and sinners was an acting-out of the message of the parable of the prodigal son. His miracles, for example his healings, his miraculous feeding of the hungry and his transformation of the water into wine, were pictures of the kingdom of God, although also more than pictures, being actual samples of that kingdom in action. Jesus' parables were therefore not just a convenient teaching method which Jesus happened to hit on. They were part and parcel of his whole ministry; they were a forceful and visual demonstration of what he had come to do.

## Understanding the parables: (a) context

If Jesus' parables were such a significant part of his ministry, then it is obviously important to seek to understand them, both for the historian and even more so for the Christian who sees the teaching of Jesus as having continuing relevance and authority today. How then are we to understand Jesus' parables?

The major obstacle in the way of our understanding is our distance from Jesus and his situation. We are chronologically distant from Jesus – almost two thousand years away; we are socially and politically and religiously distant. This means that the full force and flavour of Jesus' sayings may often elude us. Most of us, for example, are not familiar with the disastrous effect of putting new wine into old wineskins, or with the dangers of the Jericho road described in the parable of the good Samaritan, nor with the political and religious background to the story of the nobleman going to get a kingdom in the parable of the pounds.

Interpreters have often ignored the problem of historical distance, and, in keeping with their convictions about the ongoing authority and relevance of Jesus' teaching, have explained the parables in terms of their own context and experience and convictions. Thus the parable of the good Samaritan has been taken by some as a summary of Christian doctrine – describing the fall of man, the work of Christ (= the good Samaritan) and the role of the church (= the inn). By others it has been interpreted psycho-analytically, the good Samaritan being the model counsellor, unobtrusively meeting the needs of the unfortunate sufferer.

The trouble with such unhistorical interpretations is that they are often more a reflection of the ideas of the Christian interpreter than of the ideas likely to have been in Jesus' own mind. And although it is admirable to interpret the teachings of Jesus in ways that speak to us today, it is obviously important that it is the teaching of Jesus that is so interpreted, and not just his words taken out of context. It is dangerously possible to make words mean almost anything if we ignore their context. If we cut off a branch from a tree, we can carve it into anything we want, but it is no longer part of that tree; similarly, if we take Jesus' words out of their context, we can make them mean almost anything we want, but such interpretation has little claim to be Jesus' teaching in a significant sense. Sound interpretation of Jesus' teaching must be historically rooted.

The word 'context' is probably the key to the proper

interpretation of the parables of Jesus. We need to understand the parables of Jesus, first within their overall historical
context, second within the context of Jesus' teaching and
ministry, and third within the context of the gospels in which
they are found.

First, before we apply the parables to ourselves and our
situation, we must seek to put ourselves into the historical
context of Jesus and his hearers and to hear the parables
with their ears. Such a historical understanding, however
imperfect it may be, must then be the basis and the measure
of our contemporary understanding. Thus we need to
understand what the terms priest, Levite and Samaritan
meant in the first century in Palestine, as well as something
of the history of Jewish/Samaritan relations, if we are to
appreciate the full force of Jesus' parable of the good
Samaritan. We need in particular to be alert to the Old
Testament background to many of the parables, since Jesus'
hearers will repeatedly have made connections between his
teaching and the Scripture that was so important to them:
for example, Jesus' parable about the vineyard in Mark
12:1–12 will immediately have reminded his hearers of Isaiah
5, where Israel is compared to a vineyard. This is a vital clue
to the interpretation of that parable.

As well as paying attention to the historical, literary,
cultural, religious, social and linguistic context of first-
century Palestine, we need also to understand the parables
within the context of Jesus' teaching as a whole. The
parables must be understood within the context of Jesus'
proclamation of the coming kingdom, and not in the context of twentieth-century psychoanalytic theory or whatever.

Paying attention to the context of the parables within the
gospels is also important. The evangelists often give us clues
about the setting and meaning of the parables, as does Luke,
for example, when he indicates that the parable of the good
Samaritan was given in reply to a lawyer's question about
what it means to 'love your neighbour as yourself'. Some
scholars doubt if the gospels are a reliable guide to the
original meaning of the parables, arguing that the writers of

the gospels have reinterpreted Jesus' teaching in the light of their own later Christian experience. However, scholarly scepticism is often exaggerated, and the evangelists' hints about the interpretation of the parables should be taken very seriously. At the very least the gospels are our earliest evidence about how the parables of Jesus were understood and used shortly after Jesus' ministry.

Having said that, we should perhaps qualify it slightly, since some of the New Testament epistles, for example the letters of Paul, have possible echoes of Jesus' parables from time to time, and may be even earlier evidence than the gospels. However, the gospels specifically set out to record Jesus' teaching, whereas someone like Paul makes use of it in the context of his own teaching; so, although it is always worth seeing if the epistles give us clues as to how Jesus' teaching was understood, the evidence is less directly useful than that of the gospels themselves.

## Understanding the parables: (b) form

If 'context' is one key word for the understanding of Jesus' parables, 'form' is another. The interpreter needs to be sensitive to the particular shape and structure of the parable being studied. It has been a common assumption among scholars and preachers for some years that Jesus' parables all had one main point, and that they should be interpreted accordingly. But that is at best an over-simplification and at worst an arbitrary theory which results in artificial and distorted interpretations. Jesus, like other Jewish teachers, used different sorts of parables – some simple, some more complex. The interpreter must not force them into one mould, but must seek to identify the particular points of emphasis and to distinguish the points that are significant from the narrative details which simply add colour to the story.

Thus in the parable of the good Samaritan it is undoubtedly significant that the hero of the story is a Samaritan, and probably significant that his disappointing predecessors

are a priest and a Levite, but the Samaritan's oil, wine and
donkey, while contributing to the picture of the Samaritan's
generosity, are not significant in themselves. Recognising the
relative importance of such things within a parable is not
always easy: a combination of literary and historical sensitivity is needed.

## Applying the parables today

Although I have emphasised the importance of a historical
understanding of the parables of Jesus, it would be a mistake
to suppose that a purely historical approach is either possible
or desirable. Every interpreter of history is influenced by his
or her own situation and questions, and every Christian must
want to appreciate the meaning of Jesus' parables for today.
However, it is important to distinguish the historical task
and the task of application, and to emphasise the importance
of both. The interpreter's role may be compared to the role
of a translator. A good translator requires two things: an
accurate appreciation of the original language and its idioms,
and a similarly accurate grasp of the language into which he
is going to translate. Similarly with the exposition of Jesus'
parables, sensitivity to Jesus' situation and sensitivity to
today's world are both essential.

Despite the importance of applying the parables to today's
world, this book will be concentrating on the historical side
of interpretation, both because it is fundamental – obviously
if we get this wrong, we cannot get the application right –
and also because our historical distance from Jesus makes it
the more difficult part of the equation for us to get right. But
the book will be a wasted effort if its readers are content to
stay with the historical meaning and fail to make the
connections to today. Jesus' teaching is as exciting and
important today as it was in his own time, if we will
listen. He said: 'He who has ears to hear, let him hear'
(Mk 4:9).

## A note on the interpretative method being followed in this book

This book takes the parables of Jesus in the form in which they are found in the gospels, and seeks to make sense of them in the context of Jesus' ministry and teaching, drawing also on the broader context of New Testament thought to illuminate their meaning. There is not an extensive discussion of the critical issues which dominate many scholarly treatments of the parables, important though these are. Nor is there a strong emphasis on the distinctive perspectives of the different evangelists, though differences between the gospels have often been noted. In the appendices at the end of the book there is a brief discussion of critical issues and method.

I have been conscious that almost any selection of parables is arbitrary to some degree, and that I have included some sayings of Jesus that others would not regard as parables and have excluded others which could qualify. I have included discussion of two parables from John's gospel – that of the good shepherd in John 10 and that of the true vine in John 15. Although scholars have seen John's figurative sayings as in a different category from the parables in the synoptic gospels, I am unpersuaded that they are significantly different or less authentic.

# 2 SETTING THE SCENE: JESUS' REVOLUTION

Imagine a small Middle Eastern country: its people looked back to times when their country was strong and free, but now they were depressingly weak, poor and under the thumb of foreign imperialists. They longed for release and for a better future. And, being a religious people, they prayed for it, though not always with much optimism. Nationalist leaders came and went, promising great things and yet not in the end delivering them. But now at last it seemed different: this man told them, 'The revolution is here!', and he seemed to be someone who might actually deliver the goods. Crowds were out on the streets; they thronged him and listened with excited curiosity to his speeches . . .

What are Jesus' parables all about? The simple answer to that question is that they are all describing some aspect of the 'kingdom of God'. The 'kingdom of God' was the central theme of Jesus' preaching and indeed of his whole ministry, and the parables should all be seen and understood in that context.

But to say that is not necessarily very helpful to modern readers of the gospels, since many of us have only a very hazy understanding of what Jesus meant by the 'kingdom'. Part of our problem is that the word 'kingdom' itself has different connotations now from those it had in Jesus' day: whereas the word 'kingdom' often suggests a place to us, Jesus used the term in a broader sense to refer to a state of affairs – to God ruling as king – as well as to the realm where God rules. More important, for us today words such as 'king' and 'kingdom' tend to have a less forceful feel to them than they

had in Jesus' day. There are still some kings (and queens!)
and kingdoms in our world, but they are mostly constitu-
tional monarchs and monarchies without great power; and,
if anything, we tend to regard royalty as a rather old-
fashioned institution (much as we may love it).

In Jesus' day, however, kings were far from being constitu-
tional figureheads: a man like Herod the Great, who was in
power at the time of Jesus' birth, was an effective and (to his
enemies) extremely dangerous military and political ruler. He
gained his power by a combination of political astuteness
and military force. He then ruled ruthlessly and magnifi-
cently, eliminating any whom he saw as a threat to his
throne (including members of his own family) and making a
name for himself by his marvellous building projects (including the restoration of the Jerusalem temple) and by his lavish
way of doing things. 'Kingship' was then something very
contemporary and very powerful. So when Jesus announced
the coming of God's kingdom or kingly rule, he was not
explaining an interesting theological theory; rather he was
claiming that something of enormous importance and practical relevance was taking place, of which people needed to
take urgent account.

He was in fact announcing God's final intervention in
history. The Old Testament prophets looked forward to the
time when God would impose his kingly rule on the world.
They believed that in one sense God had always ruled the
world from the time of creation, and so the psalmists joyfully
exclaim 'The Lord reigns' (*e.g.* Ps 93:1; 96:10); and yet at the
same time it was quite evident that God was not exerting his
rule in a total sense: the sin and suffering and oppression
that were such a painful reality in the Old Testament world,
not least among God's chosen people of Israel (to whom he
had made great promises), were the reflection of a world out
of tune with its maker and in rebellion against God's kingly
rule. So the Old Testament prophets looked forward to a
future time when God would intervene, put things right and
rule – so Zechariah 14:9, 'The Lord will be king over the
whole earth.'

The Old Testament looks forward to that time in many

different ways, speaking sometimes of the restoration of the people of Israel to greatness, and of the coming of a new king like the great Old Testament king David, and sometimes more broadly of God healing the sicknesses and enmities and hatreds of the world. Isaiah 11, for example, speaks of the coming of a 'shoot from the stump of Jesse' (*i.e.* of a new Spirit-filled king from the family of David), and then of restored harmony in nature: 'The wolf will live with the lamb, the leopard will lie down with the goat, the calf and the lion and the yearling together . . . They will neither harm nor destroy on all my holy mountain, for the earth will be full of the knowledge of the Lord as the waters cover the sea' (Isa 11:6–9). Other passages speak of God's people being freed from foreign oppression, of renewed prosperity and of justice for the poor, of war and weapons of war being abolished, of death being swallowed up and tears wiped away, of the estrangement between God and mankind being removed, of God's Spirit being poured out in a new way, and so on. (Some notable passages are Isa 2, 25, 61; Jer 31; Dan 7, 12; Mic 4; Joel 2.)

Today we might describe the Old Testament hope as a hope for a divine 'revolution'. We are all familiar with the Marxist hope of revolution, and, although some Christians may not like the thought, there is something important in common between the Old Testament hope and the Marxist vision of a new society characterised by new economic relationships; the Marxist hope may indeed have its roots in Old Testament teaching. The important difference is, of course, that the Marxist revolution is characteristically man-centred and man-made and thus something limited, whereas the Old Testament prophets looked forward to a cosmic revolution with the whole world being at peace again with God and under his kingly control. Jesus announced the coming of this greater revolution. When he told people that 'The time is fulfilled; the kingdom of God has come near' (Mk 1:15), he was saying, in effect, 'The longed-for revolution is now under way.'

To paraphrase 'kingdom of God' with the phrase 'revolution of God' may help us to appreciate something of the excitement of Jesus' message. He was announcing a dramatic, forceful change in society to people who – unlike many in our complacent modern world – really longed for such a change: God was at last intervening to put things right. Not surprisingly Jesus' contemporaries understood Jesus to mean that the Roman imperialists and their unprincipled and unpleasant lackeys such as the Herods were about to be driven out of Palestine: 'kingdom' to many of them, like 'revolution' to many of us, suggested something primarily political and military. But Jesus had in mind a bigger revolution than that: God's revolution was to be a total revolution overthrowing Satan and evil and bringing earth and heaven back into harmony, and this would not be accomplished by force of arms, but – unbelievably so far as the disciples were concerned, and who blames them? – through suffering and death.

But, although God's revolution was not quite as the disciples expected, it was something powerful and down-to-earth, not just a heavenly reality. Modern readers of the New Testament may be misled by the phrase 'kingdom of heaven', which we find in Matthew's gospel, and suppose that in speaking about the kingdom Jesus was talking about 'getting to heaven'. But the phrase 'kingdom of heaven' is just an alternative way of saying 'kingdom of God' (the expression used by Mark and Luke in their gospels). Matthew, writing his distinctively Jewish gospel, uses the alternative expression because it refers to God indirectly (as Jews often did) rather than directly, and perhaps because it makes it clear that the kingdom in question is not a purely this-worldly kingdom. And yet the kingdom which Jesus proclaimed was not just up in heaven; it was more like an invasion of earth by heaven!

Jesus' extraordinary miracles were evidence of this. He explained them as a fulfilment of the Old Testament promises and as tangible evidence of the overthrow of Satan's evil empire: so when John the Baptist had doubts about Jesus, Jesus said to John's disciples, 'Go back and report to John what you hear and see: The blind receive sight, the lame walk, those who have leprosy are cured, the deaf hear, the dead are raised' – a revolution indeed, and a fulfilment of Old Testament passages such as Isaiah 35:5–6; 61:1 (see Mt 11:2–6; Lk 7:18–23).

Jesus' revolution affected not only people's diseases, but also their relationships with each other: Jesus broke through social barriers, bringing together Jew and Samaritan, man and woman, rich and poor. It was no accident that on meeting with Jesus the rich Zacchaeus gave half his goods to the poor (Lk 19:8), because God's revolutionary rule is not something affecting only people's minds or their relationship with God, but also their life in society and their relationships with each other. The revolution of God entails the establishment of a revolutionary society. Indeed the word 'kingdom', when used by Jesus, often suggests not just the process of revolution, but also the new world and society that God is bringing.

Of course, a most important part of the revolution that Jesus brought had to do with divine–human relationships. God's new society includes God – not surprisingly! Thus Jesus proclaimed forgiveness to sinners, thereby bringing people out of the darkness of Satan's rule into the light of God's favour and into the experience of God as 'Abba', Father. 'Abba' was a revolutionary word to use of God: it was the intimate family word used by children to address their father – a little like 'Daddy' in English, though without the juvenile feel that the English word often has. Jews did not ordinarily address their holy God with this word; but Jesus brought a revolution, expressing his own close relationship with God through this word and inviting his followers to do so too (see Mk 14:36; Lk 11:2; Jn 17:1–26; Rom 8:15; Gal 4:6, *etc.*).

To announce the coming of a revolution is calculated to stir people up. The question on many lips is: What's involved in joining the revolution, and what must I do to get into the new society ('to enter the kingdom')? Some people, especially those who have suffered under the old regime, will be stirred up in enthusiastic support, and will often be prepared to commit themselves in a very costly way to the cause; others, especially those who are comfortably content with the status quo, will see the revolution as a threat to be resisted. Jesus' announcement of the kingdom, of God's revolution, had precisely the same effect: some responded enthusiastically, others did their best to suppress the revolution.

Few revolutions are established overnight; there is often a long and fierce struggle with drawn-out resistance from 'reactionary' elements. Jesus' revolution was no exception, nor did he suppose that it would be. He, in his ministry, death and resurrection, established a decisive bridgehead in the occupied territory; but it would be a long struggle with many casualties before Satan was completely ousted and God's legitimate rule restored. Jesus taught his followers to look forward to his return at the end of time, when he would bring the revolution to completion and when God's new world and society would be finally and fully established. In the meantime he called his followers to live for the revolution and in the spirit (or rather 'Spirit') of the revolution, and to keep alive their confident expectation of the final liberation and victory.

To sum up: in proclaiming the kingdom of God, Jesus was announcing the coming of God's revolution and of God's new world, as promised in the Old Testament. God was at last intervening, Jesus declared, to establish his reign over everything, to bring salvation to his people and renewal and reconciliation to the world. But fortunately Jesus did not announce his message in such general theological terms; he announced it primarily through vivid, concrete parables.

To summarise Jesus' teaching about the kingdom at the outset of this book is to some extent to anticipate its findings. But it is helpful to have some idea of the broader context of Jesus' teaching before plunging into a study of particular parables. The study of the parables themselves will in turn fill out and clarify our understanding of the kingdom.

# 3 THE REVOLUTION IS HERE!

It is hard to know where to begin or how to arrange a study of Jesus' parables: almost any arrangement has its advantages and disadvantages! We plan to take Mark as our guide in the first instance, looking briefly at the short parabolic sayings of Mark 2:18–22, then at the saying about Satan being bound in Mark 3:22–27, before going on in later chapters to other parables. In each case we shall also have in mind the parallel passages in Matthew and Luke, but readers may like in the first instance to have Mark's gospel open in front of them. (Readers are strongly urged to follow the biblical passages as we go along, and not to fall into the well-known trap of paying more attention to theories about the Bible than to the inspired text of the Bible itself!)

### *The bridegroom's guests, the children playing, the unshrunk cloth, the new wine, and the Christian scribe* (Mk 2:18–22; Mt 9:14–17; Lk 5:33–39; Mt 13:52)

The opening chapters of Mark's gospel describe the coming of God's revolution into the world through Jesus. Jesus announced, 'The time is up: the kingdom of God has come near' (Mk 1:15), and he not only announced the revolutionary event; he also demonstrated it, by his powerful exorcism of demons (Mk 1:21–28), by his touching and cleansing the unclean (Mk 1:40–45), by his pronouncing a man's sins forgiven (Mk 2:1–12), by cutting through traditional religious taboos and ministering to the irreligious outcasts of society (Mk 2:13–17).

People reacted with astonishment at the new thing that

was happening, making remarks such as, 'What is this? A new teaching – and with authority! He even gives orders to evil spirits and they obey him' (Mk 1:27) and 'We have never seen anything like this!' (Mk 2:12). The astonished response was not all friendly: in particular, the religious leaders found the unconventional Jesus uncomfortable, and questioned his actions: 'Why does this fellow talk like that? He's blaspheming. Who can forgive sins but God alone?' (Mk 2:7), 'Why does he eat with tax collectors and "sinners"?' (Mk 2:16). Like most revolutions, Jesus' revolution stirred people up.

One of Jesus' departures from tradition which upset some people was his breaking with the tradition of regular fasting. Other groups of Jewish religious enthusiasts at the time fasted regularly. The Pharisees were one such group: they were a highly committed and widely respected group of Jews who stood for holiness. The name 'Pharisees' quite probably means 'separated ones', and they sought to separate themselves from evil and evildoers. Jesus himself recognised them as 'top' people when it came to religious righteousness (see Mt 5:20). They were very particular about keeping themselves pure and about observing the sabbath day, and they used to fast from dawn to dusk on two days every week. Another highly committed group were the followers of John the Baptist, who had been noted for his disciplined and abstemious life (see Mt 11:18; Lk 7:33). Jesus and his followers had, of course, close connections with John and his movement. But Jesus departed from the tradition of both John and the Pharisees, in that he was known more for feasting than for fasting. His critics went so far as to call him 'a glutton and a drunkard' because of this (Mt 11:19; Lk 7:34). (It is a testimony to the reliability of our Christian gospels that they record this derogatory estimate of Jesus!)

It is in this sort of context that Jesus' sayings about the bridegroom, the unshrunk cloth and the new wine fit. Jesus is questioned by people about his followers' failure to fast, and he replies: 'How can the guests of the bridegroom fast while he is with them? They cannot, so long as they have him with them' (Mk 2:19).

*Fasting during a wedding?* (Mk 2:19–20)

The picture is of a wedding. Today we usually think of a wedding as a religious ceremony held in church (or as an equivalent legal ceremony), with some sort of meal following. In New Testament times the meal was not an addition to the wedding ceremony; it was the ceremony itself, with no preceding synagogue service, and so it was highly significant. The normal procedure seems to have been for the guests to gather at the bridegroom's house on the day appointed for the marriage. The bridegroom would go to the bride's home to claim her, and then he would bring her in joyful procession to his own home. The eating and drinking would then begin, and would often go on through the night. The coming of the bridegroom with his bride was thus the signal for the wedding feast to begin. It would obviously be quite inappropriate for the guests to fast at that point (as Jewish custom indeed recognised: regular fasting was not expected during weddings). Jesus claims that it would be similarly inappropriate for his disciples to fast during his ministry. The implication is that something joyful and significant, like a wedding, is taking place in Jesus' ministry and, furthermore, that Jesus is like the bridegroom at the wedding, being the reason for the joy and the celebration.

For Jesus to explain his followers' failure to fulfil the religious duty of fasting in these terms is, to say the least, remarkable; but it makes sense in the context of his announcement of the kingdom. He was conscious of having brought God's revolution into the world, and this was a cause for great rejoicing and for the abandonment of religious fasting. Fasting was appropriate for the previous period of longing and waiting; but now things were different, and feasting was appropriate.

Jesus' comparison of the kingdom to a feast, not only here but also elsewhere in his teaching, is not surprising in the light of the Old Testament and later Jewish thought. Isaiah 25:6, for example, after speaking of God destroying death and wiping away every tear says: 'On this mountain the Lord Almighty will prepare a feast of rich food for all peoples, a banquet of aged wine – the best of meats and the finest of wines.'

What is perhaps more surprising is Jesus' comparison of himself to the bridegroom, since in the Old Testament it is God who is portrayed as the bridegroom of his people. The book of Hosea, for instance, is full of the idea. God says to his people: 'I will betroth you to me for ever; I will betroth you in righteousness and justice, in love and compassion' (Hos 2:19). Was Jesus, then, identifying himself with God in speaking of himself as the bridegroom? It seems quite probable that this is exactly what he was doing. The neighbouring story in Mark's gospel, about Jesus declaring a paralysed man forgiven (Mk 2:1–12), suggests that Jesus saw himself as having divine authority (to the horror of his opponents, who saw this as blasphemy). And, since the Old Testament vision of God's coming salvation includes the idea of God coming to his people to be with them, it is very likely that Jesus understood this to be happening when he announced the coming of the kingdom (see Isa 40:3–5; Zech 2:10–11; 8:3; Mal 3:1; and *cf.* Mt 11:10). John's gospel is quite explicit that this was Jesus' view of his ministry (*e.g.* Jn 8:58). John is sometimes thought to have gone beyond the other gospels and beyond Jesus himself in what he has Jesus say, but the other gospels share his view that Jesus was 'God with us' (Mt 1:23), and Jesus too understood the coming of the revolution to be the coming of God himself to save his people.

After explaining in these terms his disciples' failure to fast, Jesus goes on to say that 'The days will come when the bridegroom is taken away from them, and then they will fast in that day.' The reference is probably to the forcible taking away of Jesus in his passion and death: that would be a time of sadness for Jesus' followers and in one sense a time of Satanic rule; it would therefore be a time in which fasting rather than feasting would be appropriate (*cf.* Jn 14:30 and the story of Gethsemane in Mk 14:32–42, esp. v. 38).

Do the words of Jesus have any implications for the question of fasting in the church? They could be taken either to exclude Christian fasting on the grounds that we continue to live in the time of the 'wedding' of the kingdom of God, the temporary sorrow of the passion having been displaced by the joy and victory of the resurrection; or they could be taken to justify the practice of Christian fasting on the grounds that we continue to live in the age when the bridegroom is away from us (cf. the parable of the wise and foolish girls in Mt 25:1–13). The latter interpretation has in its favour the fact that the early church did practise fasting (see Acts 13:2–3; Mt 6:16–18); on the other hand, it is doubtful if 'the days' when the bridegroom is taken away refer to the time after the passion, since the post-resurrection period of the church's life was a period characterised less by the painful absence of the Lord than by joy at his victory and at his spiritual presence; this could favour the former interpretation and argue against Christian fasting.

However, to use the verses in either way is almost certainly to misuse them: the sayings about the bridegroom are not intended to be guidelines in Christian piety. What they are intended to do is vividly to describe the kingdom and Jesus' role in it. Jesus' coming is the coming of a joyful revolution, of God's great party for the end-times. A feast was a more significant occasion for the average Palestinian of the first century than it is for those of us who live in the well-fed affluence of the twentieth century (in the West at least): it was something really to be looked forward to and enjoyed. The coming of the kingdom in Jesus' ministry was such an occasion, only much more so because the feast which Jesus announced was God's great and final feast, *the* party to end all parties, the one not to miss at any costs.

*The children playing* (Mt 11:16–19; Lk 7:31–35)

The parable of the bridegroom contrasted Jesus' failure to fast with the fasting of the Pharisees and John the Baptist. A similar contrast is made in Jesus' sayings about the children sitting in the marketplace, sayings which are found only in Matthew and Luke, not in Mark. The marketplace or centre of the village was a natural place for children to congregate

and play; in the era before television and modern toys,
children's games were the sort of open-air games that still go
on in school playgrounds.

Jesus pictures a scene familiar to all parents – namely
children arguing about what game to play and complaining
about their companions' refusal to join in. The games
probably involved playing at weddings and funerals, or
dancing wedding and funeral dances, and the complaint is
that the other children will not play along with either the
wedding or the funeral option!

Jesus uses this picture as a comment on people's attitudes
to himself and John the Baptist. 'For John came neither
eating nor drinking, and they say, "He has a demon." The
Son of Man came eating and drinking, and they say, "Here
is a glutton and a drunkard, a friend of tax collectors and
'sinners'."' People called John demon-possessed because of
his austerity, but then went on to complain of Jesus – we
shall discuss the expression 'Son of Man' later (in chapter 4)
– and of his eating and drinking and socialising with the
outcasts of society. Like obstinate children, nothing would
satisfy them. 'But,' Jesus comments, 'wisdom is justified on
the basis of its deeds' (Lk 7:35, 'by all its children'). In other
words, for those willing to see it there was perfectly good
evidence of God's wisdom at work in Jesus' own ministry.
The signs of God's revolution were there.

These sayings re-emphasise the distinctiveness of Jesus'
ministry. John the Baptist and Jesus had much in common:
there were family links between them (Lk 1:36), Jesus
associated himself with John's mission by being baptised,
and John identified Jesus as the coming one of God,
directing people to him (Mk 1; Mt 3; Lk 3; Jn 1, 3); they
both baptised people, and they both spoke of the coming
'revolution of God' (Jn 3:22–36; Mt 3:2). But for all their
similarity, they were remarkably different in their respective
lifestyles, John being austere, Jesus being notable for his
enjoyment of the good things of life and his sociability. The
explanation of this difference is that their lives were reflections of their respective messages: whereas the sombre focus
of John's preaching was on imminent judgement, the joyful

focus of Jesus' preaching was on God's offer of life and love. (See further in chapters 6 and 7.)

*The unshrunk cloth and the new wine* (Mt 9:16–17; Mk 2:21– 22; Lk 5:36–39), *also the Christian scribe* (Mt 13:52)

In the same context of discussion about fasting, Jesus goes on to give two further parables, the first about not patching an old garment with a new patch, the second about not putting new wine in old wineskins.

The point of the parables is simple, though it could be lost in our twentieth-century context of synthetic fibres, throw-away clothes and bottled wine. The first parable pictures someone patching a torn piece of clothing, and it points out the folly of patching an old damaged garment with a piece of new unshrunk cloth. The patch may be ever so carefully stitched and may look ever so good; but at the first washing (or soaking) the new patch would shrink and tear away from its stitching, and the tear would probably be worse at the end than it was at the beginning.

The second picture is of wine being bottled, except that the 'bottles' in those days – as in some places today – were made of animal skins, not of glass. A great merit of such skins was that they could expand with the wine as it fermented. At least a fresh skin could expand. Skins do, however, dry out and lose their flexibility, and if new wine were stored in such skins the result would be disastrous, with the expanding wine bursting the skins and all being lost.

Luke's parable of the new patch on the old cloth is slightly different from that in Mark and Matthew. His picture seems to be of someone cutting a bit out of a new garment in order to mend and preserve an old one. In this case the folly is twofold, since the new garment is damaged and the old is not effectively repaired. But the main point about the in-compatibility of the old and the new is the same as in Mark's parable. Luke also has a saying about people who have drunk old wine not wanting to change to new wine (Lk 5:39); this is probably an ironical comment by Jesus on people's resistance to his ministry. The conservative 'old-guard' who are unwilling to receive the revolution of God are like people extolling the virtues of old wine; but this time it is the new 'wine' which is far superior!

Both the parables of the patch and of the wine and the wineskins are about new things in old things, about new things bursting out of old things. The context of the parables is Jesus' failure to fit into expected patterns of Jewish piety, and through the parables Jesus is asserting the revolutionary nature of his coming and ministry. He is indeed unconventional, because the kingdom of God which he has brought is a new reality which cannot be contained in the old forms of Judaism: when God's rule is established, this is something exciting, even explosive, not just a new version of an old theme.

That is not to say that Jesus saw himself as starting something completely new, having no connection with the past. On the contrary: 'Do not think that I have come to abolish the Law or the Prophets; I have not come to abolish them but to fulfil them' (Mt 5:17; *cf.* Lk 24:44, *etc.*). Jesus saw himself as building on and bringing to fulfilment God's plan and purpose revealed in the Old Testament and in the history of the people of Israel. In his intriguing short parable of the 'Christian scribe' in Matthew 13:52, he speaks of 'every teacher of the law who has been instructed about the kingdom of heaven' (lit. 'every scribe who has been discipled for the kingdom of heaven') being like a householder 'who brings out of his storeroom new treasures as well as old'. The picture is of a wealthy man with a collection of precious things – we can imagine silver bowls and cups and the like – some of them ancient and some newly made. Jesus implies that Christian teachers are similar to the Jewish theological experts in some ways, and yet, whereas the Jewish teachers looked back to the past, to the great figure of Moses above all, Jesus' disciples had not only the old but also great new treasures as well – in Jesus and his message of the kingdom, being the fulfilment of Moses and the prophets.

So, to return to the parables of the cloth and the wine, Jesus was not an iconoclastic revolutionary, smashing everything that had gone before, but he did see his coming as bringing a decisively new stage in God's purpose. Once the space rocket's motors have fired and the rocket lifts off the launch-pad, the space mission moves into a quite new and most exciting stage for which everything else has been preparation. So Jesus' ministry represented the 'lift-off' of God's revolution, and things could never be the same again. As with Jesus' parable of the bridegroom and the feast, so with the parables of the patch and the wine Jesus makes a remarkable claim for himself: he has brought God's promised revolution into the world. God has worked in the history of his people in wonderful ways, but now something of a decisively new order was taking place.

Modern scholars sometimes speak of Jesus' movement as one of a number of 'renewal' movements within Judaism, comparable, for example, to the Pharisees and to the Qumran community who lived by the Dead Sea. But, although it may be possible for sociologists to categorise the Christian movement in these terms, it is quite clear that neither Jesus nor his followers would have been satisfied with such a view. Jesus' coming represented a quantum leap forward: it was the coming of the revolution, and the Pharisees, the Qumran community and the disciples of John were still living in pre-revolutionary Judaism.

Another interesting passage in which the same thought is differently expressed is in Matthew 11 (also Lk 7), where Jesus speaks about John the Baptist. He says:

> Among those born of women there has risen no one greater than John the Baptist; yet he who is least in the kingdom of heaven is greater than he. From the days of John the Baptist until now the kingdom of heaven has been coming violently, and men of violence take it by force. For all the prophets and the law prophesied until John, and if you are willing to accept it, he is Elijah who is to come. (Mt 11:11–14)

The perplexing references to violence in this passage are probably Jesus' vivid way of expressing the forceful and exciting nature of the revolution that was coming in his ministry. Before the revolution, Jesus says, was the time of 'the Law and the Prophets'. John the Baptist was the final prophet of that old age (the new 'Elijah' of Mal 4:5–6): he was greater than all others born of women in that it was his privilege to announce the 'great and terrible day of the Lord' (to quote Malachi), *i.e.* the coming of the new age of revolution. And yet he himself belonged to the 'pre-revolutionary' age, and as such was less privileged than even the least in the kingdom. The implication of this passage, as of the parables we have been looking at, is that Jesus' coming was a dramatically significant revolution, marking a turning-point between one age of world history and another, between the time of preparation and the time of fulfilment. With Jesus' coming the period of engagement was over, and the wedding had come!

Something similar is also implied in the best-known wedding story of the New Testament, the wedding at Cana, when Jesus turned the water into wine (Jn 2:1–11). John, who records the miraculous event for us, probably intends us to see Jesus' miracle as an acted parable of the revolution Jesus brought. For the plain water of Judaism, Jesus gives the expensive and excellent wine of the kingdom of God – 'eternal life' as John would call it. Wine was not the normal drink of ordinary people in Palestine; it was something special for feasts (and in biblical thought something good and to be enjoyed, though in moderation). Although Jesus' followers in the church have often seemed anything but like joyful revolutionaries, he himself brought the new wine of revolution, the new wine of the kingdom of God.

### The divided kingdom and house, the strong man bound, and the return of the evil spirit (Mk 3:22–27; Mt 12:22–30; Lk 11:14–23; Mt 12:43–45; Lk 11:24–26)

The nature of Jesus' revolution is further explained in the next group of mini-parables found in Mark 3:22–27.

In the preceding chapters Mark has described something of the ministry of Jesus and the great impact that this had on people. People were astonished at the power seen in Jesus – in his teaching, his healing of the sick, his casting out of demons, and his whole conduct. But people reacted differently to this unprecedented, phenomenal person: whereas some responded enthusiastically, others were cautious or even openly hostile.

Jesus' family, according to Mark 3:21, were in the second category: Mark explains that they doubted Jesus' sanity and actually resolved to 'seize' him, in order no doubt to calm him down or simply to keep him out of harm's way. It is instructive for those of us who tend to think of Jesus as a decent, reasonable sort of person who did good to realise that he was actually an uncomfortable person to have in your family.

The religious leaders went so far as to explain his activity as demonic. This was a logical enough explanation, given his undoubted powers and given his religious attitudes which contradicted conventional Jewish notions of piety (see Mk 2:16, 18, 23–28). They suggested that Jesus was himself possessed by Beelzebul – not by any ordinary demon, but by the chief of demons, hence no doubt his powers. And they suggested that his exorcisms, which to judge from the gospels were a particularly striking part of his ministry, were not the work of God but the work of the devil. The implication of this accusation is that Jesus' critics recognised the unusual supernatural power of Jesus, though they refused to acknowledge it as divine power.

It was in the context of this accusation – which according to Matthew and Luke itself occurred in the context of an exorcism of a dumb demoniac – that Jesus spoke 'in parables', first about the divided house and the divided kingdom, then about entering a strong man's house. What did he mean?

First, he is ridiculing the idea that his exorcisms could be the work of Satan, since that would be a case of Satan warring against himself. Jesus points out how a divided nation or a divided household or family cannot stand. He is not suggesting that every political or family tension is fatal (happily!), but he is generalising about the effect of serious division and infighting on a people or a family; and he and his hearers had to look back only a little way into their own history to recognise the truth of Jesus' words. The Roman takeover of Palestine in 63 BC, for example, was in the first instance at least the result of infighting within the Jewish nation and within the then ruling family. Hyrcanus, leader of one of the warring factions, invited the famous Roman general Pompey into the situation, doing himself some good in the process but handing his country over to the foreign power. Jesus' point is simple: to explain his powerful exorcising ministry as inspired by Satan is logically to imagine Satan's kingdom involved in such fatal infighting. But that, Jesus implies, is not a likely scenario, and not at all a plausible explanation of what is going on in his ministry.

What then was the correct explanation of his exorcisms? Jesus gives this in the parable of the strong man's house being burgled. I was reminded of this parable by a recent newspaper report of a seventeen-year-old burglar climbing through a kitchen window into the arms of the muscular owner of the house, and thence being passed on to the police. That burglar failed to reckon with the strong man, and so failed to get away with any stolen goods! Jesus explains that his exorcisms are the opposite of that: they are the ransacking of the house of the supremely strong man (*i.e.* Satan), and reflect the fact that, far from being in collaboration with him, Jesus has successfully tied him up. The coming of God's revolution is the coming of God's rule, which means the ending of Satan's illegitimate rule. Jesus' exorcisms are Satan's goods being taken away and his captives being freed.

In Matthew and Luke, Jesus responds to the accusation that he casts out demons by the prince of demons in the same way as he does in Mark, but he also asks: 'If I cast out demons by the prince of demons, by whom do your sons cast them out?' (Mt 12:27; Lk 11:19). Jesus was not the only exorcist in Palestine, and he knew that his opponents looked with favour on the exorcisms of others; so he suggests that their position, in explaining his exorcisms as demonic, is inconsistent. In saying that, however, Jesus is not suggesting that his exorcisms are no different from those of other exorcists: his exorcisms seem to have been of a different order from those of others (*e.g.* Mk 1:27), and even his opponents recognised them as such (hence their ascription of them to the chief of demons). Jesus' explanation of the difference is straightforward: 'If I drive out demons by the Spirit of God, then the kingdom of God has come upon you' (Mt 12:28; Lk 11:20).

In this context Jesus' saying (found in only Matthew and Luke's gospels) about the expelled demon who returns to the house from which he has been expelled with seven worse demons is worth mentioning (Mt 12:43–45; Lk 11:24–26). The saying is a warning of the dangers of getting rid of evil without filling the vacuum with good. Jesus may be contrasting other people's exorcisms with his own, but he may be speaking more generally of his opponents' ministry. They, like Jesus, are in favour of 'exorcising Satan', but in rejecting God's revolution in Jesus they are leaving themselves exposed to increased Satanic attack. Jesus, on the other hand, brings the revolution of God's Spirit, expelling evil and filling 'the house' with good, so that it can be kept 'clean' and 'in order'. The revolution of God is the defeat of Satan and the coming of God's cleansing and renewing presence.

Jesus' ministry did not of course mean the complete overthrow of Satan immediately. We shall see in chapter 4 that Jesus' ministry represented the start of the revolution, not its completion: there were crucial battles ahead, not least at Jesus' crucifixion (see Jn 12:31). Nevertheless the revolution had really begun, and there were unmistakable signs of Satan's downfall.

Before concluding this chapter, it may be worth commenting on the whole idea of Satan and demons. Jesus himself clearly believed in the reality of both. Ronald Wallace says about Jesus' belief in Satan:

> No one can deny that to Jesus the enemy was a most concrete and sinister personal reality. Jesus Christ did not speak of Himself as one who was fighting against fate, or against man, or against bad social conditions, or against wrong ideas, but as one who was fighting against a single personal will which had defied God in a sphere far greater than this earth, and whose widespread activity has seriously called in question the sovereignty of God. He called this one 'Satan'.

Wallace notes the considerable number of passages where

Jesus speaks of the devil – including Luke 10:18; 13:16; 22:31–32, 53; John 2:4; 8:44 – and says 'John summed up the whole purpose of [Jesus'] ministry when he said, "For this purpose the Son of God was manifested, that He might destroy the works of the devil"' (*Many Things in Parables*, pp. 27–28).

Many modern Christians find this idea of Jesus bringing an anti-Satan revolution a difficult one, because Satan and demons feature so much less prominently in the thinking of many of us than they did in first-century Palestine. This difference is partly due to the fact that we live in a secular world where we tend to explain things in non-supernatural ways, but also probably because demon-possession was more frequent in first-century Palestine than it is in the societies that some of us live in today.

We should, however, be very slow to regard our own materialistic world-view as superior to the more 'spiritual' world-view of Jesus and his contemporaries. Even if some of the New Testament teaching about the spirit-world is pictorial, the idea of a menacing and pervasive power of evil at work in our world continues to be thoroughly credible, and there is plenty of evidence of the reality of spirits and of demon-possession, even (and increasingly) in the secular and so-called 'developed' countries of the world. It is an illusion to think that political, economic and educational changes are adequate to release society as a whole from its destructive and unjust tendencies or to release individuals both from obvious forms of 'possession' (whether by demons, drugs or drink) and from less obvious forms of Satanic oppression such as deep-seated selfishness and unfaithfulness. The problem is more fundamental, as Jesus recognised. He saw as the primary target of God's revolution a far stronger and more sinister 'strong man' than the Roman emperor Tiberius Caesar. That is not to say that he condoned political oppression, let alone that he saw the kingdom of God as something 'spiritual' rather than social; the revolution of God was for him something total. It is to say that Jesus saw his work as going to the roots of evil rather than only dealing with the symptoms. He saw evil as having a cosmic and spiritual dimension (*i.e.* Satan and his hosts), and, as we shall see in chapter 4, a deeply personal dimension in the human heart (see Mk 7:20–23). The Old Testament had looked forward to God rescuing 'captives' from 'fierce warriors' (Isa 49:24–25). Jesus saw himself as fulfilling this promise and as rescuing people from the fiercest warrior and the most profound captivity of all.

# 4 ON THE WAY TO THE NEW WORLD

It is all very well to say that Jesus proclaimed and brought the kingdom of God, the divine revolution. But of what value is such a claim when we look at the world around us, or even at the church? It hardly looks as though Satan is out for the count; it does not feel like the new age of God.

This problem is not a new one. There is evidence that Jesus' contemporaries had the same sort of questions: John the Baptist, for one, sent messengers to Jesus to ask if he really was the 'coming one', because from John's position in Herod's jail it did not feel like the kingdom of God (Mt 11:2–3; Lk 7:18–19). The kingdom of God would surely mean the end of the oppressive rule of corrupt people like Herod, but Jesus showed no sign of achieving that. John was not the only person who felt such frustration over Jesus; Jesus' disciples felt similar impatience over his lack of decisive action (e.g. Lk 19:11; Acts 1:6).

Jesus' reply to John the Baptist was to point to the evidence of the divine revolution in his own ministry, for example in his healings, which were the fulfilment of Old Testament promises. His parables about seeds and sowing, which we find in Mark 4 (and Mt 13; Lk 8), may also be seen in part at least as a response to this concern.

*The sower* (Mt 13:1–9, 18–23; Mk 4:1–9, 13–20; Lk 8:4–8, 11–15)

In our world of big supermarkets, agricultural surpluses and mechanised farming we are far removed from the fragile agricultural economy of first-century Palestine. The peasant farmer sowing his plot of ground was a very familiar sight then, and everyone will have been conscious of the importance of his work. On the results of his sowing everyone's livelihood depended; only the very rich would be unaffected by a poor harvest.

In his parable Jesus describes one such farmer's sowing. Jesus' hearers will immediately have pictured the scene – the farmer, with a supply of seed (probably of wheat or possibly of barley) in a bag hanging from his neck or in a fold of his outer-garment, walking up and down his field, dipping his hand into the seed and scattering it evenly across the soil.

But the focus in Jesus' parable is less on the man doing the sowing than on what happened to the seed. Some of it was lost almost as soon as it was sown, since it fell on the beaten paths around the field, where it lay on the surface, only to be picked up by birds. It is no discredit to the farmer that this happened; it was inevitable if the sower was to sow to the edges of his field. Some of it fell on places where there was only a thin covering of soil over rock – a very familiar feature of the rocky Galilean hillsides; it grew for a little in the rainy season, but the roots could not go deep, and when the hot weather came it withered. Some of it fell in places where there were thistles growing. The thistles may have been quite invisible to the farmer when he sowed his seed, but in due course they grew up with the wheat, and it was an unequal battle, with the vigorous weeds choking the wheat. Finally, other seed fell into good soil, grew steadily, and produced the all-important fruit, the yield being thirty, sixty or even a hundred times the amount of grain sown.

Jesus' hearers will have identified with the scene. Many of them will have had farmers in the family and have known the frustrations as well as the joys of farming in Palestine. There was nothing very extraordinary or unexpected about the story. A number of modern commentators have worried over what they have seen as the carelessness of the farmer in the story in scattering so much seed on unproductive soil: some have seen this as a clue to the parable's meaning; others have explained it in terms of then-current agricultural methods. Thus one particular idea is that the sower would have ploughed the seed in after completing the sowing, and that the path on which he sowed, apparently carelessly, was a track across the field that would have been ploughed up.

Such explanations are unnecessary. The best farmer then, as the best farmer today, experienced the sort of agricultural problem described in the parable, and there is nothing in the parable to suggest that the quantity of seed lost was enormous. We need not suppose that three quarters of the seed fell into unproductive soil and only one quarter into good soil, or even that half of the seed fell into poor soil and half into good, although three unproductive categories and three productive categories (thirty, sixty, and a hundred) are described in Matthew and Mark. The point of the parable is to describe types of growth (or absence of growth), not to give a statistically accurate breakdown of the yield of the field.

Scholars have also got excited over the figures thirty, sixty and a hundred, arguing that these are miraculously high, since it has been calculated that the average yield of a field was approximately sevenfold. But the figures thirty, sixty and a hundred describe the yield of productive parts of the field, not the overall return on the total seed sown, and so, although the picture is indeed of a good yield, there is no need to see miraculous significance in the figures.

But what significance then had this parable, with its description of a familiar scene? The answer suggested by the gospels themselves is that it is (1) about the kingdom, (2) more specifically about the preaching of the kingdom, and (3) more specifically again about people's response to that preaching. Let us look at these points in turn.

*The kingdom*

The parable of the sower is about the kingdom, about the revolution of God announced by Jesus. It does not start with the words 'The kingdom of God is like . . .'; in fact the word 'kingdom' occurs only once in the parable and its interpretation, and then only in Matthew's version of the interpretation (Mt 13:19). But in all the gospels the general context of the parable is Jesus' ministry in Galilee, with its focus on the kingdom. It is accompanied by other parables or sayings explicitly about the kingdom (*e.g.* Mt 13:11, 24 *etc.*). And the immediate context is the gathering of a huge crowd around Jesus: Matthew and Mark describe Jesus retreating to a boat and using that as his pulpit. The people's enthusiasm is, no doubt, because of their excitement over Jesus' message.

Given this context, the parable must be a parable about the revolution and its coming. We have seen that a problem to Jesus' contemporaries, as to many Christians since, was Jesus' failure to bring the kingdom in the forceful way they anticipated. Instead he had met with strong opposition, even from his nearest and dearest (Mt 12:46–50; Mk 3:31–35; Lk 8:19–21). The parable addresses this situation.

The sowing metaphor is a particularly potent one as applied to Jesus' ministry, and it is no accident that the gospels contain several parables about sowing. Sowing is, on the one hand, something that seems quite weak and unimpressive at the time, and the seed is very vulnerable. On the other hand, the sowing of seed is the initiation of something of the greatest importance and power. Jesus' ministry was such a sowing: apparently ineffective, certainly vulnerable to rejection, yet still the initiation of the kingdom of God.

## The preaching of the kingdom

The parable of the sower is not simply making a general point of that sort, though some commentators have read it that way. The parable is about four seed-in-soil situations, and it is accordingly interpreted in the gospels themselves in terms of four categories of response to 'the word' (Mk 4:15).

The explanation of the seed as the 'word' or, as Matthew has it, 'the word of the kingdom' (Mt 13:19) makes a lot of sense. Why was the coming of God's revolution in Jesus' ministry not totally and immediately successful? Answer: because Jesus depended not on military force or even on supernatural power for the bringing of the kingdom, but on the 'word', in other words on telling people about the revolution and calling them to join it ('to repent and believe', to use the Bible's terminology). Of course there were marvellous signs of the kingdom in Jesus' ministry, but nothing to force belief. People had to decide whether to respond to Jesus' message of revolution or not.

The importance of 'the word' to Jesus is clear from elsewhere in the gospels. He was tempted to use political or spiritual force to bring the revolution – tempted by the devil and tempted by his own followers (*e.g.* Mt 4:1–11; Lk 4:1–11; Mk 1:36–39; 8:31–33). But he saw his calling as being to 'preach the good news' and also to die, in other words as a calling to conquer by love, not force. Sowing is something gentle; Jesus' ministry was sowing. It is interesting that John the Baptist spoke of the coming one as a harvester, as someone who brings things to completion (*e.g.* Mt 3:12); Jesus in his ministry was a sower who did not bring the kingdom of God completely, and so mystified people like John.

Sowing, though weak and vulnerable, is also something powerful and life-giving. As the seed brings a harvest of life-sustaining grain, though not overnight, so Jesus' word would produce the longed-for revolution of God. It has been said that the parable of the sower is a parable about parables. It may not be exactly that, but it is about Jesus' preaching of the kingdom, of which parables were an important part. Precisely the same thought is expressed in the parable of the two houses, where the wise man who builds his house on rock is the person who hears and does Jesus' words (Mt 7:24–27; Lk 6:47–49).

The idea of the transforming power of the word is not just the idea that propaganda is effective in motivating people to action: every revolutionary believes that. It is rather the idea that the message Jesus brought was, like seed, something creative, producing new life – the new life of the kingdom of God. As for how it does this, the reference to the word being sown 'in the heart' may be a clue (Mt 13:19; Lk 8:12, 15). Jesus, as we mentioned in the last chapter, diagnosed the human problem as having to do with Satan on the one hand and with the human heart on the other. By the 'heart' in this context is meant not the body's blood-pumping system, but the inner life of thought and will; so in Mark 7:20–23, where Jesus is discussing cleanness and uncleanness, he says: 'For from within, out of men's hearts, come evil thoughts, sexual immorality, theft, murder, adultery, greed, malice, deceit, lewdness, envy, slander, arrogance and folly. All these evils come from inside and make a man "unclean".' This was a radical statement to make in a context where people tended to think in terms of religious cleanness and uncleanness having to do with keeping one's body ritually pure, and it helps us to see where the 'word' comes in. The effectiveness of the 'word of the kingdom' is that it has the power to bring cleanness and renewal to the heart, producing that inward revolution which is the key to any real revolution.

The prophet Jeremiah looked forward to such a revolution when he spoke of God making a new covenant (or agreement) with his people: 'I will put my law in their minds and write it on their hearts' (Jer 31:33). The old covenant, described in the Old Testament, involved animal sacrifice and the giving of the written law of God through Moses (see Exod 24). Jesus proclaimed the coming of the new covenant, involving (1) his sacrificial death for the sins of the world, (2) the preaching and hearing of 'the word', and (3) the indwelling Holy Spirit.

Jesus' view of the 'word' as life-giving seed is echoed in various passages in the New Testament; quite likely the authors have been influenced, consciously or unconsciously, by the parable of the sower. James 1:21 says: 'Humbly accept the word planted in you, which can save you.' 1 Peter 1:23 says: 'You have been born again, not of perishable seed, but of imperishable, through the living and enduring word of God,' and Paul in Colossians 1:5–6 speaks of 'the word of truth, the gospel that has come to you. All over the world this gospel is bearing fruit and growing . . .' This understanding of the saving power of the word of the gospel was reflected in the priority given to their preaching and teaching ministry by the apostles, when they commented that it would not be right to 'neglect the ministry of the word of God in order to wait on tables' (Acts 6:2). Waiting on tables and social concern are the work of the kingdom, but the bringing of the good news of the kingdom is a priority, since it generates revolution in people and the world. The word is the 'sword' of God's revolution – the sword of the Spirit, as Paul puts it in Ephesians 6:17 – because it pierces the human heart, challenging and changing it (see Heb 4:12).

The idea of a powerful creative 'word' does not appear for the first time in the New Testament. The psalmist speaks for the whole Old Testament when he says: 'By the word of the Lord were the heavens made, their starry host by the breath of his mouth' (Ps 33:6). Isaiah comments:

> As the rain and the snow come down from heaven, and do not return to it without watering the earth and making it bud and flourish, so that it yields seed for the sower and bread for the eater, so is my word that goes out from my mouth: It will not return to me empty, but will accomplish what I desire. (Isa 55:10–11)

The Old Testament writers are speaking of God's word. In Jesus' parable of the sower he is speaking of his own word. The implied claim is clear, and is made explicit by Luke, who identifies the seed not simply with 'the word' (as does Mark) or 'the word of the kingdom' (as does Matthew), but with the 'word of God' (Lk 8:11).

## People's response to the kingdom

The parable of the sower is, then, about Jesus' preaching of the kingdom. But in particular it is a comment on the variable success of his preaching. Sometimes Jesus' word is like the seed on the path, meeting with no response or understanding and being immediately rejected or forgotten, snatched away by Satan. Sometimes there is enthusiasm at first, but the hearers immediately give up when things get hot, *i.e.* 'When there is pressure or persecution for the sake of the word'. Sometimes there is response, but then the word is gradually strangled by competing forces, 'the cares of the world, the deceit of wealth and desires for other things'. But finally 'those on the good soil' are those who listen to the message, receive it, and in due course bear fruit, living out in practice the life of the revolution.

The four-part interpretation of the parable given in the gospels is a brilliant analysis of the experience of Christian ministry. Some scholars have seen it as a reflection of the church's experience rather than of Jesus' own experience. But in fact it fits very well indeed with what we know of Jesus' ministry. He faced blind Satanic rejection from some (see the preceding story of Mk 3:20–30). He encountered many others who were interested in him, but who were eventually not prepared for the cost in terms of suffering or material sacrifice. It is no accident that precisely these barriers to discipleship are referred to elsewhere in Jesus' teaching, for example in his emphatic words about the need to take up the cross, which were so difficult for the disciples to accept (Mk 8:34–38), and in his call to the rich young ruler and others to 'give up all' (Mk 10:17–31), a call which the young man was unwilling to face up to. But Jesus also saw the 'revolution of God' take root in his disciples, and with painful slowness grow and bear fruit.

In analysing people's response to the message of the kingdom in this way, Jesus was explaining something about his ministry and its apparent 'ineffectiveness', but at the same time he was challenging the great crowd who were around him to consider their position and to ensure that they were producing fruit. The parable is an invitation to see the kingdom in Jesus, despite the disappointments that could lead the reader to doubt Jesus; but it is also an exhortation to the reader to consider where he or she fits into the picture. The parable is about the preaching of the kingdom, but it is also itself preaching of the kingdom which looks for a response. Thus Jesus concludes the parable: 'He who has ears to hear, let him hear' (Mk 4:9; Mt 13:9; Lk 8:8).

## *The lamp and the measure* (Mk 4:21–25; Lk 8:16–18)

The parable of the sower is followed in Mark and Luke by sayings concerning a lamp and a measure. A lamp, according to the first saying, is not designed to be put under a bowl or a bed, but on a lampstand; the picture is of a small oil lamp containing a floating wick, the usual form of lighting in a Palestinian home. By our standards it gave out very little light, but it was an important piece of domestic equipment, as even in the daytime houses would often have been dark, having only small unglazed windows. A typical house would have niches in the walls where lamps could be put when they were lit. This is probably what Jesus means when he refers to the 'lampstand' where the lamp should be put. Mark and Luke go on to speak about things being hidden with the purpose that they may subsequently be brought out into the open.

It is not easy to be certain what point is being made in this saying. Does the lamp refer to Jesus' parables, the meaning of which was at first concealed but which would one day be clear to all? Some scholars take the saying in that way and see it as a qualification of Mark 4:11–12: 'The secret of the kingdom of God has been given to you. But to those on the outside everything is said in parables, so that "they may be ever seeing but never perceiving…".' But it is doubtful if Mark 4:11–12 means that parables were meant to conceal (see appendix 3 for a discussion of those verses), and even more doubtful if Mark 4:21–23 should be read as putting a time limit on Mark 4:11–12.

A more probable view is that the saying is referring more broadly to Jesus' ministry and to the revelation of God that had come in Jesus. The idea of Jesus as a light is familiar to us from John's gospel (Jn 9:5), and it is attractive to take this saying as referring to Jesus as the 'lamp that comes' (as the Greek of our parable puts it): the mystery of his identity is hidden from most people at present, and known only to the disciples (Mk 4:11), but one day will be known to all.

Yet another possibility is that the parable is a follow-up to the parable of the sower and is a call to obedient hearing of the word. The saying may be an encouragement to people to 'let their light shine', or, in terms of the preceding parable, to 'bear fruit'. The last sense is that suggested by Matthew 5:14–16, where Jesus speaks of the city that cannot be hidden and of 'letting your light shine before men, so that they see your good deeds and glorify your Father in heaven' (see further on this in chapter 8 and compare Lk 11:33).

The saying about the measure is also not easy to interpret. The picture is clear enough: in biblical times commodities such as oil and flour were not bought off supermarket shelves in neatly labelled packets, but were weighed or measured out by the merchant to the purchaser. Although there were standard-sized containers (made of pottery, wickerwork or metal), the merchant could be honest or even generous in his measurement, or he could be the opposite. Jesus has this sort of situation in mind when he says: 'With the measure you measure it will be measured to you, and more will be added.' He goes on with the paradoxical-sounding statement: 'For whoever has, to him will be given; and whoever does not have, even what he has will be taken away from him.' It helps make sense of these sayings if we recognise that one of the typical ways that a Jew spoke of God was to use a passive form of the verb, as in the phrase 'it will be measured to you'. (Christians do the same today when they say 'I was led' to do something, meaning 'God led me'.) So the saying about the measure is a promise that God will reward people according to and in proportion to their actions.

In the context of the parable of the sower, with its reference at the end to people producing fruit thirtyfold, sixtyfold and a hundredfold, the probability is that the saying about the measure is promising God's blessing to people according to their response to the word. The point is much the same as that made in the parables of the talents and the pounds in Matthew 25:14–30 and Luke 19:11–27, where the saying about a person being given or deprived according to what he has is also found. The saying should not be taken to mean that entry into the kingdom is on the basis of human effort: we will see later that this is far from Jesus' view. But the saying does reinforce the importance of obedient response, as explained in the parable of the sower: the blessings of God's revolution are for those who commit themselves seriously and practically to the revolution.

### *The seed growing secretly* (Mk 4:26–29)

If the parable of the sower answers the question: How can

Jesus claim to have brought the kingdom of God and yet have been so unsuccessful?, the next parable answers the question: How can Jesus proclaim the kingdom of God and not be more active in bringing it? Jesus' followers had high hopes for Jesus' ministry, and they were impatient over his failure to bring the kingdom in the way they anticipated. We need only remind ourselves of their abortive attempt to make Jesus king after the feeding of the five thousand and of their high hopes for the completion of the revolution when Jesus entered Jerusalem for the last time in order to get a feel of their impatience (Jn 6:15; Lk 19:11, 37–38, *etc.*). They wanted to know why he did not do more. Modern Christians sometimes wonder the same thing when their ministry is frustratingly slow.

Jesus answers that question by comparing the kingdom of God to a farmer who, after he has sown his seed, does nothing until harvest, when he again goes to work, bringing in his crop. The parable is effectively in three scenes: scene 1 is the farmer sowing his seed; scene 2 has the farmer doing nothing, except going to bed and getting up each day. There is no need to accuse the farmer of laziness or neglect of duty in this scene: the point being made is that in this period (between sowing and harvest) he is relatively inactive; he simply waits. There is, of course, activity in scene 2, but it is the seed that is actively and steadily growing, and the farmer has nothing to do with it. It grows 'automatically', in a way that the farmer does not understand or control. In scene 3 the farmer swings back into action, putting in his sickle and gathering the ripened corn.

The last words of the parable, 'he puts in the sickle, because the harvest has come', are strongly reminiscent of the description of God's final judgement in Joel 3:12–13: 'I will sit to judge all the nations on every side. Swing the sickle, for the harvest is ripe.' It seems likely that the echo is deliberate. Jesus is explaining in this parable that he has indeed brought the kingdom of God, but he is like a farmer who sows his crop and then waits patiently for the harvest. It would be silly for the farmer to hurry or anticipate the harvest. So Jesus implies that his work will lead to the harvest of divine judgement on the last day, but in the meantime there has to be patient waiting in the confidence that the work of the kingdom will come to harvest.

There are a number of significant implications in the parable. First, if we are right in seeing this parable, like the parable of the sower, as an explanation of Jesus' own work – or of his lack of work! – then Jesus is not only the one who 'sows' and inaugurates the kingdom of God, but also the one who will bring the process to completion, putting in the sickle of divine judgement. We are reminded of Jesus' teaching about the future, where he speaks of the Son of Man coming on the clouds of heaven to gather his elect (Mt 24:29–31; Mk 13:24–27; Lk 21:25–28).

But, second, Jesus does not have total control over the coming of the kingdom. Like the farmer, he has to wait for the sown seed to come to fruition. In Jesus' teaching about the future there is the same note: 'No-one knows about that day or hour, not even the angels in heaven, nor the Son, but only the Father' (Mt 24:36; Mk 13:32). Just as the farmer 'does not know' how the seed grows – that is God's business! – so Jesus, having sown the seed, leaves the growth process to God. It is interesting to see how the parable implies the divine authority of Jesus in the kingdom, and yet distinguishes Jesus from the Father.

Third, the parable implies the growth of the kingdom. The emphasis on the process of growth is unmistakable in the parable: 'it sprouts and grows ... first the shoot, then the ear, then the full corn in the ear'. This does not mean that Jesus expected the world to get steadily better and better by a process of spiritual evolution until everything was wonderful. That was a popular view among Christian interpreters of the parables in the optimistic years before the two world wars; but it was not the view of Jesus, to judge from his teaching about judgement day, when the wicked will still be flourishing (*e.g.* Mt 24:37–39; Lk 17:26–29). But, although Jesus did not believe in evolutionary progress, he did teach that the work of the kingdom begun in his ministry would grow and one day be completed – the harvest would come. Part of what is involved and intended by this growth process is evident in Matthew 24:14: 'This gospel of the kingdom will be preached in the whole world as a testimony to all nations, and then the end will come.' As we saw, the revolution of God comes and grows, according to Jesus, primarily through the 'word of the kingdom': the harvest will come when the task of proclamation is complete. Until then it may seem that the Lord is being slow. But in fact, 'The Lord is not slow in keeping his promise, as some understand slowness. He is patient with you, not wanting anyone to perish, but everyone to come to repentance' (2 Pet 3:9).

### The mustard seed (Mt 13:31–32; Mk 4:30–32; Lk 13:18–19)

Another parable of growth in Mark 4 is that of the mustard seed. It is found also in Matthew and Luke, who in both cases combine it with the parable of the leaven. There are minor differences between the three versions of the parable: the biggest of these is that Mark and Matthew have explanatory phrases about the smallness of the mustard seed and the large size of the grown mustard plant which make the point of the parable clearer.

The mustard plant in question is probably the

Brassica nigra, source of the most important condiment black mustard, which has long been extensively cultivated and was in biblical times the source of mustard-seed oil and a medicament ... The black mustard is an annual herb with large leaves clustered mainly at the base of the plant. Its central stem branches abundantly in its upper part and produces an enormous number of yellow flowers and small, many-seeded linear fruits. (So Michael Zohary, the Israeli botanist, in his *Plants of the Bible*, p. 93.)

The seed of the plant is tiny – about a millimetre in diameter. And 'like a mustard seed' was a proverbial way of referring to something very small. Thus, when Jesus wants to speak of having just a tiny amount of faith, he speaks of 'faith as small as a mustard seed' (Mt 17:20), and when the rabbis spoke of a minute amount of blood, they spoke of a drop like a mustard seed. From this tiny beginning the mustard plant would grow, reaching a height of six feet (or even twice that) within a season and becoming quite sturdy enough for birds to perch in its branches. One commentator refers to goldfinches and linnets coming in flocks to perch in this tree-like herb and to eat its seeds (B Matthews, *A Life of Jesus*, OUP, London, 1934, p. 203).

What is this parable all about? Jesus introduces a number of parables with an opening attention-catching question. He introduces this parable as follows: 'What shall we say the kingdom of God is like, or what parable shall we use to describe it?' (Mk 4:30). The question makes clear that this is another kingdom parable, and the probability is that through this parable Jesus was once again addressing the doubts of those who had difficulty in recognising the kingdom of God in his ministry. They expected the kingdom to be massively powerful and all-embracing, but the Jesus revolution was nothing of the sort; it was tiny. Jesus' parable acknowledges this, but compares the kingdom to the tiny mustard seed, which so remarkably grows up into a handsome plant.

In Matthew and Luke the mustard seed is actually said to become a 'tree', an understandable piece of hyperbole. In the Old Testament there are several passages where powerful earthly kingdoms are pictured as trees with birds in the branches. For example, in Ezekiel 17:22–23 God speaks of his plans: 'I myself will take a shoot from the very top of a cedar and plant it . . . it will produce branches and bear fruit and become a splendid cedar. Birds of every kind will nest in it; they will find shelter in the shade of its branches' (see also Ezek 31:1–14 and Dan 4:11–12). It is possible that Jesus' parable is deliberately reminiscent of these passages as it looks forward to the time when God's kingdom, inaugurated in Jesus' ministry, will be such a powerful kingdom, offering shelter to the nations of the world. Church history has at least partially illustrated the truth of Jesus' words: the seed has grown amazingly. The parable continues to be an encouragement in contexts where the work of Christ is still as small as a mustard seed.

## *The leaven* (Mt 13:33; Lk 13:20–21)

It makes sense while thinking about the parable of the mustard seed to think also about the parable which accompanies it in Matthew and Luke, namely that of the leaven. There are a number of 'parable pairs' in the gospels, for example the parables of the treasure and the pearl in Matthew 13:44–46 or the parables of the lost sheep and the lost coin in Luke 15:1–10. The mustard seed and the leaven are such a pair, the one parable taken from the sphere of men's work (sowing) and the other from the sphere of women's work (cooking in the home). The same male–female balance is there with the parables of the lost sheep and the lost coin and in the sayings of Jesus about his second coming dividing 'two men in a field' and 'two women at the mill' (Mt 24:40–41). We should not necessarily see much significance in this, though it is striking that Jesus did not share the prejudices of many of his contemporaries about women: the revolution of God means the breaking down of divisive prejudice, whether against Samaritans, tax-collectors, women or children. We recall Paul's words: 'There is neither Jew nor Greek, slave nor free, male nor female, for you are all one in Christ Jesus' (Gal 3:28). Of course, the twelve whom Jesus chose as his apostles were men, and Paul taught that men and women have different roles in church and family. But both Paul and Jesus believed in the equality of men and women within marriage, the church and in the sight of God. The revolution of God does not mean the suppression of the God-given differences between men and women – being part of God's good creation; it does mean transformed relationships and true liberation for all.

To return to the parable of the leaven: bread was the staple food of the time, and was made from wheat or, particularly in the case of poor people, from barley. The bread was leavened not with fresh yeast, but by keeping a piece of fermented dough from the previous baking and mixing it with the new batch. (The fermentation process could be begun from scratch in various ways, *e.g.* by letting barley and water ferment or by mixing bran and wine.) The poor would probably bake their own bread in the home, and so the mysteriously powerful process of leaven at work and dough bubbling and rising would be well known.

Jesus speaks of a woman 'hiding' the leaven in three *sata* (Greek) of flour – a huge quantity, reckoned to be about fifty pounds – enough to make bread for a hundred people. The actual figure may have been taken from the story in Genesis 18:6 of Abraham and Sarah baking bread for their angelic visitors, but the point being made is simple and clear: that a little hidden leaven can have a remarkably big effect. Paul says almost exactly that in his first letter to the Corinthians when he urges them to get rid of the old leaven of malice and wickedness (1 Cor 5:6–8).

Paul uses the picture of leaven to refer to the pervasive effects of sin. Jesus, on the other hand, uses it positively to make a point similar to that of the parable of the mustard seed. The kingdom of God, which Jesus brought, seemed unimpressive to many people, but Jesus was setting in motion a powerful process which, though hidden at present, would as surely reach its intended goal as does the leaven in the dough.

The picture of the leaven leavening the whole lump might seem to suggest an evolutionary understanding of the kingdom of God and the associated idea that the world will get progressively better and better as time goes on, until the revolution of God is total. The difficulty with this view is not just that it does not correspond to our experience – it has rightly been said that as the human race leaps forward technologically, it remains as backward as ever morally – but also, as we have seen and will also see in the next parable, that it does not fit with other teaching of Jesus. How then should we understand the leavening of the whole lump? Perhaps simply as a statement that the work of the kingdom will one day be complete. On the other hand, the kingdom of God in Jesus' understanding was something total and world-embracing, and the parable may plausibly be seen as looking forward to the time when, as Paul puts it, all God's enemies are defeated and when God's purpose of 'bringing all things in heaven and on earth together under one head, even Christ' is fulfilled (1 Cor 15:28; Eph 1:10; *cf.* Rom 8:20–21). In other words, Jesus' parable does not teach evolutionary progress, but it does teach that Jesus' present work is the beginning of a powerful process which will eventually lead to the reconciliation and renewal of all creation.

## The wheat and the weeds (Mt 13:24–30, 36–43)

Although Matthew has more parables in his parables chapter (Mt 13) than does Mark, he does not have the Markan parable of the seed growing secretly. Instead, at the same point in the chapter, he has his own parable of the wheat and the weeds. It has things in common with Mark's parable, both in terms of the vocabulary used and the ideas expressed, but at the same time it is significantly different. The similarity and difference remind us that Jesus must have used similar teaching on many different occasions, sometimes repeating himself word for word, sometimes varying his wording and emphasis.

Matthew's parable, like Mark's, is about sowing and harvesting, and about 'inactivity' in between. But the context of the inactivity is a dastardly action by an enemy, who comes at night and sows weeds in the middle of the farmer's field. It is usually supposed that the weed concerned is darnel (*Lolium temulentum*), which is 'a member of the Grass family and resembles wheat-like grass. A weed in whose grains lives a poisonous fungus, it grows exclusively in grain fields through the Middle East. Its grains have been found in a 4,000 year-old Egyptian tomb' (Zohary, p. 161).

We are not told what sort of grudge provoked this first-century equivalent of modern industrial sabotage, but its seriousness is recognised by the man's servants when, presumably after some months, they discover what has happened. They want to act immediately to pull up the weeds. Sometimes such weeding-out of weeds was done, but in this case the quantity and/or type of weed was presumably such that the roots of the different plants will have been intertwined, and the master fears that pulling out the darnel would endanger the corn. He insists that nothing be done until harvest, when the wheat can be gathered in, and the darnel left on the ground, later to be collected up for burning as fuel.

If Mark's parable was addressing the doubts and questions of those followers of Jesus who wanted him to do more and to act faster in bringing the kingdom, Matthew's parable spells out what sort of action they were looking for, namely the weeding out of evil and evildoers. Jesus' answer in Mark was simply that the seed must be allowed to grow and that at harvest the 'man' will put in the sickle and reap. In Matthew his answer is similar: that the wheat must be allowed to grow without disturbance until harvest, and that then the sorting of good and bad will take place. Premature action will damage the crop and curtail the growth. The most obviously new ingredient in this parable is the idea of good and evil coexisting in the present but being separated in the future.

The parable of the wheat and the weeds is given a fairly detailed interpretation in Matthew's gospel, in which Jesus is identified with the sower of good seed, the devil with the enemy, the field with the world, the harvest with the end of the world, the reapers with the angels, *etc*. After giving this key to the parable, the interpretation then dwells on the thought of the final harvest and judgement (vv. 36–43). Various significant things are made explicit in the interpretation about the nature of 'the revolution of God', and they are worth exploring in some detail.

First, the revolution is *a plan for the salvation of 'the world'*: thus 'the field is the world' (v. 38). This field belongs rightfully to the sower (v. 24), who sows in it 'sons of the kingdom' (v. 38); but it is encroached on by an enemy, and 'the sons of the evil one' (v. 38) have to be weeded out of the kingdom (v. 41). Some scholars have detected a confusion in the interpretation, with the field being identified at one moment with 'the world' (v. 38) and at another with 'the kingdom' (v. 41). But there is no confusion: the point is that the world belongs properly to God as king, and the revolution is the restoration of that rule. Just as the parable of the leaven spoke of the whole lump being leavened, so this parable speaks explicitly of the world-embracing scope of the revolution. Revelation 11:15 is an apt commentary: 'The kingdom of the world has become the kingdom of our Lord and of his Christ . . .'

Second, the revolution is *an anti-Satan revolution*: 'the enemy . . . is the devil' (Mt 13:39). Just as in the parable of the strong man and in many other passages, so here it is a case of Jesus versus the arch counter-revolutionary, the devil.

Third, the conflict is not played out on a purely spiritual plane, but *in the world of people*, and there is division between 'the sons of the kingdom' and the 'sons of the evil one'. The expression 'son of . . .' in this sort of context is a familiar phrase in Hebrew or Aramaic, and means 'someone who belongs to . . .'

What divides those who 'belong to the kingdom' and those who 'belong to the evil one'? We notice four things about 'those who belong to the kingdom'.

(1) They are the seed sown by the sower (vv. 37, 38). In other words, they owe their position in the revolution of God to the work of Jesus himself. We are reminded of the teaching of the parable of the sower about the life-giving effects of Jesus' word of the kingdom, and of the whole emphasis of the New Testament on forgiveness and life being through the mercy and love of God. We shall return to that theme when we come to parables such as that of the prodigal son.

(2) God is described as 'their Father' (v. 43): the mention of the parable of the prodigal son reminds us that the idea of God as Father and of us as his children is a central and distinctive theme in Jesus' teaching (see also Jn 1:12). The revolution of God is not an impersonal or hard revolution, but is a loving, family affair. Joining the revolution is not becoming a number in an army, but joining Jesus in a relationship of intimate sonship.

(3) They are called 'the righteous' (v. 43). The Old Testament vision of God's revolution is of a time when God will establish righteousness and his people will be righteous, for example Isaiah 45:24–25: 'In the Lord all the descendants of Israel will be found righteous . . .' (also Jer 33:15–16; Dan

12:3, *etc.*). The New Testament sees Jesus as the one through whom this promised 'righteousness of God is revealed' (as Paul puts it in Rom 1:17). The revolution of God is all to do with 'righteousness' (*cf.* Mt 6:33; Rom 14:17). Jesus himself 'fulfils all righteousness' (Mt 3:15) and he calls his followers to 'righteousness' (Mt 5:20). What does it mean to be 'righteous'? The word is used first as a relational term, meaning right with God, second as an ethical term, meaning living a good and godly life; the two senses are seen as closely related within the New Testament, with the right relationship leading to right living. Either or both meanings could be intended in the parable of the wheat and the weeds, though perhaps the contrast with the 'doers of lawlessness' (v. 41) favours the ethical interpretation in this passage: being in the revolution means upright living.

(4) The promise to the 'sons of the kingdom' is that they will shine like the sun in the kingdom of their Father (v. 43). The Old Testament picture of God's revolution is of a time when 'the glory of the Lord will be revealed' (Isa 40:5) and when his people will live in the brightness of that glory. The parable of the wheat and the weeds may be an echo particularly of Daniel 12:2–3: 'Multitudes who sleep in the dust of the earth will awake: some to everlasting life, others to shame and everlasting contempt. Those who are wise will shine like the brightness of the heavens, and those who lead many to righteousness, like the stars for ever and ever.' The same picture of eternal glory is found elsewhere in the New Testament, most obviously in the book of Revelation, which speaks of the new Jerusalem as shining with the glory of God (Rev 21:10–11; 22:5).

Contrasted with the 'sons of the kingdom' are the 'sons of the evil one'. We note three things about them.

(1) They are seed sown by the devil (v. 39), or 'sons of the evil one' (v. 38). To our modern ears this sounds rather strong language for unbelievers. But it is not unique in the New Testament: the most obvious parallel is John 8:44, where Jesus says to those who reject him: 'You belong to your father, the devil.' Paul diagnoses the human condition similarly in 2 Corinthians 4:3–4, when he comments that 'our

gospel . . . is veiled to those who are perishing. The god of
this age has blinded the minds of unbelievers, so that they
cannot see the light of the gospel of the glory of Christ . . .'
Such passages as these emphasise two things, first the
seriousness of belief and unbelief, and second the power of
evil. Unbelief is not a respectable option, but is to be under
the power of the devil, even though he may disguise himself
as an angel of light (2 Cor 11:14).

(2) They are characterised as 'those who do evil' (v. 41).
The Greek word used is not evil in general, but 'lawlessness'.
The opposite of 'righteousness' is disobedience to the law of
God. Lawlessness is rebellion against God and is counter-
revolutionary activity. This is clear from Paul's writings,
particularly from 2 Thessalonians 2, where he speaks of 'the
lawless one' who will come in the power of Satan and set
himself up against God, and of the 'secret power of
lawlessness' that is already at work in the world. Paul speaks
in that context of the Lord Jesus destroying the lawless one
at his coming. The thought is the same in the parable of the
wheat and the weeds, with its description of judgement on
those who do lawlessness. One clarification of this point may
be needed. If 'lawlessness' is anti-revolutionary, then does
the revolution of God involve 'keeping the law', despite
Paul's apparently contrary teaching about Christ as the end
of the law? The answer is yes and no: the righteousness of
the revolution of God is not the righteousness of the
Old Testament law, but the higher righteousness of Jesus,
who fulfilled and surpassed the old legal standards and
whose Spirit inspires his followers (Mt 5:17, 20; Rom 8:4;
13:10).

The parable also speaks of the angels weeding out 'everything that causes sin' (v. 41): this is another important New
Testament word, *skandalon* in the Greek. It means something
that causes people to stumble; it is the word used when Jesus
warns that 'if anyone causes one of these little ones who
believe in me to sin, it would be better for him to have a
large millstone hung around his neck and to be drowned in
the depths of the sea' (Mt 18:6). It is, in other words,
counter-revolutionary activity.

(3) The destiny of 'sons of the evil one' is described as 'the fiery furnace, where there will be weeping and gnashing of teeth' (v. 42). The book of Daniel, as we saw, spoke of people being condemned to shame and everlasting contempt; Jesus' words are a vivid pictorial description of the same terrible reality of judgement. The book of Daniel, of course, describes a 'burning fiery furnace', prepared by King Nebuchadnezzar for disloyal or supposedly disloyal citizens (Dan 3); the parable uses that picture of final judgement. Paul speaks somewhat similarly in 2 Thessalonians 1:7–9:

> This will happen when the Lord Jesus is revealed from heaven in blazing fire with his powerful angels. He will punish those who do not know God and do not obey the gospel of our Lord Jesus. They will be punished with everlasting destruction and shut out from the presence of the Lord.

Modern Christians find it hard to come to terms with this sort of language which speaks about divine judgement, sometimes because of a failure to recognise pictorial language (such as the fiery furnace) as pictorial, sometimes because of an unwillingness or inability to believe in the serious and awful reality of judgement. But there is no doubt that Jesus had such a belief, and that for him the revolutionary message of God's love was good news and urgent good news precisely because he believed that a time would come for the destruction of all the works and workers of 'the evil one'.

Fourth, the parable of the wheat and the weeds, like others of the parables, makes it clear that *the revolution of God comes in two stages*, with a period of growth being followed by a decisive intervention at harvest time. What this parable adds to the others is the understanding, on the one hand, that the period of growth is a period when revolution and counter-revolution coexist uncomfortably together and, on the other, that the judgement and final triumph of the revolution will come only at the 'end' of the age.

A diagram which some scholars have used is quite helpful.

Jesus' contemporaries expected the kingdom to come explosively and totally, thus:

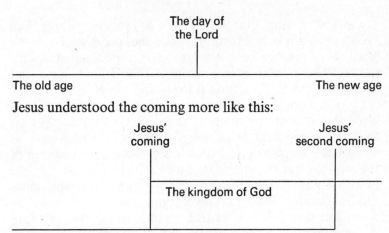

Jesus understood the coming more like this:

The old age of Satan

The kingdom had come with Jesus, but the old age had not been eliminated. The weeds were still very much present, and only at the end of the age will they be destroyed and the kingdom be the total reality. This understanding of the 'overlap' of the ages is a valuable clue to understanding various parts of the New Testament, for example Paul's teaching about 'Spirit' and 'flesh'. For Paul the Christian believer has the revolutionary Spirit of Jesus – an anticipation of the full revolution to come – but he always has to resist the counter-revolutionary 'flesh', which wars against the Spirit and from which he will be released only at the Lord's return.

Fifth, the interpretation spells out in no uncertain terms *Jesus' crucial role in the bringing of the revolution.* Thus we note the following four points.

(1) Jesus is explicitly identified with the sower of the good seed (v. 37); this is implied in the other parables of growth, but is explicit only in this parable. The thought is similar to that which we find in John's gospel, for example when Jesus says, 'I am the light of the world', or when he says, 'I am the good shepherd' of the sheep and contrasts himself with the false shepherds; we could paraphrase Jesus' words in the interpretation of the parable of the weeds: 'I am the sower of the good seed in the world.'

(2) The sowing that Jesus does is bringing people into God's revolutionary kingdom. Thus the 'good seed' are the 'sons of the kingdom'. We are again reminded of John's gospel, where Jesus' role is to bring life: 'I have come that they may have life, and have it to the full' (Jn 10:10).

(3) The association of Jesus with the kingdom is in fact so close that it is at one moment called God's kingdom (v. 43) and at one moment Jesus' kingdom (v. 41). This is not, as some have suggested, an indication of inconsistent editing of the parable, but something that we have already seen implied in other parables, namely that Jesus is in a strong sense God's agent in bringing his revolution.

(4) The way Jesus refers to himself is as the Son of Man. This mysterious phrase, which means literally 'the human being', is one of the most important expressions in the gospels, as it is the way Jesus usually seems to have referred to himself. The probable background to this phrase is in the strange vision of Daniel 7, which portrays four ferocious animals and then speaks of one 'like a son of man', to whom authority and kingdom is given (Dan 7:14, 27). In Daniel the beasts stand for the pagan empires of the world and the human figure stands for the people of God, who after their sufferings will receive God's salvation. In using the title 'Son of Man' of himself Jesus probably claims to be the one in whom and through whom God's promised salvation and 'kingdom' have come to his people.

It is clear that the interpretation of the parable of the wheat and the weeds contains a wealth of theological ideas and fills out our understanding of 'the revolution' considerably. Many of the ideas have Old Testament roots, notably in the book of Daniel, including Son of Man, kingdom, lawlessness, righteousness, the fiery furnace, the radiance of the saints, and the whole idea of judgement dividing the righteous and the lawless. The revolution of God is the fulfilment of Old Testament promise.

The interpretation also has strong links with other parts of the New Testament: the stark contrast between the 'sons of the kingdom' and the 'sons of the evil one' and the explicit emphasis on Jesus as the sower of good seed are reminiscent of John's gospel, with its equally sharp contrast between Christ and Satan and between the 'sons of light' and 'of darkness' and its emphasis on Jesus as giver of life to the world. (John prefers to speak of 'life' rather than of the kingdom.) There are also parallel ideas in Paul, for example in 1 Corinthians 15:25, where he speaks of Christ putting his enemies under his feet.

The richness of ideas and the parallels have led many scholars to conclude that in the interpretation of the parable we have the mature reflections of the church rather than the simple teaching of Jesus. But the intepretation fits the parable brilliantly. There is nothing in it that is out of keeping with the Palestinian context of Jesus' ministry – indeed the Danielic flavour of the interpretation makes good sense in that context – and there is nothing in it that is out of keeping with the content of his kingdom teaching as we find it elsewhere in the gospels. On the contrary, it is much more likely that the parallel ideas in Paul and John are derived from teaching of Jesus such as we find in the parable of the wheat and the weeds and its interpretation than vice versa.

In conclusion, the parable is an assurance that despite the ambiguity of present experience the kingdom of God is at work and will ultimately triumph. It explains that the revolution does and will coexist with the counter-revolution of the devil until the day of judgement. This is an encouragement when we are tempted to be depressed by the power of evil in the world, the church and in personal experience. The implication is not, of course, that evil does not matter: it is the work of an enemy, which will one day be judged. Nor is it implied that it is not imperative to resist evil. Jesus urged taking drastic action against evil, both on an individual level, for example in his vividly expressed commands about getting rid of the eye or hand that lead into sin (Mt 5:27–30), and on a church level, where the brother who refuses to listen to reason is to be excluded from the Christian fellowship (Mt 18:15–17). But, although personal and church discipline are important (and often neglected in the modern church), the parable of the weeds warns of the contrary danger, *i.e.* of expecting perfection this side of judgement day. The parable is thus an antidote, on the one hand, to unrealistic idealism, whether on the part of the social revolutionary who expects utopia in this age or on the part of the Christian who hopes to find or found a perfect church, and, on the other hand, to loss of idealism on the part of those experiencing failure and opposition.

## *The net* (Mt 13:47–50)

The parable of the net, to which we now come, and the parable of the wheat and the weeds have been seen as a 'parable pair' because of their similarity. But here we move from agriculture to something almost as important in Jesus' Galilee, fishing. One of the most interesting archaeological finds of recent years was the discovery in 1986 in the Sea of Galilee of a still intact fishing boat dating back to New Testament times: the boat is ten metres long and three metres wide, and may well be the sort of boat Peter and Jesus' other disciples worked from. It is evident from the New Testament that fishing was big business – hazardous and hard-going at times, but also profitable.

The picture in Jesus' parable is of a big trawling net weighted down at the bottom – a weight was found in the recently discovered boat – and with floats at the top; this would either be pulled through the sea between two fishing boats or taken out to sea by one boat going out from the land, swinging round in a semi-circle and returning to shore, where the net would be pulled into land with long ropes. In either case fish would be enclosed within the net, brought to land, and then sorted out. Certain categories of fish were designated unclean in the Old Testament (*e.g.* Lev 11:9–12). These and others that were regarded as inedible would be discarded on the beach, and the rest would be taken in baskets for sale.

Whereas the parable of the wheat and the weeds is probably about the coexistence of God's revolution and Satan's counter-revolution in the world generally, the casting of the net in this parable may plausibly be seen as the 'fishing for men' of which Jesus spoke (*e.g.* Mt 4:19), and those in the net therefore as those caught up in Jesus' revolutionary movement. The parable speaks of 'all kinds of fish' being caught in the net, and there may possibly be a hint here that the mission of Jesus and his followers will be international in its scope. But the main point of the parable is that the net contains good and bad fish. The parable thus speaks of the church as a mixed (or mixed-up!) community. The gospels are clear that of those Jesus attracted to himself some were deceptive wolves in sheep's clothing and that it is possible to say 'Lord, Lord' and yet not to be true 'revolutionaries'. The parable of the net reflects this, and promises that judgement day will sort out the true and the false.

Like that of the wheat and the weeds, the parable of the net by implication encourages realism (a realism at odds with two opposite modern tendencies – on the one hand to regard everyone in the church as true sons of the kingdom by virtue of their profession, and on the other hand to try to identify and sort out all the good and bad 'fish' prematurely). It also encourages patience and hope. The revolution, as it came in Jesus, was a great and in some ways indiscriminate gathering in of people, as indeed his opponents complained. But Jesus is as clear as his opponents that the revolution of God will mean judgement when the present time of gathering is over. For, as the author of Revelation puts it in speaking of the new Jerusalem, 'Nothing impure will ever enter it, nor will anyone who does what is shameful or deceitful, but only those whose names are written in the Lamb's book of life' (Rev 21:27).

# 5 THE GREAT DAY OF THE LORD'S COMING

Jesus announced the coming of the divine revolution in his ministry, but he spoke of its coming as a process. How would the process end, and the revolutionising work be completed? In the previous chapter we saw something of the answer to this question in the parables that look forward to the time of harvest, for example the parables of the wheat and the weeds and of the net. It would be a time of joyful reaping, but also a time of sombre reckoning. These themes are developed in other parables in all three synoptic gospels.

### The budding fig tree (Mt 24:32–36; Mk 13:28–32; Lk 21:29–33)

The last parables in Mark's gospel come in Jesus' great discourse about the future, and the first of them is a saying about the appearance of leaves on a fig tree being a sign of summer's imminence. The explanatory comment in the gospel is: 'Even so, when you see these things happening, you know that it is near, right at the door' (Mk 13:29; Mt 24:33; Lk 21:31).

In order to understand this, we must obviously look back into the preceding discourse to find out what 'these things' and 'it' are. The discourse is teaching of Jesus given shortly before his death. The teaching was provoked by a statement of Jesus to the effect that the Jerusalem temple (which was one of the wonders of the world – one of Herod the Great's architectural masterpieces) would be destroyed. The disciples,

who were eagerly (and rightly!) looking for Jesus to complete
the task of revolution, probably guessed that the destruction
of the temple of which Jesus spoke would be the signal for
the end, and they asked him: 'Tell us, when will these things
happen? And what will be the sign that they are all about to
be fulfilled?' (Mk 13:4). Jesus in his answering discourse gave
them something like a map of the future (see Mk 13:1–37;
Mt 24–25; Lk 21:5–36).

The map is not all that easy for us to interpret. But
broadly speaking we can summarise it as follows. First, Jesus
spoke of a period of disturbances during which his followers
would have to suffer and the good news of the revolution
would be preached to all nations. This is evidently the period
of waiting and growth which we read of in the last chapter,
when the 'word of the kingdom' is preached.

Second, Jesus spoke of a catastrophe hitting Jerusalem. He
used the phrase 'the abomination that causes desolation'
(Mk 13:14). This phrase will have reminded his hearers of the
horrific time in 169 BC when the pagan emperor Antiochus
Epiphanes set up a pagan altar in the temple and tried
forcibly to abolish the Jewish religion. That abomination
sparked off the heroic Maccabean rebellion which was to be
an inspiration to Jews throughout their subsequent history.
Jesus expected a similar abomination to come on Jerusalem
again, but this time including the destruction of the temple.

Third, Jesus spoke of the Son of Man coming 'in clouds
with great power and glory' and gathering his elect (Mk
13:26–27): this reminds us of the harvest in the parable of the
wheat and the weeds, and is a picture of judgement day,
when the longed-for revolution would finally and completely
be established.

If this is Jesus' teaching, what are we to make of his
parable of the fig tree and of the saying 'When you see these
things happening, you know that it is near'? Jesus here
speaks of one set of events being an indication that something
else (or someone else: the Greek for 'it' in Mk 13:29 could
be understood 'he') is near, 'at the very doors'. The most
likely explanation is that 'these things' = the catastrophe
that will hit Jerusalem, and that 'it' or 'he' = the coming of

the Son of Man in judgement. In other words, Jesus says that, as the coming of fig leaves heralds summer, so the destruction of the Jerusalem temple heralds the coming of judgement day and the coming of the revolution of God in its totality.

There is an obvious problem for the modern Christian reader with this interpretation, since the destruction of Jerusalem came in AD 70 and judgement day has still not come. Was Jesus then mistaken? Many people have argued that he was. But several things tell against that conclusion. First, when Jesus spoke of the coming disaster in Jerusalem, he warned that at that time there would be 'false Christs and false prophets' who would say, 'Look, here is the Christ!' or, 'Look, there he is!' (Mk 13:21–23). Second, after the parable of the fig tree Jesus speaks of 'all these things' happening in 'this generation', but then he says: 'No-one knows about *that* day or hour, not even the angels in heaven, nor the Son, but only the Father' (Mk 13:30, 32). Jesus thus distinguished between the Jerusalem catastrophe, which would happen in a generation (as indeed it did), and 'that day', *i.e.* the day of judgement, the time of which is unknown. These two pieces of evidence show that Jesus did not make a tight chronological connection between the Jerusalem catastrophe and the day of judgement.

Nevertheless he did see the judgement on Jerusalem as a sign of the coming of the universal judgement (like the leaves on a fig tree pointing to the coming of summer). We may helpfully think of God's plan – his plan of revolution – being a drama: the judgement on Jerusalem is the penultimate act of the drama, and we now await the final act. Judgement is near in terms of the structure of the drama, though the exact timing is unknown. Meanwhile we are called to carry on enduring in suffering and proclaiming the good news.

### The watchman (Mk 13:34–36; Lk 12:35–38)

After mapping out the future in the way we have described, Jesus ends his discourse by exhorting people to 'keep awake'.

This exhortation takes rather different forms in Matthew, Mark and Luke. Matthew has a big group of parables (the thief, the steward, the wise and foolish girls, the talents, the sheep and the goats), Luke has a few sentences of exhortation, and Mark has something in-between, with what sounds like the beginning of a parable and various exhortations. Thus after the exhortation: 'Be on guard! Be alert! You do not know when that time will come' (Mk 13:33), Mark continues: 'It's like a man going away: He leaves his house and puts his servants in charge, each with his assigned task, and tells the one at the door to keep watch.' Those sentences sound like the start of a typical parable story. But the story of the watchman on the door does not continue any further. Instead there is an exhortation applying the half-parable: 'Keep awake then; for you do not know when the master of the house comes, whether at evening or midnight or at cock-crow or early.'

The probable explanation of the differences between Matthew, Mark and Luke here is that Matthew with his group of parables has the fullest record of Jesus' teaching; Mark and Luke have given abbreviated extracts from the teaching. Interestingly, Luke shows that he knows all the parables, but he has put them at an earlier point in his gospel (in Lk 12:35–48).

All this helps explain Mark's half-parable of the watchman, since it is quite probably half of the parable also found in a slightly different form in Luke 12:36–38, where Jesus speaks of servants awaiting their master's return from a feast so as to be able to open the door to him when he arrives and knocks, and of the blessedness of such servants, since the master himself will welcome them and entertain them to a meal.

Whether or not this explanation is correct, we can take Mark's and Luke's parables together. They both speak of a wealthy man with servants, going out and coming back at an unknown hour of the night. When he comes back, the house will be bolted and barred from the inside. He will need to be let in by his servants. The good servant will be awake at however unearthly an hour the master arrives.

In this parable we are back in the world of the relatively wealthy. Not that you had to be enormously wealthy in those days to have servants. The economy was labour-intensive, and it was relatively cheap to employ people, as it still is in some parts of the world today. Servants were of two main types: the first category were 'slaves' who were actually owned by their master, having sold themselves or been sold into slavery because of debt or for some other reason. Slaves had relatively few rights and could be badly treated. But they were often well treated. They had some security as members of their household, and they were sometimes able to buy their freedom. Under Jewish law in particular slaves were protected, and a Jewish slave had an automatic right to release in the 'jubilee' year (see Lev 25:40–41). The second category of servants were 'hired servants' who hired themselves out, often as day labourers; they were free, but sometimes worse off than a well cared-for slave.

The watchman of our parable (like most of those called 'servants' in our English translations of the gospels) was a slave. To have such a watchman was the ancient equivalent of having elaborate locks and burglar alarms these days. The task of the watchman was to guard the house at night, to watch out for intruders, but to open the door of the house – or more likely the gate to the courtyard of the house – to those with a right to enter, including, most importantly, to the master when returning home. The usual failing of such a watchman was to fall asleep on the job, understandably enough given the nocturnal and often solitary nature of his job and the warmth of some evenings. But to be caught asleep by the master was obviously a serious matter.

The main point of the parable is unmistakable: it is about the importance of 'keeping awake' – a better translation of the Greek word than 'watch' – and being ready to welcome the master when he comes and knocks. Jesus thus urges his disciples to keep awake at all times for the 'coming of the Son of Man', *i.e.* for his own return. The danger is that the disciples may 'fall asleep' and not be ready to welcome him.

Whereas others of the parables which we shall look at emphasise the need for good work in the master's absence, the focus of this parable is specifically on being expectant and ready. It is a first-century warning against a familiar twentieth-century phenomenon, *i.e.* servants of Christ who would be most surprised if he returned. Although Jesus strongly discourages speculation about the time of his return, because the time is unknown, he also for that very same reason urges his disciples to keep awake lest they be found unprepared. The point of the parable is echoed by Paul in a passage where he may well be drawing on this and other parables of Jesus:

> So then, let us not be like others, who are asleep, but let us be alert and self-controlled. For those who sleep, sleep at night, and those who get drunk, get drunk at night. But since we belong to the day, let us be self-controlled, putting on faith and love as a breastplate, and the hope of salvation as a helmet. (1 Thess 5:6–8)

The implications of the parable of the watchman for our understanding of the 'revolution of God' are worth exploring a bit further.

First, we note Jesus' use of the master/servant picture in many parables. As we have seen, masters with servants were a common feature of everyday life, and so Jesus' use of the idea is no surprise. We have also seen that the master/servant relationship in a household was a close one, often very much a family affair rather than an impersonal employer/employee relationship, although the master was the boss, of course, and the servants were responsible to him and dependent on his favour. Given this background, it was natural enough for Jesus to speak thus of himself and his disciples. But the implied claim is a significant one, comparable to that made in the growth parables: Jesus claims to be the sower of the field and the master of the house, in other words the Lord of the revolution to whom his disciples were responsible as servants.

Second, we notice the idea of the master going away and leaving his servants. There was barely a hint of this in the parables we looked at earlier; but now, shortly before his death, Jesus speaks not just of an apparently inactive or ineffective farmer, but of a master who actually goes away before the revolution is complete, leaving his followers to carry on his work in his absence and until his return. It is clear from a parable like this that Jesus both anticipated a period when he would leave his followers long enough for some of them to be tempted to 'fall asleep', and also that he expected to return himself to bring in the kingdom. He did not just look forward to a general intervention of God in the future (as some scholars have suggested): he believed that the kingdom was coming during his ministry and would finally come through his returning. Although the kingdom is 'of God', it is also the kingdom of Jesus the Lord.

Finally we must observe Luke's fascinating conclusion to his form of the parable, which describes the returning master sitting his servants down and himself serving them (Lk 12:37). This is an extraordinary, but most significant, end to the story. It is extraordinary because it would be almost unthinkable for an oriental master to act thus towards his slaves, but significant because this is exactly how Jesus portrays the kingdom of God elsewhere, notably through his acted parable of washing the disciples' feet at the last supper (in Jn 13:1–17) and also through his words explaining his own death as the model of Christian service and the antithesis of worldly styles of leadership (see Mt 20:25–28; Mk 10:42–45; Lk 22:25–27). The kingdom of God is all to do with the unbelievable generosity and condescension on the part of 'the Lord' to his servants. Our parable speaks of this in looking forward to the coming feast of the kingdom; Jesus demonstrated it at the feast of the last supper and in his death, and he called his disciples to do the same.

### The thief (Mt 24:42–44; Lk 12:39–40; cf. 1 Thess 5:2; 2 Pet 3:10; Rev 3:3; 16:15)

Matthew knew Jesus' parable of the watchman (see Mt 25:13), but he chose to give in his gospel four or five other parables, all about the future and the second coming of Jesus.

Jesus' parable about the thief coming in the night is found in both Matthew and Luke. It is evident from the New

Testament that crime was common in Palestine: the man in the parable of the good Samaritan is mugged and robbed (Lk 10:30); Jesus warns against laying up treasure on earth ... 'where thieves break through and steal' (Mt 6:19); and, of course, he speaks of breaking into a strong man's house, as we saw in chapter 3. No doubt the economic hardship of the time encouraged theft. So when Jesus compared the Son of Man's coming to the unpredictable coming of a thief, this will have rung uncomfortable bells with his hearers.

But what was Jesus intending to teach through this parable? We suggest three related points.

First, the break-in of a thief is a classic example of something that is unpredictable. So Jesus says: 'If the owner of the house had known ... he would not have allowed his house to be broken into.' In fact he did not know. So 'the Son of Man will come at an hour when you do not expect him'. Jesus uses a thief as an illustration of his own coming, because a thief's coming is a paradigm of something unexpected.

Second, it is desirable to be prepared against the burglar, as the mushrooming of burglar alarms in modern cities attests. Jesus says that if the house-owner had known of the burglar's coming, 'he would not have allowed his house to be broken into', and this thought of anticipating the burglar is what is brought out in the application of the parable: 'You too be ready, for you do not know the hour when the Son of Man comes.' The unpredictability of the coming of the Son of Man is not a cause for despair, or even alarm, as the comparison of the thief might suggest. On the contrary, the disciples are to do just what the householder cannot do for the thief, *i.e.* to keep awake and ready for the Lord's coming. The point is in effect the same as that of the parable of the watchman: the unknownness of the time makes spiritual alertness essential.

Third, perhaps the most obvious thing about a thief is the unpleasantness of his work for those on the receiving end. A break-in is often a shocking and distressing experience, hence the growth of 'victim support' schemes in modern society. Is Jesus then suggesting that the coming of the Son of Man will be a bad experience? Obviously not in general. But Jesus is forthright about the reality and seriousness of judgement, and, although it is not spelled out, there may well be an implication in our parable that the coming will be bad – like a thief – for those who are unprepared.

Paul, who makes use of the parable of the thief in 1 Thessalonians 5:2 and is thus a very early witness to it, exploits the negative connotations of the picture of a thief by warning that the day of the Lord will come as destruction and judgement on those 'in darkness' and those who are 'asleep' (cf. Rev 3:3); but he urges his Christian readers to keep awake and sober, commenting that then the day will not come on them like a thief. In one sense the day will come like a thief for everyone in that its timing is unknown; in another sense it will not be like a thief for believers who are expecting its coming at any time and so are spiritually awake; for unbelievers, on the other hand, it will be as traumatic as a break-in, only more so. The parable is thus a threat as well as an encouragement.

Before leaving the parable, we may observe that it is unlikely that the Christian church would have compared Jesus' second coming to the coming of a thief had Jesus himself not done so. Here is evidence of the gospels' reliability. The same thing applies also to others of Jesus' 'crime parables', as we might describe them, such as that of the burgling of the strong man's house and the parables of the unjust judge and of the unjust steward, as well as to the parable of the pounds, in which Jesus compares himself to an unpopular king hated by his citizens (Mk 3:23–27; Lk 16:1–9; 18:1–8; 19:11–27). It is remarkable that Jesus draws on such a gallery of rogues to illustrate his ministry, but of course in none of the parables concerned is Jesus commending the morality of the characters concerned, but simply using lively stories to make his point.

### The steward (Mt 24:45–51; Lk 12:42–46)

Matthew and Luke both follow the parable of the thief with

that of the steward. We are back in this parable with a householder and his servants, the spotlight this time being specifically on the servant who was given charge of the household and responsibility for looking after his fellow servants in his master's absence. Luke uses the word 'manager' or 'steward', and we are to think of a senior and presumably capable member of the household who is entrusted with considerable responsibility. He is his master's right-hand man.

The parable of Jesus contrasts two ways of carrying out the job. A faithful and sensible servant conscientiously fulfils his responsibility and is accordingly rewarded by his master on his return by being made manager of the whole estate, not just of domestic affairs. A bad servant, calculating that his master will be away a long time, maltreats his fellow servants and lives it up himself; his reward is the unexpected arrival of his master and severe punishment – the parable speaks of him being cut to pieces, probably a reference to a severe beating, and put with the 'unfaithful' (Luke) or the 'hypocrites' (Matthew). The picture is of demotion or dismissal and of miserable disgrace, hence Matthew's vivid wording, 'there will be weeping and gnashing of teeth'.

The general force of the parable is quite clear: the disciples are servants awaiting their Lord's return, the time of which is unknown. The choice is to be prudent and faithful servants, doing the Lord's will and ready for his return at any time, or to be disobedient and dissolute, reckoning on the master's absence; the outcome will be great reward or fearful judgement.

The theme of reward and punishment is a prominent one in Jesus' teaching as a whole. It is prominent in the Sermon on the Mount, for example, where Jesus says that if you 'do your acts of piety before men . . . you will have no reward from your Father in heaven' (Mt 6:1). Modern Christians are often uncomfortable with ideas of reward and punishment and of heaven and hell; the very idea of reward is regarded as unworthy – whether because it suggests so-called works-righteousness, or a sort of bribery! But the teaching of Jesus is unequivocal on the matter: the gospel is all about the narrow way that leads to life and the broad way that leads to destruction, and the life at the end of the narrow way is not a bribe; it is God's great purpose – to establish the kingdom of God. Entering the narrow way is by invitation, not something earned; but accepting the invitation entails walking on the way, bearing fruit, being a faithful manager.

Such a message is relevant to every Christian disciple. But is there any significance in the description of the manager's task as feeding and providing for his fellow servants? It may well be that the thought is especially of the responsibility of Christian leaders to those in their care. According to both Matthew and Luke, Jesus is speaking to Peter and others, and in Luke the parable of the steward follows a question from Peter about the preceding parable: 'Lord, are you telling this parable to us, or to everyone?' (Lk 12:41). Following that question, Jesus' reply may well be saying something about the apostles' particular responsibility to the wider group.

This may be confirmed by a comparison of the promise in the parable, that the faithful steward will be set over all his goods, with Jesus' promise to the apostles in Matthew 19:28 that they will sit on thrones with him. It may also be confirmed by Paul. He sees the church as God's 'household', with Jesus as Lord (*e.g.* Gal 6:10; Eph 2:19; 1 Tim 3:4–15), and in 1 Corinthians 4 he speaks of himself and Apollos as 'stewards'. Paul says there: 'Men ought to regard us as servants of Christ and as stewards of the mysteries of God. Now it is required of stewards that they be found faithful ... wait till the Lord comes ... At that time each will receive his praise from God' (1 Cor 4:1–5). It seems quite likely that Paul is here echoing Jesus' parable, and his application of it to his apostolic ministry may well be a reflection of its original thrust. The same interpretation may be reflected in Titus 1:7, where the overseer of the church is called 'God's steward' – the Greek word *episkopos*, or overseer, is very similar in sense to the word steward; he is not to be 'overbearing, not quick-tempered, not given to drunkenness,

not violent, not pursuing dishonest gain . . .' And it is not just
Paul: Peter refers to Christians using their gifts in service of
one another 'as good stewards of God's varied grace' (1 Pet
4:10). We also find the idea of the leaders of the Christian
church being called to 'feed' the flock in John 21:15–17 and
in 1 Peter 5:2.

If such is the original sense, then the parable shows Jesus'
concern for the pastoral care – the feeding – of his people.
Some Christians, including scholars, do not like the idea that
what we might call church organisation originated with
Jesus, partly no doubt because of the glaring failings of the
church over the centuries. We can sympathise with this
allergy to ecclesiastical organisation. But there is no reason
to suppose that Jesus expected the coming 'revolution' of
God to be carried on without leaders. On the contrary, he
appointed and carefully trained the twelve to have responsibility and to carry on his work of revolution (*e.g.* Mt
10:5–8; Jn 20:21).

The style of leadership he looked for was, of course, very
different from the hierarchical and bureaucratic and often
corrupt style that has been characteristic of so much of
church life. The parable of the steward may give us some
clues as to what Jesus expected: the faithful leader is one who
(1) honours his master in his absence and is ready to give
account to him at any time; (2) does so positively by feeding
his fellow servants at the proper time – we are reminded of
Paul's instruction on the pastor's teaching responsibility to
Timothy and Titus; (3) does so negatively by not exalting
himself over his fellow servants or indulging himself. This
style of leadership is that directly advocated and exemplified
by Jesus (as we saw in discussing the parable of the
watchman). Peter, who according to Luke asked the question
that led into the parable of the manager, learnt the lesson
well, as is clear from his words to church elders in 1 Peter
5:1–4:

> To the elders among you, I appeal as a fellow-elder ... Be
> shepherds of God's flock that is under your care, serving as
> overseers – not because you must, but because you are willing, as
> God wants you to be; not greedy for money, but eager to serve;

not lording it over those entrusted to you, but being examples to
the flock. And when the Chief Shepherd appears, you will
receive the crown of glory that will never fade away.

## The wise and foolish girls (Mt 25:1–13)

The folly of the bad steward was in reckoning that the
master would not return soon; the folly in the next parable in
Matthew is that of the five silly girls who were unprepared
for the length of the bridegroom's absence.

Weddings were, then even more than now, great occasions
– with many guests, lots of food and drink, and lasting a long
time. The celebration would begin when all was ready, and
sometimes that could mean the guests having to wait. There
was not only the food to be prepared, but even sometimes
last-minute negotiations between the groom and his in-laws
about the terms of the marriage. When everything was set,
the groom would come to his bride's home to claim her, and
to bring her in procession to his parental home for the
wedding and the feast. Jesus' story is of a group of ten girls
waiting for the bridegroom to come and for the wedding to
begin. They were all equipped with oil lamps, and probably
had a particular part to play in the wedding: one scholar has
suggested that it was torches, not lamps, that they were
carrying, and that their role was to do a colourful torch
dance. Perhaps more likely their job was to provide light for
the feast: they would accompany the bridal party in procession into the feast and provide much-needed illumination for
the festivities.

In Jesus' story the wait is unusually long, and the girls nod
off as they wait in the warm evening. It is midnight when
eventually the shout comes to them to come out and meet
the groom. The great moment has come, but five of the girls
are in dire trouble since the oil in their lamps has run out.
This is a disaster, because (we have suggested) their job was
to give light in the feast. The foolish girls fail to persuade the
prudent five to share their oil, which would presumably have
meant that no one would have been able to do the job

properly. So they have to go off to try and buy more oil – in the middle of the night.

The result is that the five sensible girls go into the feast; the other five arrive after the feast has begun, and the bridegroom refuses to let them in. After all, they have failed in their responsibility, missing out on the procession, and the wedding has got under way without them.

The story contains many of the ingredients that we have come across in other parables. First, there is the comparison of the kingdom to a joyful wedding feast and of the bridegroom to Jesus. We came across these ideas in chapter 3 when discussing the controversy about Jesus' disciples not fasting. Only there it was Jesus' present ministry which was compared to a wedding; here it is the future kingdom which is the wedding feast. This could at first sight seem surprising and even contradictory. But in fact a characteristic of Jesus' kingdom teaching is that he sometimes speaks of the kingdom being present in his ministry and yet at other times he urges his disciples to pray, 'Your kingdom come.' The explanation of this is not, as some have suggested, that the gospel record has mixed up and confused what Jesus said, but rather that Jesus did indeed believe that in one sense the revolution had come in his ministry and that in another sense it was still to come. The growth parables help to explain this: sowing and reaping are part of the same process and yet quite distinct from each other.

Second, the parable of the girls speaks of waiting for the coming of the master – in this case the bridegroom – and of being prepared or unprepared for one's appointed task and of being rewarded or punished. In this case the reward is entry into the wedding feast with the bridegroom, and the punishment is to find the door shut in one's face and to be left outside. This is a particularly suggestive picture of the outcome of final judgement: colourful pictures of heaven and hell undoubtedly have their place in making vividly clear the glory and awfulness of heaven and hell. But the essence of heaven is to be 'with the Lord for ever', as Paul puts it in 1 Thessalonians 4:17 (cf. Phil 1:23). Hell is, to quote Paul again, to be punished 'with everlasting destruction and shut out from the presence of the Lord and from the majesty of his power on the day he comes to be glorified in his holy people' (2 Thess 1:9–10).

Third, the idea of keeping lamps burning is another one that we have met before in Jesus' parables (see chapter 4). At least in Matthew 5:15–16 the burning lamp is 'good works', and it is probable that the same thought is implied in the parable of the ten girls. The wise ones are ready in that they are actively bearing fruit. In the story the foolish girls are caught out by the master's lateness, and the intended meaning is probably that they have not persevered in the good deeds to which they are called. Just as the parable of the manager was reminiscent of the seed among the thistles in the parable of the sower – of those who allow themselves to be distracted from the word – so this story may remind us of the seed on the rocky ground – i.e. of those who fail to endure when things grow difficult. Joining Jesus' revolution is not a recipe for instant and total happiness, though there is great joy in it; it involves patient waiting and keeping the lamp of faith and love burning even through the night.

A similar saying about keeping one's lamps burning is Luke 12:35: 'Let your loins be girded and your lamps burning . . .' Having the loins girded means having one's belt on and being ready to go, as distinct from taking off one's belt for sleep. It is possible that this saying was in fact part of Jesus' parable of the girls which Matthew has not reproduced. In any case it makes the same point as the parable: Jesus calls his disciples to be alert for the coming kingdom and faithful in good works.

One difference between this parable and some of the others we have looked at is that this parable portrays sleeping people getting into the feast, whereas in the parable of the watchman it was precisely not sleeping that was important! Noticing this, some commentators have said that Matthew 25:13, 'Keep awake, because you do not know the day or the hour,' does not fit after the parable of the girls. But, although it is possible that the saying did not originally follow the parable, Matthew has not made a mistake in putting it here, since spiritual wakefulness is precisely what the wise girls displayed.

An interesting possibility is that Paul knew the parable and saw it as an answer to the worries of the Thessalonian Christians who were anxious about their loved ones who had died before the Lord's return. Paul assures them 'according to the Lord's own teaching' that Christians who fall asleep will 'rise up', as the sensible girls did, to 'meet the Lord', as the sensible girls did, and 'to be with him', as the sensible girls did (see 1 Thess 4:15–17). Whether Jesus had any such idea in mind when referring to 'sleeping' servants is uncertain, but it is at least a legitimate application of a parable which emphasises the need to endure to the end.

### The talents and the pounds (Mt 25:14–30; Lk 19:11–27)

The last parable about a journeying master and his servants is the parable of the talents; both Mark and Luke may have known the parable, but we will look first at how Matthew relates it.

It is a story, rather like that of the steward, of a wealthy man going away on a long journey and leaving his affairs in the hands of his employees. In this case the man's wealth is enormous, since he gives to his servants five talents, two talents and one talent respectively, a talent being roughly equivalent to the wages of a working man for ten years. It is impossible to give anything like an accurate modern equivalent, but if we think of a talent as something between £50,000 and £100,000 British pounds (in 1989!), we will probably not be too far out.

The parable describes how the master entrusts his wealth to his servants 'according to their ability', and how the first two servants set to work and double the money entrusted to them. The third servant, by contrast, digs a hole and hides the money in the ground – a recognised way of preserving something, and a guaranteed way of not increasing it! The master returns after a long time, and calls the servants to account. The first two servants are commended: 'Well done, good and faithful servant, you have been faithful with few things, I will appoint you in charge of many things. Enter into the joy of your lord.' The 'few things' with which they had been entrusted were not, of course, few by most standards, but this emphasises the man's greatness and the implication is that great responsibility will be replaced by even greater responsibility, and by a special position in the master's favour and friendship. We are reminded of the rewards given to the steward (in that parable) and to the five wise girls (in that parable).

The story then turns to the third servant, who explains his unproductive inactivity as due to fear of his master's 'hardness' – 'reaping where you did not sow and gathering where you did not scatter' (*i.e.* taking the fruits of others' labours for himself). The master in his reply picks up the servant's words about his rapaciousness, not, of course, to agree with them, but to make the point that the servant should have done what he knew was expected, at least putting the money into the bank and earning interest. The servant excuses himself as frightened; the master calls him 'wicked and lazy' and 'useless'. His reward is the opposite of that of the first two servants: his one talent is taken away from him and is given to the servant who had ten, and he himself is thrown into 'outer darkness'.

In this parable the focus is not on the unexpectedness of the time of the master's return, but simply on the responsibility and accountability of the servants. The parable underlines points made in the other parables, but, if the parable of the steward emphasises the need for faithfulness as opposed to self-indulgence, the parable of the talents emphasises the need for work and productivity rather than laziness and timidity. The man who hides his talent under the ground is reminiscent of the one who hides his lamp under a jar when it ought to be used to give light (Mt 5:15), and the taking of the talent from the lazy one and the giving of it to the one with ten talents is reminiscent of the saying about the measure one gives and gets (Mk 4:24).

How is the talent to be understood? The reference could be literally to financial provision, and the parable could be taken as a parable about stewardship of money. But it is probably more broadly intended to refer to the various resources that the Lord entrusts to his people. It is notable that it is said that the master gives to each 'according to his ability', and he expects every servant to put what he is given to use. The thought is closely similar to the understanding of spiritual gifts found in the epistles: thus Paul in Romans 12:3–8 speaks of the differing gifts given to each and urges that they be put to use; and in Ephesians 4:7–8 he speaks of Christ at his ascension giving gifts – 'to each one of us grace has been given as Christ apportioned it' (cf. 1 Pet 4:7–11).

Luke's parable that resembles Matthew's parable of the talents is his parable of the pounds or minas. This is like Matthew's parable in certain respects: servants are given money to trade with by a master when he goes away; two servants do very well, and are rewarded with increased authority – in fact they are put in charge of cities. The third wraps his money up and returns it to the master unused, excusing himself by describing his master's harshness and being rewarded by the loss of what he had. Both Matthew and Luke end the parable with the saying of Jesus: 'To everyone who has, more will be given, but from the one who has nothing, even what he has will be taken away.'

The differences from Matthew include the amount of money entrusted to the servants – in Luke each servant receives one mina only, being a very modest amount, equivalent to about a hundred days' wages. More significantly Luke's parable calls the master a nobleman, and explains that he was going away to get a kingdom for himself. When he does so, Luke's story describes how the citizens of the country send a delegation after him asking that he not be made king. But in vain. When he returns, he not only calls his servants to account for the money they were given, but he has 'these enemies of mine' killed in front of him.

The differences between Matthew's parable and Luke's have been variously explained. Jesus surely told parables many times and in different forms, and we may have here two of his variants on a theme. Or another possibility is that Luke has woven two parables together, one like Matthew's parable about the servants' responsibility, the other about enemies of the aspiring king.

The story of the aspiring king would have rung very loud bells with Jesus' contemporaries, because Herod the Great's son, Archelaus, who is mentioned in Matthew 2:22, did almost exactly what the parable describes in 4 BC. His father, the Herod of Matthew 1 and 2 who tried to eliminate the infant Jesus, died in 4 BC, and in his will left his mini-empire to three of his sons. He left Galilee to Herod Antipas, the man who killed John the Baptist and tried Jesus; but he left Judea (including Jerusalem) and Samaria to Archelaus. He also bequeathed to him the title of king. But Herod's bequests were all subject in the long run to the approval of the Romans; Herod the Great had been subject to them and supported by them. And when he died, Archelaus went off to Rome, a very long journey, to get his position as king and ruler of Judea and Samaria confirmed. The Jews had not liked the ruthlessness of Archelaus' father, Herod, and they knew Archelaus to be a chip off the old block. Accordingly they sent a delegation off to Rome to petition against Archelaus. In the event the Romans confirmed Archelaus' position, though they did not grant him the title 'king', and within ten years they removed him from office because of his conspicuous maladministration.

The similarity between the historical event and the story of the parable is striking, and it has rightly been said that no one but Jesus himself would have used the rather unsavoury Archelaus for comparison with himself!

The story complements that of the servants with the pounds. If that story explains that the servants of Christ the Lord will have to give account of their service when he returns, receiving reward or punishment, the other story speaks of judgement at the same time on those who are not servants and who reject the kingship of Christ. It is possible that the thought is of the Jews in particular being the 'citizens of the country' who reject their appointed king; but it is probably a broader warning of judgement on unbelievers. The Lord will be absent for a while, but he will return and bring in the kingdom, rewarding faithful servants, but judging his enemies and unfaithful servants.

Before leaving the parable, we should return briefly to

comment on another difference between Matthew's parable
and Luke's. As we saw, in Matthew the servants are given
differing amounts to trade with, five talents, two talents and
one talent respectively; when they return them to the master,
the two faithful servants have made proportionate profits
(five and two talents), and they are rewarded equally. In
Luke's parable the servants are given equal amounts, one
mina each; and when they return them the two faithful
servants have made ten and five minas more respectively,
and they are rewarded proportionately with rule over ten
and five cities.

The difference may be insignificant, but it is possible that
the two forms of the parable are expressing complementary
truths. Luke's parable suggests that all who join the revolution are equal before God and will be judged according to
their faithfulness. We may compare Paul's teaching: 'We
were all baptised by one Spirit into one body – whether Jews
or Greeks, slave or free – and we were all given the one Spirit
to drink,' and: 'We must all appear before the judgment seat
of Christ, that each one may receive what is due to him for
things done while in the body, whether good or bad' (1 Cor
12:13; 2 Cor 5:10).

Matthew's parable suggests that all who join the revolution
are different, and will be judged equally according to how
they have used their particular gifts. Again Paul's teaching in
1 Corinthians 12 comes to mind, where he speaks of people
who have different gifts, some more prominent than others.
The principle that 'from everyone who has been given much,
much will be required' is expressed both in Luke 12:47–48,
which speaks of the servant who knowingly disobeys his
master's will being punished more severely than the servant
who ignorantly fails in his duty, and also in the words of
James about teachers in the church being judged with greater
strictness than others (Jas 3:1).

Where Matthew and Luke come together is in the
paradoxical-sounding comment on the lazy servant: 'To everyone who has, more will be given, but as for the one who has
nothing, even what he has will be taken away.' The point is a
straightforward one, which we met before in chapter 4: the

rewards of the revolution are for those who work for the revolution, not for those who, like the lazy servant, have nothing to show the master.

Ideas of judgement, reward and punishment are rather out of fashion in modern Christianity, but they were important in Jesus' thinking. Two observations on this are in order. First, our parables do not teach that entry into the revolution of God is through human effort or worth. They are about those in the revolution being judged on the basis of their faithfulness. There is an implication that Christian disciples can bring judgement on themselves by disobedience, but not that people enter the master's service other than by his mercy (which is what other parables make clear). Second, although the parables give no comfort to those who view God as a harmless and benevolent father-figure who will let everyone into the kingdom whatever their belief or conduct, the master is harsh only to those who are deliberately rebellious or lazy. To others he is a good master who gives gifts to his servants and rewards them generously for their faithful service.

A last comment: Christians have sometimes pictured heaven as a state of rather passive adoration. Jesus in the parables of the pounds and the talents, as in that of the steward, speaks of the faithful being rewarded in the kingdom with the privilege of greater service and responsibility. The perfect peace of God's revolution is not sleep, but is life wonderfully renewed and relationships restored (the *shalom* of the Old Testament) – a life of joy and service in God's presence (*cf.* Rev 7:15).

### The sheep and the goats (Mt 25:31–46)

Many parables, such as that of the sower, consist of a story which is followed by an interpretation. But in some parables the story and the interpretation are interwoven with each other to a greater or lesser degree. The parable of the sheep and the goats is a good example of this, being a mixture of straight description (*e.g.* 'when the Son of Man comes') and of the pictorial (*e.g.* 'as a shepherd separates the sheep from the goats'). Even that may be too simple a way of putting it, since there are two pictures in the parable – the picture of a king on his throne, as well as that of the herdsman with his herd. The parable portrays the Son of Man coming and sitting on his glorious throne. The nations are gathered before him, and he separates the gathered multitudes into two categories – like a shepherd separating a mixed flock of sheep and goats. Such mixed flocks were common enough, both because it was economical to work with one herd, but also, apparently, because the more restless goats tended to keep the herd on the move and so to produce more effective grazing in sparsely vegetated areas. But at night the herdsman would divide up his herd so that the hardier sheep could be left outside and the goats be brought in overnight. Judgement day will be like that, the story explains: there will be a sorting out of sheep and goats, or (in the terms of the earlier parable) of wheat and weeds. On that day some will be invited by the king to 'come here, blessed of my Father, and inherit the kingdom prepared for you from the foundation of the world'; others will be told: 'Go from me, you cursed ones, into the eternal fire prepared for the devil and his angels.' The thought is like that of the other parables of the end in that some are invited into the joy of the kingdom in the presence of the king, and others are sent away to punishment.

It is interesting and significant that the Son of Man is described as the king 'sitting on a throne', and also that the kingdom is said to have been prepared for the 'blessed of my Father'. The background to these ideas is probably in the Old Testament. First, we recall the vision of Daniel 7 where the 'Ancient of Days' (*i.e.* God himself) is described as judging the nations and giving rule (or kingdom) to the people of God, represented in the vision by 'one like a son of man'. Second, there are all the passages which speak of God bringing salvation to his people through a new king in the family of David who will rule in justice and righteousness (*e.g.* Isa 9:1–7). Third, we note that the king can be spoken of as 'son' of God in the Old Testament (*e.g.* Ps 2:7). Jesus, as we have seen, understands himself to be the fulfilment of Old Testament prophecy, and in the parable of the sheep and the goats he looks forward to the time when God will finally give the kingdom to his people in and through him as Son of Man, and when as God's promised king and Son of God he will judge the nations, saving and caring for his needy people.

But, if this is the background to the parable, what is the difference between the sheep and the goats in the story? It is, as in the previous parables, the difference between faithfulness and unfaithfulness to the Lord. But this time this faithfulness is defined for us as caring for those whom the king calls 'his brothers': 'I was hungry and you gave me something to eat, I was thirsty and you gave me something to drink, I was a stranger and you took me in, I was naked and you clothed me, I was ill and you visited me, I was in prison and you came to me ... In as far as you did it to one of the least of these brothers of mine you did it for me.'

If we were in some doubt about the meaning of 'using one's talent' well for the Master, there is no such obscurity in this case. Specific down-to-earth examples of caring service are given. We are reminded of the equally practical parable of the good Samaritan, expressing Jesus' understanding of 'loving one's neighbour'. Serving the Lord means loving in that practical down-to-earth way.

One striking feature of the story is the way the king (*i.e.* the Son of Man) identifies himself with the hungry, the thirsty, the stranger, the naked, the sick and the imprisoned. He speaks of them as 'my brothers' and explains to his surprised hearers: 'Whatever you did for one of the least of these brothers of mine, you did for me.' Many recent scholars have argued that Jesus is here identifying himself specifically with his disciples, not with the poor in general. It is argued that elsewhere in Matthew Jesus speaks of his disciples, and not others, as his 'brothers', and also of them as 'little ones' (see Mt 10:42; 12:50; 18:10); this is seen as a clue to the meaning of the phrase 'the least of these brothers of mine'. It is also argued that Jesus elsewhere identifies

himself with the disciples in a way that parallels the parable
of the sheep and the goats: so, for example, in Matthew
10:40–42 we find a strikingly similar passage to the parable in
a context that is all about the disciples' mission: 'He who
receives you receives me . . . And if anyone gives even a cup
of cold water to one of these little ones because he is my
disciple, I tell you the truth, he will certainly not lose his
reward.' In the light of these parallels the parable of the
sheep and the goats is seen as a description of the nations
being judged according to their reception of the gospel and
its ambassadors.

This view is plausible at first sight. And yet there is a
significant difference between Matthew 10:40–42, where the
service done to the needy is specifically 'because he is my
disciple', and the parable of the sheep and the goats, where
those helping the needy are surprised to find their work
claimed by the king as done to him. There is nothing in the
parable to suggest that the poor and needy referred to are
specifically disciples, unless the words 'the least of these my
brothers' are taken that way. But the words by themselves
are not a very obvious indication that it is specifically Jesus'
followers who are in mind: within the parable they are a
natural enough way for the king to express his identification
with even his least favoured citizens.

It seems likely, then, that the traditional view that Jesus is
here identifying with the needy in general is correct. There is
plenty of other evidence in Jesus' teaching, as in his ministry
as a whole, of his particular concern for the oppressed and
distressed of society. The parable is, then, correctly seen as
Jesus' classic statement of Christian social responsibility:
judgement will be on the basis of whether we love our
neighbour as ourselves, and our neighbour is defined in the
parable of the good Samaritan as anyone in need. The test of
whether someone belongs to those who are 'blessed by my
Father' or to those who are accursed and of the devil is
whether that person is living the life of the revolution, as
Jesus did; the thought is closely similar to that of the parable
of the wheat and the weeds, with its distinction between the
'righteous', sown by the Son of Man, and the 'workers of

lawlessness', sown by the evil one. But now righteousness and lawlessness are illustrated. The revolution of God is seen clearly through this parable to be something practical, not purely a matter of belief. In this respect too the revolution of God is the fulfilment of Old Testament righteousness, as expressed, for example, in the famous words of Micah: 'What does the Lord require of you? To act justly and to love mercy and to walk humbly with your God' (Mic 6:8). In the New Testament James puts it as follows: 'Religion that God our Father accepts as pure and faultless is this: to look after orphans and widows in their distress and to keep oneself from being polluted by the world' (Jas 1:27).

There are two common misconceptions about the parable of the sheep and the goats. The first is that the parable teaches that acts of mercy done outside of the context of faith may bring salvation. This is a popular view in the secular West, where being a nice person who helps others is seen as more important than religious commitment. The parable is thought to show that service to the poor is service to Christ, even when it is not intended as such, and that it will be judged as such on the last day.

This is, however, to read into the parable a twentieth-century view that is in contradiction to the strong emphasis on belief found elsewhere in Jesus' teaching. It is always important to recognise the limitations of individual parables. None of the parables of judgement which we have been looking at in this chapter teaches justification by human goodness or achievement; they are all about how the disciple should live for his Lord. It is interesting that the phrase 'blessed by my Father' is used in the parable of those showing compassion to the needy, and that a very similar phrase is used in Matthew 16:17 of Peter when he recognised and confessed Jesus as Messiah. Putting two and two together, we may justifiably conclude that it is those who have faith in Jesus and live it out in practical action who are 'blessed'. The parable of the sheep and the goats is thus a description of how those who call Jesus 'Lord' (see Mt 25:37, 44) should live. It is making the same point as those awesome words of Jesus in Matthew 7:21–23:

Not everyone who says to me, 'Lord, Lord' will enter the kingdom of heaven, but only he who does the will of my Father who is in heaven. Many will say to me on that day, 'Lord, Lord, did we not prophesy in your name, and in your name drive out demons and perform many miracles?' Then I will tell them plainly, 'I never knew you. Away from me, you evildoers!'

Another modern misapplication of the parable is to take the king's words, 'I was hungry and you gave me something to eat . . .' etc., to mean that Jesus is somehow 'in' the poor of the world because of their poverty. But this is again to read a modern notion into the parable. The parable does speak of the king seeing service to his needy citizens as service to himself, but this does not imply that he is 'within' the poor. Similarly Jesus identifies with the poor: but this is because he is a king who cares for his people, not because he is 'in' them, and the poor like the rich have to repent and believe in order to enter the revolution.

We have criticised those who use the parable improperly in emphasising the Christian's social responsibility. The parable does nevertheless stress that responsibility in a vivid way, making clear how much the Lord cares for those who suffer. The parable is a severe warning to those who see the revolution of God as something purely spiritual and to do with 'my personal relationship with God', and who fail to see that the kingdom is a practical down-to-earth revolution and that no amount of spiritual gifts, or fervour in calling Jesus Lord, will be persuasive on judgement day. Jesus calls his followers to be a revolutionary, caring community, not comfortable conservationists protecting the status quo.

# 6 GOOD NEWS FOR THE NEEDY

*Doctor to the sick* (Mt 9:12; Mk 2:17; Lk 5:31–32)

Human revolutions are usually good news for some people and bad news for others. Jesus' announcement of the coming of God's revolution also cut two ways. But it was first and foremost good news. We saw this in chapter 3, for example in the saying about the children in the marketplace, which contrasted John the Baptist's sombre ministry with its focus on judgement and Jesus' ministry with its focus on God's mercy. That saying was a comment on the accusation that Jesus was 'a friend of tax-collectors and sinners'.

The accusation was not unjustified, since it was indeed one of the striking characteristics of Jesus' ministry that he not only proclaimed the love of God for sinners but also expressed it in practice. The sight of Jesus, a religious leader, sitting down to table with corrupt tax-collectors, immoral prostitutes and other known bad characters set his critics buzzing with disapproval. Eating with people meant a lot in the first-century Jewish world; it meant acceptance and recognition. In the context of Jesus' announcement that the kingdom of God had come, his eating with conspicuous sinners suggested that the kingdom was open to such people. How could that be?

The answer is that God's revolution, proclaimed and brought by Jesus, was a revolution bringing deliverance. That idea of the kingdom was, of course, well understood by Jesus' contemporaries, but whereas they thought in terms of national deliverance from foreign oppression and of personal deliverance for the righteous, Jesus had a bigger concept; God's revolution meant deliverance for the needy, the oppressed and the depressed, for the sick, the demon-possessed and the sinners. Jesus' opponents expected sinners to be judged in the coming kingdom, and, although they subscribed in theory to the desirability of getting sinners to repent, in practice they tended to keep away from evildoers and they expected God to endorse their condemnation of the unclean and ungodly. When Jesus mixed with such people and announced the coming of God's kingdom to them, this contradicted what his opponents stood for and was very uncomfortable to them. Jesus seemed to be undermining their high standards, and they protested vocally.

A good number of Jesus' parables are in response to such protests. We have to look to Matthew and especially to Luke for these parables. But Mark too has Jesus' pithy saying: 'It is not the healthy who need a doctor, but the sick. I have not come to call the righteous, but sinners' (Mk 2:17). In this mini-parable Jesus justifies his distinctive ministry to the obvious sinners of society very forcefully. He does not mean to imply that his religious opponents are actually righteous in the sight of God, but only to explain how ministry to the irreligious has a very clear rationale, even on their premises. He was not in the business of lowering the standards of the kingdom of God, or of identifying with people for the sake of it, but of healing people for the kingdom.

This understanding of the kingdom may have seemed strange to his contemporaries, but it was the fulfilment of the Old Testament vision of God's revolution (as he made clear). We might compare Jesus' work to the modern eye-camp in countries like India, where a team of doctors descend on a village or town for a week or more and invite all who need help to come for free care and treatment: crowds of needy people are helped. Jesus' revolution was such a healing campaign.

The point was demonstrated, of course by Jesus' own healing of the physically sick. But his mission was one that involved physical, social and spiritual healing, because that is the nature of the kingdom of God.

## The two debtors (Lk 7:41–50)

Luke has a particular interest in Jesus' ministry to the disadvantaged. It comes out at the beginning of his gospel in his description of Jesus' infancy, for example in Mary's song, the 'Magnificat', in which she speaks of God scattering the proud, lifting up the humble, filling the hungry with good things and sending the rich away empty (Lk 1:46–55). It comes out in his description of Jesus' programmatic sermon at Nazareth, with its text from Isaiah 61: 'The Spirit of the Lord is on me, because he has anointed me to preach good news to the poor . . . to proclaim freedom for the prisoners and recovery of sight for the blind, to release the oppressed . . .' (Lk 4:18–19). It comes out in his version of the Beatitudes: 'Blessed are you who are poor . . . Woe to you who are rich' (Lk 6:20, 24). It comes out in his description of Jesus' ministry to outcasts like Zacchaeus, with its striking concluding sentence, 'For the Son of Man came to seek and to save the lost' (Lk 19:10).

It comes out too in his parables. Thus in Luke 7, Luke describes Jesus having dinner in a Pharisee's house. (It is notable that, for all the hard things he has to say about the rich and the religious, Jesus does not stay away from them or refrain from fellowship with them.) While dinner is going on, a woman who is a known sinner, presumably a village prostitute, comes to the house and goes over to where Jesus is reclining for the meal.

We may guess that it was a big meal, with a lot of coming and going of servants and with others from the village looking on. At formal meals the custom was to recline on couches to eat: guests would lean on their left elbows with their legs tucked behind them and eat with their right hands from dishes placed in front of them, probably on low tables. Luke describes the woman coming behind where Jesus was reclining, weeping profusely over Jesus' feet and wiping them with her hair, then kissing his feet and pouring expensive perfume over them. It is an extraordinary scene, and not surprisingly it caused embarrassment and comment.

The comment of the host at the feast was that this disproved Jesus' claim to be from God. Perhaps he had invited Jesus to his house out of critical curiosity to see what the controversial teacher was really like, and hoping to catch him out. Certainly he did not go out of his way to make Jesus welcome, as becomes clear later in the story. He comments that, had Jesus been a real prophet, he would have recognised the woman as a sinner and he would have had nothing to do with her: the Pharisees prided themselves on keeping themselves separate from anything impure; in the eyes of his host Jesus was allowing himself to be defiled by physical contact with this particularly unclean woman.

In this context Jesus tells his parable of the two debtors who were unable to pay their debts and who were both let off free by a remarkably generous money-lender; the one was excused a debt of five hundred denarii – well over a year's wages – and the other fifty denarii. Jesus ends this parable, like others such as the good Samaritan, with a question that gets the person to whom it is directed to bring out the point of the story: 'Which of them will love him more?' The answer is obvious.

Jesus then goes on to apply the point to the cases of his host and the sinful woman: he compares her emotional and extravagant welcome with the cool reception he received from his host. His host's hospitality did not even extend to courtesies such as providing water for Jesus to wash his feet. People entering a house would leave their shoes at the entrance, and it was a special courtesy for someone, most likely a slave, to wash the dust from guests' feet. The Pharisee did not do that. Nor did he greet Jesus with a kiss, though it would be normal to kiss a friend on the cheek, or a teacher on his hand. Nor did he anoint Jesus' head with olive oil, the commonest and cheapest oil. In fact he did not go out of his way to do anything.

It is possible that he was being deliberately insulting, and that the woman and others present noted the insult. If she did, then she may have wished to make up for what Simon the host had failed to do. But it is probable that her actions were more spontaneous expressions of love. She had presumably came to this unlikely place – a Pharisee's house – because she knew of Jesus or perhaps had heard him. Joachim Jeremias thinks that Jesus may have been asked by

his Pharisee host to preach a sermon before the meal, and
that the woman heard that. In any case, we may guess that
she had been touched by his message of God's love for
sinners such as herself – note Jesus' comment on 'her faith'
in verse 50 – and she came to express her gratitude. She
brought with her a stone flask of perfume: some women
apparently wore such a flask around the neck to enhance
their attractiveness; the prostitute now has another use for
her flask. Perhaps she wanted to anoint Jesus' head with it.
But when she comes up behind him, she breaks down, and
her tears fall on Jesus' feet. She has no towel to dry them,
and so she takes off her head-covering and lets her hair fall
down, using that to dry Jesus' feet. For a woman to undo
her hair in public was a disgrace – grounds for divorce
according to some rabbis! But she is oblivious to convention:
she pours kisses on Jesus' feet and uses her perfume –
something much more costly than the olive oil that Simon
did not use – to anoint Jesus' feet. The feet were for obvious
reasons the dirtiest part of the body, and to minister to
someone's feet was the lowliest of tasks. She expresses her
humility and love in a dramatic and moving way.

The Pharisee completely fails to see the extraordinary
significance of the action by the woman, and what had
happened to her. He continues simply to see her as the local
prostitute, and accuses Jesus of spiritual blindness in letting
himself be touched by such a woman. Jesus does not let this
go, and, even though it was not the done thing for a guest to
question his host's hospitality, he explains that the difference
between Simon's minimal welcome and her generous welcome
is the difference between the two forgiven debtors: the one
forgiven much is the one who will love much. The remarkable
implication is that the woman has been forgiven by or
through Jesus. And, to the astonishment of the other guests,
Jesus says exactly that: 'Your sins are forgiven.' Jesus, it
turns out, is not condoning sin by his actions, but expressing
the forgiveness of God. And he brings that forgiveness not to
the upright Pharisee, but to a woman and a prostitute. A
revolution indeed.

In one respect the Pharisee was correct: he saw sin as

something serious, not lightly forgiven (contrast much modern thinking). Jesus interestingly pictures sin as 'debt' both in the parable, but also in the Lord's Prayer: 'Forgive us our debts, as we forgive those indebted to us' (Mt 6:12, literally translated). Our English translations follow Luke's lead in preferring words such as 'trespass' or 'sin' rather than debt (*cf.* Lk 11:4). But the concept of 'indebtedness' has value in making it clear that 'sin' is not something vaguely unpleasant, but is something that comes between people and, with potentially fatal consequences, between us and God.

Jesus brought the good news of God's forgiveness of those unable to pay their 'debts'. The revolution of God is a revolution of forgiveness. Those in the revolution are those who have received that forgiveness through Jesus, and whose lives are (or should be) marked by grateful love for Jesus, such as the woman showed, and by a forgiving spirit towards others, such as is described in the Lord's Prayer. (We shall return to this point when looking at the parable of the unmerciful servant in chapter 8.)

### The lost sheep and the good shepherd (Lk 15:1–7; Mt 18:12–14; Jn 10:1–18)

The classic chapter for Jesus' good news for sinners is Luke 15, where we find the parables of the lost sheep, the lost coin and the lost son (usually known as the parable of the prodigal son). The chapter is introduced with the now-familiar protest of his opponents about his fraternising with the sinners of society.

By way of reply Jesus first compares the situation of the man who loses a sheep from his flock and then goes out to find it. Sheep and shepherds were very much a part of everyday life in rural Palestine. Some people looked down on shepherds, but the profession had an honourable history. King David was shepherd of the family flock, and God is often spoken of as shepherd of his people in the Old Testament, for example in that best-known of psalms, Psalm 23. Other notable passages speaking of shepherds and sheep include Isaiah 40:11, which speaks of God's salvation coming to Zion and says: 'He tends his flock like a shepherd: He gathers the lambs in his arms and carries them close to his heart...' In Ezekiel 34 God denounces the faithlessness of the leaders of Israel, who were meant to be the people's shepherds, and promises both that he will be their shepherd – 'I will search for the lost and bring back the strays' – and also that 'I will place over them one shepherd, my servant David, and he will tend them' (Ezek 34:16,23). The thought of a coming Messiah-king is also found in the famous Christmas passage about one arising out of Bethlehem, and 'he will stand and shepherd his flock' (Mic 5:4). The idea of straying sheep comes out in another well-known passage, Isaiah 53:6: 'We all, like sheep, have gone astray, each of us has turned to his own way; and the Lord has laid on him the iniquity of us all.'

Jesus' parable speaks of a shepherd with a hundred sheep, quite a sizeable flock, maybe belonging to several people but cared for by the one shepherd. The shepherd would care for the flock, leading them across the often dry hillsides to suitable grazing pastures and bringing them back to the village at night, if he was near enough to do so. Discovering the loss of one of the hundred, the shepherd of the parable gives all of his attention to finding the lost one, leaving the ninety-nine.

We need not suppose that he leaves the ninety-nine wandering free in the open country for any length of time. Quite likely he has a boy with him, or he gets another shepherd to take the ninety-nine back to the village for him. An interesting modern example of this is the Arab goatherd who discovered in previously unknown caves the famous Dead Sea Scrolls in 1947. He did so when looking for a lost goat, having left the remainder of his flock with two fellow shepherds. The shepherd of the parable may have made similar arrangements for his flock. But what the parable emphasises is that he leaves the ninety-nine and gives himself to looking for the one lost sheep. Although it might seem insignificant – only one in a hundred – the lost sheep is his priority.

When he finds it, the simplest way for the shepherd to get

the probably terrified animal back to the flock is for him to carry it, heavy though it is. Accordingly he puts it on his shoulders with the legs around his neck, and, holding the legs, makes his way back to the village, where people will probably have heard of his loss. There he shares his good news with his friends and neighbours. In the small village community such joys and sorrows are shared. To lose a sheep was no small loss, and the shepherd is naturally very happy at finding the wanderer.

The focus of the parable is on the effort expended and the joy experienced because of just one lost and found sheep. The point of the parable is explained in Luke 15:7: 'I tell you that in the same way there will be more rejoicing in heaven over one sinner who repents than over ninety-nine persons who do not need to repent.' In the context of the controversy over his ministry to sinners, Jesus explains that his ministry is one of seeking the lost, and claims that it indicates God's priorities (reflected in the 'rejoicing in heaven').

There is, again, no need to infer that Jesus' reference to 'ninety-nine righteous persons who need no repentance' means that he saw the Pharisees and their ilk as really righteous. It is obvious from other things he said, for example from the parable of the Pharisee and tax-collector (which we shall shortly look at), that he did not. But Jesus' words are both an explanation of his ministry to those who saw themselves as the ninety-nine – which was logical on their own premises – and also an explanation of God's priorities as they truly are, since he really does rejoice more over the bringing back of the lost than over anything else.

Some people have argued that the explanation of the parable in Luke does not fit, since it refers to the 'sinner who repents' and the parable does not refer to the sheep 'repenting'. But that is a thoroughly unpersuasive argument. The emphasis of the parable is certainly not on the sheep repenting; but it is on the shepherd putting all his effort into bringing the lost sheep back, and that, being interpreted, means being brought back from sin to righteousness, which entails repentance.

The significance of the parable for an understanding of

Jesus' ministry is considerable. Jesus sees himself as bringing joy to God, as God's promised shepherd – God's new David, we may infer – and as doing the work of God as described in the Old Testament. The revolution promised in the Old Testament is one in which God intervenes to rescue his lost sheep; Jesus claims to have brought that revolution.

In Matthew 18 there is a parable very similar to that of Luke 15. But in this context it is applied not to the ministry of Jesus to sinners but to the ministry of the church to its erring members. Just as in the Lukan parable Jesus speaks of 'rejoicing in heaven' over repentant sinners, so in Matthew Jesus says: 'your Father in heaven is not willing that any one of these little ones should be lost'. Many people believe that both Matthew and Luke's parables derive from a common original which has been differently applied in the different gospels. This may be so. But there is every probability that Jesus used the idea of finding a lost sheep more than once. It would be natural enough for Jesus to use the same picture as a description of his ministry to the 'lost sheep of the house of Israel' as well as of his ministry to the 'little flock' of his disciples (Mt 15:24; Lk 12:32; Mt 26:31), and to use it to describe both his own ministry and that of his followers (Mt 10:6; 15:24). Indeed it is characteristic of Jesus' instructions for his disciples that he calls them to be like him, to have his priorities (reaching out to the lost in this case, rather than feeding the ninety-nine or mending the fold!), and to carry on his work (see chapter 8).

Before moving on to the parable of the lost coin, we will digress to look briefly at John's parable about the shepherd and his sheep (Jn 10:1–18). Here the thought is not of the shepherd bringing back a lost sheep, but more generally of the shepherd's care of his flock. As with Matthew's parable of the sheep and the goats, so in John 10 the picture and its interpretation are interwoven with each other. To be more precise, there are several distinct sheep/shepherd pictures in the passage.

The first picture is of sheep in a sheepfold. We may imagine a walled courtyard attached to a village house, having a gate and a watchman on duty at night, where a number of flocks could be kept together. In the morning the different shepherds would come and call their sheep out, leading them to pasture. Shepherds knew their own sheep and gave them names (such as 'Long-ears' and 'White-nose'!), and the sheep would recognise their owner's voice, following him and not others. The danger to sheep in a sheepfold was from thieves and burglars climbing over the wall to grab some valuable prey for themselves.

Jesus uses this picture to describe his relationship with his followers; he is the shepherd who cares for his flock, knowing them personally and being known by them. Jesus contrasts himself with others – the thieves and robbers; in the context of his ministry he probably has in mind the Jewish religious leaders who opposed his ministry and tried to prevent people following him. We may recall his comment in the temple: 'Is it not written: "My house will be called a house of prayer for all nations"? But you have made it "a den of robbers"'' (Mk 11:17).

The second picture is of Jesus as 'the gate' through which the sheep enter and leave the fold, finding protection inside at night and pasture outside by day. An ingenious suggestion is that the picture is of the shepherd lying across the gateway of the fold at night – a known practice – and thus literally being 'the door'. We would thus still be thinking of the good shepherd, but in the role of door. But there is no need to reconcile the different pictures in John 10 in that way. It is just as likely that the picture has changed, and that Jesus is now being portrayed not as a shepherd to whom a door keeper would open, but actually as a door – a door giving access to 'life'. A similar idea is expressed in the parable of the narrow gate and the narrow way (see chapter 10); the narrow gate, according to Matthew 7:14, 'leads to life', i.e. to the life of the kingdom of God. John 10 has the same picture, speaking of life in all its fullness, i.e. life in the revolution of God.

The third picture is again of the shepherd, this time as one who cares for his sheep self-sacrificially. The contrast is with the 'hired shepherd' who runs away to save his skin when wolves come. Sheep had two enemies: human predators and animal predators, especially in the form of wolves. Other sayings of Jesus allude to the dangers of wolves, as when Jesus ominously warns his disciples that he is sending them out as 'sheep among wolves' (Mt 10:16). The hired servant faced with wolves will run rather than risk his life for the sheep (though he may be expected to pay compensation for their loss); his relationship with the flock is not a close one. The owner of the sheep is quite different: the sheep are his, and he is willing to face danger to protect them. The caring owner is often genuinely fond of his sheep, and does give himself sacrificially to their care. Jesus is that sort of shepherd, and his self-sacrifice was not just in terms of effort expended or danger faced, but quite literally meant laying down his life for his flock.

The fourth picture is of a shepherd with some sheep in the sheepfold and others kept elsewhere, and of him bringing them together in one united flock. In Ezekiel 34 the promise was that the Lord would gather his people Israel, and Jesus speaks in Matthew 10:6; 15:24 of his mission to the lost sheep of the house of Israel. But Jesus also speaks, as we have seen, of the 'word of the kingdom' being preached to all nations, and the picture of the shepherd bringing sheep from outside the fold into one flock with those in the fold is undoubtedly a picture of the Gentiles being brought in with those from the house of Israel to make one united people. The revolution of God is something world-embracing, and God's design is for unity between God and mankind, between Jew and Gentile, under the Lordship of Jesus the good shepherd (see Jn 17:20–23; Eph 2:11–18).

### The lost coin (Lk 15:8–10)

In Luke 15 Jesus first of all compares his ministry to sinners to a man working out of doors looking after his sheep, but then to a woman in the home who loses one of ten silver coins. We are probably to think of some special coins, perhaps a string of them used as a necklace or headband which may have been given to the woman at the time of her wedding. Silver coins were not commonplace among poor people, and so losing one of them was a serious thing, and finding them in a dark peasant home was not necessarily easy. Jesus describes the woman's strenuous efforts to find the missing coin – her lighting of a lamp, her sweeping out of the house (probably with a broom made of branches), her careful searching and her joy when she meets with success. Perhaps an equivalent in our well-lit houses is looking for a contact lens that has fallen out, or for a stone from a ring – often a painfully slow task, but also often rewarded with joyful discovery.

The story, like that of the lost sheep, is said by Jesus to illustrate the 'rejoicing in the presence of the angels' over the repentant sinner. By this he means God's own rejoicing; but, as was typical of Jews who for reasons of reverence tended to avoid mentioning God too directly, he speaks of 'rejoicing in heaven' or 'in the presence of the angels'.

The parable of the lost sheep highlighted the shepherd's attitude to the ninety-nine and his concern for the one lost sheep; in this second parable the focus is more on the strenuous effort of the woman in looking for what was lost. Although we are accustomed to speak of the parables of the lost sheep and of the lost coin, in both stories the focus is less on the lost one and more on the concern of the looking one – on his priorities and on her strenuous efforts to recover her loss. Jesus thus explains his ministry: the lost are his priority, and he goes to every length in order to find and restore them. (He is no half-hearted evangelist.) His ministry may annoy his opponents, but, he explains, it brings joy to the God of heaven whom they profess to worship.

### The prodigal son (Lk 15:11–32)

From a lost sheep to a lost coin to a lost son. The parable of the prodigal (*i.e.* wasteful) son has been called 'the gospel within the gospel', and not without reason, since there is no more powerful a picture of the forgiving love of God or of the motivation behind Jesus' ministry within the Bible.

The story begins by introducing us to a father and his two sons, the younger of whom tells his father to give him his share of the family inheritance, which would have been a third of the total inheritance, so presumably a sizeable sum. This apparently blunt demand gets the story off to a dramatic start, since the boy would not normally have received his inheritance until his father's death. Even if the father made his property over to his sons in his lifetime, it was understood that he would continue to have the use of it until his death. So the younger son in demanding his share and turning it into cash was flouting convention, ignoring his God-given responsibility to care for his father and mother, and, more than that, insulting his father, saying in effect: 'I wish you were dead'.

Had he put the money to good use, the boy's offence might not have been so heinous. But the parable goes on to describe him going into a far country and wasting his inheritance. He squanders his money in wild living: we can imagine the eating, the drinking, the girl-friends, the fast cars (or camels, as a friend of mine suggested!) and so on. The story does not bother to spell that out. What is clear and what matters is that the boy has disgraced the family by frittering away the inheritance. He is in a far country in more senses than one.

But he reaps the consequences. What may be regarded as the second scene of the parable describes how, when the boy has run through all his money, he is left with nothing and no one. Then a famine comes; they were all too common in the ancient world, not least in Palestine (see Acts 11:27–30 for example). He becomes desperate, and takes work feeding pigs. To Jesus' hearers, feeding pigs for a foreigner was about as low as one could go: pigs were unclean animals according to Jewish law. As a Jewish rabbi put it bluntly, 'Cursed be the man who keeps swine'.

Even that job did not stave off his desperate hunger: Jesus describes how the boy longed to eat even the carob beans which he fed to the pigs. Commentators are not sure whether the reference is to the fleshy, brown pods of the *Ceratonia siliqua*, a sweet and perfectly edible fruit, or to the black berries of the wild carob, which were normally used as fuel rather than food, and which were particularly unpleasant to eat. Whichever it was, it was a terrible come-down from what he had been used to, and in any case 'no one gave him anything'.

It is that desperate situation which brings him to his senses and turns his mind back to his father who had given him so much. He realises that he has no claim on his father's kindness, quite the opposite. But he is dying in the far country, and so he has nothing to lose by returning home, confessing his fault, and asking not for a restoration of his previous privileges but for employment as a servant. So 'he got up and went to his father'.

So far in the story the father has hardly featured, except as the one sinned against by his rebel son. But in the next scene of the story the focus switches to him. While his son is still far off, he 'sees' him and 'has pity' on him. The word 'have pity' is one used quite frequently in the gospels of Jesus' attitude to those in need, and it suggests being inwardly moved: we might appropriately translate it 'his heart went out to him'. The fact that the father saw the boy while he was still far away is suggestive: it is not actually said that he was looking for his son, but that is certainly a possible implication. The father's response towards his runaway son could easily have been one of rejection and anger. Indeed the boy could reasonably have expected a very hostile welcome, not only from his father, but also from the rest of the family and the people of the village, who will have been outraged at his behaviour. However, his father, who had most cause for bitterness, responds quite otherwise: his heart goes out to his boy and he runs to meet him, a quite undignified action for the father of such an oriental family. When he meets the boy, he embraces and kisses him, expressing his welcome and forgiveness before his son has said anything.

Then the boy begins the speech he had prepared for his homecoming: 'Father, I have sinned against heaven [in other words: against God] and against you. I am no longer worthy to be called your son.' He planned to go on with the request that his father take him on as a paid servant. But before he

says anything further, his father breaks in and gives instructions to his servants: first, to bring 'the best robe' and put it
on his son (perhaps this was the robe that the father himself
wore for special occasions); then to put a ring on his hand –
a signet ring was a sign of authority – and sandals on his
feet, sandals being worn by a free man not a slave. So much
for the boy's intended request that he be treated as a servant!
That would have been a sufficient kindness. His father does
not stop there, however: he orders the fattened calf to be
killed and a feast to be prepared. The fattened calf was the
animal reserved for the next big family occasion, such as a
family wedding; but the father orders it to be prepared now.
He is going to have a feast for the village. (A calf was too big
for just a family meal.)

The father's welcome was undeserved and unexpected. But
he explains that rejoicing is appropriate, 'for this my son was
dead and is alive again, he was lost and is found'. We are
reminded, of course, of the parables of the lost sheep and the
lost coin; but this story is the more apposite to Jesus'
ministry, since the lost one is a person, whose lostness is
caused by sin.

But the story does not end with the feast. It has a final
scene, involving the elder brother. He was mentioned at the
start of the parable, and the story would be incomplete
without him being involved. He had been out on the estate
when his renegade brother returned and his father put the
celebrations in motion. He arrives back to find things buzzing
with excitement. On learning from one of the servants what
has happened he is extremely angry, refusing even to go into
the house. The cause and extent of his anger is made clear
when his father comes out to plead with him: he speaks of
how he has 'slaved' for his father for years without reward,
whereas 'this son of yours who has squandered your property
with prostitutes' is welcomed back with the fattened calf. His
bitterness is shown by his description of his own relationship
to his father as 'slavery', by his effective disowning of his
brother in the phrase 'this son of yours', and by his probably
exaggerated and perhaps unfounded accusation that his
brother squandered his father's property on prostitutes.

The boy's reaction is understandable, but is quite at odds with his father's attitude. People have with justification spoken of the parable of two lost sons, since the elder brother, faced with his father's generosity, shows himself entirely out of sympathy with his father. And by refusing to come into the feast he is now the one who is publicly insulting his father in the presence of others. But his father pleads with him, pointing out that the elder brother has nothing to complain about on his own account, since the whole of his father's estate is his: all the calves and goats and everything are his. The father urges on him the appropriateness of rejoicing and being glad, 'because this your brother was dead and is alive again; he was lost and is found'. We are not told if the brother responded to his father's entreaties.

This great parable has two main themes worked out in it. The clue to the first is the repetition of the joyful words about the one who was dead being alive again and the one who was lost being found. These words come at the end of both the first and second parts of the parable, and make it quite clear that the story of the two sons is a picture of Jesus' joyful life-giving ministry to the lost. The clue to the second theme is in the fact that the parable ends with the downbeat description of the elder brother's reaction, as well as in the context of the parable in Luke. The parable is about Jesus' opponents who, like the elder brother, refused to rejoice at his ministry to sinners. We will briefly consider the parable under these two headings.

*First, the parable is unsurpassed as a picture of Jesus' ministry to the lost.* To put it another way, it is unsurpassed in showing how Jesus perceived the purpose and nature of the revolution of God that was coming through his ministry. It is a picture which takes up themes that come out in other parables (notably in the parables of the lost sheep and the lost coin), but it goes beyond the other parables not only in its artistic power, but also in its comprehensiveness and suggestiveness.

What does it suggest? Very simply, that Jesus understood the revolution of God as the bringing back of people from selfish rebellion and death, through repentance, into the love and mercy of God and the joy of the kingdom.

More specifically, the parable gives us a picture of the lost before they are found. In ministering to the sinners and outcasts of society, Jesus was not (as his opponents argued and some modern critics sometimes seem to infer) minimising the seriousness of their sin. On the contrary, he portrays their position as one of outrageous, selfish rebellion against a loving father, the result of which is that they are in a 'far country', 'lost' and (strikingly) 'dead'. There is good reason to view this as Jesus' diagnosis of the human condition in general. Thus other parables also portray rebellion (*e.g.* the pounds – 'We don't want this man to be our king' – and the wicked tenants), selfish greed (*e.g.* the rich fool, and the rich man and Lazarus), being lost (the lost sheep and the lost coin), and awful judgement. The revolution of God comes to undo this deadly situation.

The parable also suggests how this situation is remedied in God's revolution. On the one hand, there is the picture of the boy coming to his senses, abandoning the far country and returning to his father to seek his mercy. This is a graphic picture of the repentance Jesus called for. It is probably significant that the boy has to be brought very low and to experience hunger and even the degradation of keeping a foreigner's pigs before he comes to his senses and sees that he is indeed dead and lost, since it was precisely the poor and the degraded (including those servants of the foreigner, the tax-collectors) who responded to Jesus' ministry. The rich who were still enjoying the temporary pleasures of the far country failed to see their true condition and their need to return. Jesus makes it clear that the way back to God and into the kingdom is to come empty-handed and seeking God's mercy (see the parable of the Pharisee and the tax-collector). On the other hand, there is the picture of the father who had been so insulted looking out for his son, running to meet him and overwhelming him with generous love and undeserved forgiveness. This is how Jesus understood his ministry: God was opening his arms of love to welcome the lost home.

Finally, the parable pictures the purpose and result of the revolution of God. It is about people who have forfeited their sonship being welcomed back as sons through the Father's astonishing love. It is about a joyful feast with marvellous food, with music and dancing; it is a family feast in the Father's home, a reunion to beat all other family reunions. The parable might appear to support the common, modern view that every human being is automatically a child of God rather than the usual New Testament view of people needing to be 'born again' through faith in Jesus in order to be made children of God (*e.g.* Jn 1:13; 3:3). But the parable does not contradict this New Testament view. The prodigal son when he is in the far country is 'dead' in his relationship to his father; he has forfeited his sonship. His coming back into the family is thus indeed being 'born again'; it is coming back to life. The revolution of God is about children coming home to their father, but it is a coming home out of death and disgrace into new life and sonship; it is this that makes the feast so unspeakably joyful (see also 1 Pet 1:3).

Various of the themes of the parable are echoed in Paul's writings, for example in his letter to the Ephesians, where he speaks of his readers as having been 'dead' in trespasses and sin, 'gratifying the cravings' of their sinful natures and being 'objects of wrath', 'But', he says,

> because of his great love for us, God, who is rich in mercy, made us alive with Christ ... and seated us with him in the heavenly realms ... in order that in the coming ages he might show the incomparable riches of his grace, expressed in his kindness to us in Christ Jesus. (Eph 2:1–7)

Those words sum up our parable; it is about God's astonishing love in bringing people back from the death of sin into the kingdom of God through Jesus. It is interesting to see how Paul expresses the idea of the kingdom as something present – we are already in 'the heavenly realms' – and as something future – 'that in the coming ages . . .'

Paul goes on in the same chapter to say: 'But now in Christ Jesus you who once were far away have been brought near through the blood of Christ' (Eph 2:13). In speaking of

his readers as 'once far away' Paul is probably thinking specifically of the fact that they were Gentiles, but the thought is not
far removed from that of Jesus' parable of the son in the far
country. Jesus was thinking of his ministry to the sinners and
outsiders of society; the church's mission to the Gentiles was
very much a continuation and extension of that ministry.

Paul, of course, sees Jesus' death as God's supremely
costly way of reconciling those who were far off and of
bringing the dead back to life. The parable of the prodigal
son does not refer directly to the cross. But the cross was the
climax and focus of Jesus' ministry to sinners, as he
explained when he spoke of himself as a servant come 'to
give his life as a ransom for many' (Mt 20:28; Mk 10:45). He
saw his death as the price paid (the 'ransom') to bring
freedom and forgiveness such as the prodigal son experienced.
He saw his death as the suffering of the servant spoken of in
Isaiah, who took the people's judgement on himself. The
connection of thought between the parables of Luke 15 and
the cross is suggested by the verse in Isaiah referring to the
servant of the Lord: 'We all, like sheep, have gone astray,
each of us has turned to his own way; and the Lord has laid
on him the iniquity of us all' (Isa 53:6). Jesus, God's servant
and good shepherd, brought the lost sheep home by laying
down his life. It was supremely in the cross that God in
Christ went out to meet the prodigal. The phraseology of the
modern eucharistic prayer is powerfully suggestive: 'He
opened wide his arms for us on the cross.'

The 'bright side' of the parable is the finding of the lost
boy. *The second, sombre side is the elder brother.* Jesus uses
the elder brother to portray his religious opponents who
objected to his ministry to sinners. The elder brother saw his
relationship to his father as correct drudgery, giving him
rights in the household, rather than as joyful membership of
the loving father's family. He says in the story: 'I have never
disobeyed your orders,' probably with some justification.
But, when his younger brother comes home, it becomes clear
that his relationship with his father is not at all what it
should be. He is now quite out of tune with his father,
because of his rejection of the father's love. Jesus has in mind

his critics who also claimed to be righteous (with some justification) and in tune with God, but whose rejection of Jesus and his ministry to sinners showed how far they were from the God they claimed to serve.

Jesus in fact regarded their righteousness as superficial and insufficient for entry into the kingdom of God (*e.g.* Mt 5:20; 15:3; 23:23); also, he did not believe that anyone had a 'right' to enter the kingdom in the way the elder brother had rights. But the point of the parable is not to question their claim to righteousness, it is to highlight another and more decisive proof of their alienation from God, *i.e.* their attitude to Jesus and his ministry. Their attitude, like the elder brother's, was cutting them off from the revolution of God. Jesus' parable is a challenge and warning to such people, an invitation to see things Jesus' way – 'We had to celebrate . . .' – and also by implication an invitation to those who know themselves to be in the far country to come home and receive the love of the Father.

## The labourers in the vineyard (Mt 20:1–16)

It is to Matthew that we turn for the next parable about Jesus' good news for the needy. His parable of the workers in the vineyard portrays a landowner with a lot of work to be done in his vineyard, presumably the job of gathering in the harvest. He leaves his house at about six o'clock in the morning and goes to the place in the town where casual labourers gather awaiting employment. He hires a team of those there, offering them the regular day-labourer's wage of a denarius for the day. They go off to the vineyard. The owner returns to the place where labourers gather at three-hourly intervals, *i.e.* at nine o'clock, twelve o'clock and three o'clock, and each time he finds people there without work, whom he takes on. Perhaps some of them have had work for just part of the day, and then have nothing to do. He returns there finally at five o'clock, one hour or so before the end of the working day; and yet again he finds some unemployed, whom he dispatches to the vineyard. Before he employs them, he asks how it is that they are still unemployed at the last hour of the day, and they explain that no one has hired them. The implication may possibly be that they are the most unpromising workers; in any case we are probably to think of the man taking on these workers out of compassion rather than because they will do much for him in the remaining hour of the day.

That this is the case is confirmed when the day's wages are paid out and at the master's orders they receive one denarius each, in other words a full day's wage. Seeing this the other workers expect, not surprisingly, to receive more. When in fact they all receive the same, those who have worked all day protest loudly about the injustice of the situation. But their protest is rejected by the master, firmly but kindly; he calls the spokesman of the protesters 'friend', but points out that they have exactly what they were promised, and he goes on to assert his right to use his money as he wishes: 'Or are you envious because I am generous?'

This last sentence of the story is the climax; the parable is all to do with the master's generosity. But the parable is preceded by the enigmatic saying: 'Many who are first will be last, and many who are last will be first' (Mt 19:30), and is followed by the almost identical saying: 'So the last will be first, and the first last' (Mt 20:16). These sayings make it clear that the parable is not just about the master's generosity, but about the surprising upside-down effects of that generosity.

This emphasis makes sense within the context in Matthew's gospel: the immediately preceding chapter contains the story of the rich young man who came to Jesus wanting to know about eternal life and who despite his religiousness 'went away sad' in face of Jesus' call to him to give up everything and to follow him. Jesus comments to his astonished disciples on how hard it is for the rich to enter the kingdom of God. Then he speaks of the disciples themselves:

> You who have followed me will also sit on twelve thrones, judging the twelve tribes of Israel. And everyone who has left houses or brothers or sisters or father or mother or children or fields for my sake will receive a hundred times as much and will inherit eternal life. (Mt 19:28–29)

The extraordinary fact is that the rich religious man, whom Luke calls a 'ruler' (Lk 18:18), does not get into the kingdom, whereas Jesus' mixed-up band of followers from Galilee are promised thrones. It is indeed a case of 'the first shall be last and the last first'.

This upside-down situation is what is portrayed in the parable of the labourers in the vineyard, and the message of the parable is that the revolution of God brought by Jesus is a marvellously generous revolution, offering a full place and reward even to the late-comer or outsider. For the rich and the religious such egalitarian salvation did not always seem good news, since it meant giving up their present advantage and special position. The rich man accordingly went away sad, and in the parable those who had worked all day complained of the master's unfair generosity. But for those in need of employment at the eleventh hour the master's generosity was good news indeed, and for the sinners whom he welcomed into his company Jesus and his revolution were wonderful good news.

We are reminded how the modern missionary movement has sometimes illustrated the same point, for example in India, where it has often been the outcastes or Harijans rather than caste-Hindus who have responded to the good news of Jesus. The revolution of God is a levelling revolution; not, however, a negatively levelling revolution bringing everyone down, but a positively levelling revolution in which God's amazing generosity welcomes even late-comers into the work of the revolution and gives them the full day's wage.

The parable of the labourers in the vineyard has evident similarities to that of the prodigal son: a master being amazingly generous to those who have not deserved it, and strong resentment at the apparent injustice of this on the part of those who have worked the full and regular stint. The parable of the prodigal son and that of the workers make sense in the context of objections to Jesus' ministry: the religious found it extremely galling that Jesus actively welcomed the outcasts of society into his fellowship, not as second-class citizens of the kingdom, but as full members.

Paradoxically the religious, who could boast of their fidelity – the elder brother's boast in the parable of the prodigal son (Lk 15:29) is strikingly like the rich young man's words, 'All these I have kept' (Mt 19:20) – were in danger of shutting themselves out of the feast of the kingdom. In Matthew 21:31, after yet another parable, Jesus makes precisely this point to his Jewish opponents: 'I tell you the truth, the tax collectors and the prostitutes are entering the kingdom of God ahead of you.'

One significant limitation in the parable of the labourers is that those who have laboured all the day earn their day's wage by their work, whereas Jesus did not believe that anyone earns his place in the kingdom by his work. Although the common opinion that parables have only one point is mistaken, it is important not to press the details of parables too far; as pictures they are limited. The point of the parable of the labourers is about God's amazing generosity to the outsider (and its offensiveness to some people), not about the worthiness of the labourers who serve the whole day. We may recall our earlier discussion of Jesus' saying about 'the righteous who need no repentance' (p. 95).

The observation about the limited scope of the parable may also help explain the apparent discrepancy between this parable, which speaks of equal reward for all the labourers, and a parable like that of the pounds, which speaks of different servants being rewarded according to their faithfulness. This apparent contradiction is explicable when the limited purpose of the different parables is recognised: the parable of the labourers, like the parable of the prodigal son, is about Jesus' ministry and his generous welcoming of sinners. Its message is: It is never too late to join the revolution, and no one is too bad. The parable does not discuss the quality of the work of the labourers in the vineyard. On the other hand, the parable of the talents and others like it are addressed to those who are Jesus' followers and are about faithfulness in discipleship and about quality of service. To put it simply: entry into the kingdom of God is through God's generosity to sinners; being in the kingdom of God entails running the race to obtain the prize (1 Cor 9:24).

There is truth in the old saying that the entry fee to Christianity is completely free, but the annual subscription is everything we've got. No one will be in the coming kingdom of God on the basis of his or her own achievements, but only on the basis of God's generosity; but everyone will be called to account on the day of judgement and will be rewarded according to his or her response to the Lord's generosity.

## The Pharisee and the tax-collector (Lk 18:9–14)

If the other parables we have looked at in this chapter have emphasised God's generosity and love as the driving force in Jesus' ministry, the brief but vivid parable of the Pharisee and the tax-collector also looks at the other side of the coin and describes the appropriate human response. It comes in Luke's gospel in the context of teaching about prayer. It describes two people praying in the temple. The temple comprised a massive complex of buildings and courtyards, and, although there was corporate prayer at nine o'clock and three o'clock each day when the morning and evening sacrifices were offered, at other times too the temple courts would have been thronged with pilgrims and other worshippers bringing their private sacrifices and praying individually, but probably out loud. Jesus in this parable gives us a glimpse of the sort of thing we might have seen and heard had we been there.

The first man in the parable is a Pharisee. The origins of the Pharisees are uncertain, but they were probably the successors of those pious Jews who joined with Judas Maccabeus and others in 169 BC in fighting against the Greek emperor Antiochus, who tried to enforce paganism in the Jerusalem temple and in all Judea. In any case, as we have seen, in New Testament times in Palestine they were an influential organised group of Jews who stood for religious purity and separation. They prided themselves on their scrupulous adherence to the law of God, and indeed they went beyond the letter of the Old Testament law in their personal lives. Although the Pharisees often get a bad press in the New Testament, this should not obscure the fact that they were an outstandingly religious group.

The second man in the parable is a tax-collector. Taxes were of two sorts in Roman Palestine: there was direct personal and land taxation, collected by state officials; and there were indirect taxes of various sorts, such as customs duties. The right to collect these indirect taxes was auctioned off each year to the person offering the authorities the most for the privilege: this 'chief tax-collector' – Zacchaeus was one such man – would pay the money to the government in advance, and then with a retinue of assistants recoup the money, making sure that he did very well for himself in the process. The tax-collectors mentioned in the gospels (including Luke's parable) were probably in the business of indirect taxation.

The tax-collectors were as bad a lot in most people's eyes as the Pharisees were good. This was not just normal popular resentment against taxes, though the combination of direct and indirect taxation was very high and a heavy burden on the weak economy of Palestine. Those who were religiously scrupulous will also have had tithes and offerings to pay, and it has been estimated that thirty-five to forty per cent of the small landowner's income might go on his civil and religious dues – a crushing amount for people living not much above subsistence level.

But the dislike of tax-collectors was particularly because they were seen as traitors and as extortioners. They were traitors to the nation because they were collaborating with the foreign imperialists, raising taxes for those who had no right to them. This was not just something political: it was also seen by many as an affront to God, whose people and land the Romans had usurped. The question of tax for Caesar was a very emotional and delicate issue: in AD 6 there was a major revolt led by a Galilean called Judas protesting against Roman rule and taxation (see Acts 5:37). In asking Jesus about the legitimacy of paying tax to Caesar, his opponents were putting him on a very hot spot, in the hope that he would fall foul either of the authorities on the one side or of the people with their hatred of the foreign taxes on the other (Mt 22:15–22; Mk 12:13–17; Lk 20:20–26). But tax-collectors were also hated because of their extortion and corruption; there were few checks on their powers, and they feathered their own nests by their rapacious exploitation of others. Tax-collectors were, for these reasons, regarded as corrupt, untrustworthy and irreligious. The verdict was probably justified in most cases.

So Jesus in his parable compares a representative of the most religious people in society with a representative of the most irreligious. The Pharisee's prayer is true enough, when he gives thanks for his moral and religious superiority to others. He mentions his fasting twice a week: Jews were required to fast only once a year, on the Day of Atonement, but the Pharisees fasted regularly, probably each Monday and Thursday. He mentions his tithing of all that he gets: again, like other Pharisees, he goes far beyond the letter of the Old Testament law. This required the producers of grain, wine and oil to give a tenth to God, but not the consumer to tithe everything. The tax-collector's prayer was also true enough in that he describes himself as a sinner.

The difference between the two is that the Pharisee is conscious of his goodness and the tax-collector of his sinfulness. The Pharisee stands where people can see him, and is pleased with himself. In describing him in this way Jesus, being a good story-teller, may be caricaturing a little, and we should not suppose that every Pharisee was as unpleasantly priggish as this. But there is no reason to doubt that Jesus is pointing to a real tendency towards smugness and arrogance among many of the religious people of his day. They did see themselves as superior to others, and thanked God for his goodness in making them so.

The tax-collector stands afar off; we are reminded of the prodigal son. The tax-collector knows his real position: he does not lift his head in prayer, as was customary, but beats his breast as a sign of mourning. Kenneth Bailey comments that beating of the breast is more characteristic of women in modern Middle Eastern culture than of men, and suggests that this is some indication of the man's deep feelings. His words are much briefer than those of the Pharisee: 'God, be merciful to me the sinner.' The original sense of the word 'be merciful' here is 'be appeased', and it is a word used in connection with atoning sacrifices (*e.g.* Heb 2:17). The tax-collector knew he deserved the anger of God – again we are reminded of the prodigal son – and begged that the temple sacrifices would be effective for him, despite his sin: 'Grant atonement for my sin.'

The parable concludes with the verdict of Jesus: 'I tell you, this one went down justified to his house rather than the other.' In other words the abject tax-collector, rather than the highly religious Pharisee, was right with God. Luke introduced the parable by saying that Jesus addressed it to those who 'were confident of their own righteousness and looked down on everybody else'. The word 'righteousness' is the same Greek root as that translated 'justified'. So the parable is seen by Luke as being about 'justification' and getting right with God. Another way of putting the same thought is in Luke's other famous story of a tax-collector, that of Zacchaeus in Luke 19. When Jesus visits the home of Zacchaeus, he proclaims to those listening: 'Today salvation has come to this house, because this man, too, is a son of Abraham' (Lk 19:9). To be justified is to be a member of the saved people of God; it is to receive and enter the kingdom of God.

The way to justification is expressed in the parable and summed up in the words at the end: 'For everyone who exalts himself will be humbled; and he who humbles himself will be exalted.' Here is the other side to the coin of God's mercy expressed and lived out by Jesus. God's generosity and mercy reaches out to the lost, and it can be received only by the person concerned acknowledging his need of that mercy, like the prodigal son and the tax-collector. Those (like the elder brother) who object to the generosity of God to sinners and who insist on their own righteousness are not only setting themselves against the purposes of God for others, but are also excluding themselves from his love. They are cutting themselves off from atonement, shutting themselves out of the joyful feast, though the father wants them to come in.

The parables shed some light on the often noted fact that in the gospels Jesus is characteristically gentle with sinners and hard on religious people: he ate with tax-collectors and prostitutes, but he denounced the scribes and Pharisees. The reason for this is not because Jesus preferred sin to religion (a modern notion!), or because the writers of the gospels were anti-Semitic and wanted to paint a black picture of the Jewish religious leaders. But it is because religion (like wealth) is often a major obstacle in the way of the revolution of God, giving people a false sense of security and preventing them from responding to the good news of God's love and revolution. In Jesus' own context it was the Jewish religion that had this effect. Not because Judaism was bad, or because there was a lack of real piety in Judaism; on the contrary. But because religion of all sorts so easily breeds pride: entry into the revolution of God, which Jesus proclaimed, requires a genuine acceptance of the prophetic diagnosis, 'We all, like sheep, have gone astray...' (Isa 53:6). The Pharisee of the parable would have known that verse and the doctrine of the grace of God; but in practice his confidence lay in his own righteousness, not in the mercy and atonement of God.

Jesus saw material, social and religious wealth as potential obstacles to entry into the revolution of God. He said: 'Blessed are you who are poor, for yours is the kingdom of God' (Lk 6:20; cf. Jas 2:5), not meaning that poverty as such is a qualification for the kingdom, but because the poor man knows his need of the revolution. The religiously impoverished tax-collector of the parable illustrates the point.

It is interesting to compare the teaching of Jesus about justification in this parable with Paul's teaching in his letters – particularly in Galatians and Romans, where it is a major concern of the apostle. He, like Jesus, makes it very clear that getting right with God is not on the basis of legal achievement or religious status, but is entirely on the basis of God's mercy received through faith, so that no one can boast. There is also a parallel between the point made in the parable and Paul's discussion in Romans 9–11 of the failure

of the Jewish nation to believe the Christian gospel. This was
a real problem to Christians: Why did the chosen people not
respond to their Messiah Jesus? Paul's answer, in a nutshell,
is that God's way of working and saving people is through
his free mercy and generosity shown in Christ, and the
rejection of the Jewish nation is precisely because they have
been unwilling to receive this mercy. Instead of accepting
God's righteousness as a gift they have sought to establish
their own righteousness. So, contrary to what might be
expected, the last (*i.e.* the Gentiles) are first and the first are
last.

We saw that the tax-collector in the parable asked: 'Grant
atonement for my sin.' Paul uses a similar 'atonement' word
in his discussion of the justification of sinners, and he sees
this atonement as achieved through Jesus' death on the
cross. The cross takes away the anger of God. The parables
we have looked at do not make that connection between the
cross and forgiveness; but they do make it clear that
salvation is God's gift, and that it is the unlikely outsiders
who are welcomed into the kingdom and put right with God,
whereas those who might be expected to be members of it
exclude themselves. This is not just a case of revolution
upsetting the status quo for the sake of it, but is a reflection
of the wonderful mercy of God that is the primary characteristic of God's revolution.

# 7 BAD NEWS FOR THE ESTABLISHMENT

The revolution of God brought by Jesus was very good news to those conscious of their need, such as the tax-collector and the prodigal son in the parables we have just looked at. But even in those parables there is a reverse side to the coin; Jesus' revolution is bad news to the religiously complacent, such as the Pharisee in the parable and the elder brother. A number of other parables bring this point home.

## The two sons (Mt 21:28–32)

The parable of the two sons in Matthew 21:28–32 is the story of one son who initially refused to do the work that his father asked him to do, but then changed his mind, and of a second son who promised to go, but then failed to keep his word. The story is applied to the Jewish opponents of Jesus on the one hand and to the tax-collectors and prostitutes who responded to the preaching of John the Baptist and Jesus on the other. The religious establishment were those who loudly proclaimed their own commitment to God and who were in theory looking forward to the coming of the kingdom of God. But, when the revolution was announced by John the Baptist, they backed down, refusing to respond. The tax-collectors and prostitutes, on the other hand, were those whose lives had so far been a rejection of God's demand, but who then reversed that rejection by their enthusiastic response to the good news of the kingdom. The religious establishment might have been expected to revise their opinion when they saw the good effects of the revolution on sinners; but in fact the reverse took place: 'Even after you saw this, you did not repent and believe' (Mt 21:32).

A point of particular interest about this parable is that it is in the first instance a parable about John the Baptist, not about Jesus. It thus throws interesting light on Jesus' understanding of John and his ministry. The modern reader of the New Testament can easily underestimate John, seeing him as a rather insignificant figure whose only role was to direct people away from himself to Jesus as his successor. But in fact a careful reading of the gospels and of the writings of the Jewish historian Josephus makes it clear that he was a powerful, prophetic figure in his own right and a leader of a popular reform movement. His influence was such that he was perceived as a threat by Herod Antipas, the ruler of Galilee, who accordingly arrested and finally executed him.

How did John and his movement relate to Jesus and his movement? There is some evidence of tension between the two movements, with some of John's followers advancing the claims of John over against Jesus and with Jesus' followers defending Jesus' superiority. (This is the likely background to Jn 1:19–21; 3:22–4:3.) But the parable of the two sons makes it clear that Jesus himself saw his work and John's as belonging together. In one sense what John started Jesus continued: John announced the coming kingdom of God; so did Jesus. John called people to baptism; Jesus underwent this baptism, and then for a time at least conducted a similar baptising ministry himself (Jn 3:22–4:3).

It would be wrong to give the impression that the ministries of John and Jesus were indistinguishable (see chapter 3). The distinction is made particularly clear in the passage where John asks if Jesus is the 'one who is to come' and Jesus speaks of John as preparing the way of the Lord and as the 'Elijah who was to come' (Mt 11:2–19; Lk 7:18–35). The distinction between John and Jesus is the difference between the police outrider in a procession and the royal or other dignitary following in his or her official car or carriage. In other words, John was a prophet looking forward, the last in the line in fact; Jesus was the one looked forward to, the fulfilment of the prophetic hopes.

But – and this is the point implied in the parable of the

two sons – John and Jesus were part of the same cavalcade, the same revolutionary movement. The context of the parable is the dispute between Jesus and his Jewish opponents over the nature and origin of Jesus' authority (Mt 21:23–27; Mk 11:27–33; Lk 20:1–8). Jesus replies to their questioning by asking his critics about John's baptism: 'Was it from heaven, or from men?' They are trapped by his reply, not wishing to endorse John but not wishing either to alienate the people who supported John. But Jesus' reply was not simply a trap; it was a very serious reply, since Jesus did see John's mission and his own as belonging together and having the same divine authority. In refusing to acknowledge this, his opponents were putting themselves in the position of the boy in the parable who said yes to his father, but then failed to go into the vineyard.

### The wicked tenants (Mt 21:33–46; Mk 12:1–12; Lk 20:9–19)

Matthew follows the parable of the two sons with two further parables which develop the same theme, that of the wicked tenants and that of the wedding feast. The parable of the tenants is found in slightly differing versions in Matthew, Mark and Luke: but the core of the parable is the same in each gospel.

The parable helps explain two things about Jesus' proclamation of the coming of the kingdom which his disciples found hard to understand. In the first place, they could not make sense of Jesus' increasing emphasis on his own coming death: how could he announce the day of God's glorious revolution and at the same time his own death? In the second place, they did not understand his failure to release Israel from bondage to foreign imperialists. The Old Testament vision of God's revolution was, almost more than anything else, a vision of God's restoration of his people Israel. Jesus' disciples not unnaturally understood his proclamation of the kingdom in those terms: 'Lord, are you at this time going to restore the kingdom to Israel?' (Acts 1:6). What was Jesus' view on this matter? The parable of the tenants explains vividly Jesus' perception both of his own death and of his relationship to the nation of Israel.

Vines and vineyards were a familiar part of everyday life: nearly everyone with their own home and land would have their own vine. However, the parable describes not the typical householder with a small plot of land, but a big absentee landowner with tenants working his property. Galilee had many such estates, and the absentee landlords, who were in some cases foreigners living abroad, were often resented. So in Jesus' parable the tenants object to handing over the portion of the crop which has been set as their annual rent. They want more, and preferably all, of the fruit of their own labours for themselves, and they refuse to honour their contract. Their refusal is not a politely worded one; far from it, they beat up the servant who comes to them on behalf of the owner. It is not just one servant who gets such an unfriendly reception: a succession of servants are sent, and they get an increasingly hostile and violent welcome from the increasingly bold tenants. The picture is thus of the vineyard owner, living abroad and trying to impose his authority from a distance (perhaps over a period of years), but being thwarted and getting back nothing except stories of atrocities.

The climax of the story is when the master plays his final card, sending the one person he has left, his son. He calculates that they will respect the superior authority of his son and heir. But he calculates wrongly, since the servants see the son's coming as their chance to finish the story and to secure the vineyard for themselves. Perhaps they guessed that the son was now owner of the vineyard, so that killing him would leave the vineyard ownerless and up for grabs; perhaps they gambled on the owner being too elderly and far away to take decisive action against them – after all he had not come so far! In Jewish law a person who could prove three years' undisputed possession of a property could claim ownership of it; the tenants may have gambled on this possibility. In any case they kill the son and symbolically throw him out of the vineyard. But this time it is they who have calculated wrongly, since the owner, having been extraordinarily patient so far, now intervenes forcefully, killing the tenants and giving the vineyard to others.

As with other parables, the story of the vineyard reflects Jesus' turbulent Galilean context. There is nothing historically implausible in the story: atrocities on the part of disgruntled tenants were not unknown. But still, the ferocity of the tenants, the owner's tolerance of their vicious treatment of his servants, and finally his foolhardiness (as it may appear in retrospect) in sending his son to the tenants are striking elements in the story which may be a clue to, and a reflection of, its meaning. The other clue to its meaning lies in the Old Testament book of Isaiah, since this speaks of Israel and Judah as God's vineyard and of his seeking fruit from the vineyard (Isa 5:1–7).

Given these clues, the general drift of the parable is plain. It is the story of God sending first the prophets and then Jesus to the people of Israel, patiently calling them to 'bear fruit'. It is the story of their violent rejection of that call, culminating in the killing of Jesus; and it is the story of God taking action to punish Israel and 'to give the vineyard' to others. The parable is describing pictorially what Jesus speaks of in Matthew 23:29–39, for example in his lament over Jerusalem: 'O Jerusalem, Jerusalem, you who kill the prophets and stone those sent to you, how often I have longed to gather your children together ... but you were not willing. Look, your house is left to you desolate' (vv. 37–38).

The parable makes it clear that Jesus sees his own death as the climax of the people's rejection of God's invitation to them to fulfil their proper role, an invitation brought first by the prophets and then by Jesus. But their rejection of the 'son' is not just one more act of selfish disobedience; it is an unparalleled and unprecedented act of rebellion against the 'father'.

The implications of the parable for our appreciation of how Jesus saw his own ministry are remarkable. He saw himself as God's last and decisive messenger to the people.

He saw himself in continuity with the prophets, bringing the word of God and calling people to serve God, and yet, strikingly, he saw himself as not just a servant like the great prophets of God, but as the beloved Son and heir of the owner of the vineyard. It is possible that the author of Hebrews had the parable in mind when writing the opening words of his epistle: 'In the past God spoke . . . through the prophets at many times and in various ways, but in these last days he has spoken to us by his Son . . .' (Heb 1:1–2), and we are also reminded of Paul's words about Christ and his church as heirs of God (*e.g.* Rom 8:17). Some people maintain that the church's Trinitarian understanding of God and its view of Jesus as divine Son of God developed only after the time of Jesus and was not part of his own self-understanding. It is true that it was the church, not Jesus, that formulated the doctrine in the form we know it; but the doctrine has its roots and origin in Jesus' teaching. We have commented before on Jesus' consciousness of his intimate Father/Son relationship with God, and this consciousness is strikingly expressed in this parable.

The parable ends with a quotation by Jesus from Psalm 118:22–23: 'Have you not read this Scripture, "The stone which the builders rejected, this has become the head of the corner. This was the Lord's doing, and it is marvellous in our eyes"?' The picture is of builders picking stones for a building: they throw out one in particular as (presumably) useless, but, contrary to expectation, that stone is eventually used in a key position, probably at the top corner of two walls (or just possibly as the stone forming the lintel of a doorway). Cornerstones were, and are, particularly important for holding a building together.

What is the connection between this stone saying and the parable? One interesting possibility is that Jesus was playing on words. In Hebrew and Aramaic – Jesus probably spoke Aramaic as his first language – the word for 'son' is *ben* and the word for 'stone' is *eben*. However, the connection is not just verbal. The saying about the stone supplements the parable and in a sense completes it, since the one rejected and killed, as the parable describes, was in due course to be the risen Lord and the cornerstone in the saved people of God. We have commented before on the limitations of parables, and Jesus' parable of the vineyard is limited precisely in the fact that it leaves the son dead. To have had the son of the story rise from the dead would have altered the character of the parable as a picture taken from everyday life. (It is hard to envisage any parable about people combining the ideas of death and resurrection.) So, in using the stone saying, Jesus, who regularly spoke of his death and resurrection together, supplements the parable of the vineyard with another parable of resurrection, as we may regard it.

Before leaving the parable of the vineyard, can we explain more specifically what it implies for Jesus' understanding of his own mission in relation to the Jewish nation? Matthew in his gospel is most helpful here: on the one hand, he comments that the 'chief priests and the Pharisees' recognised that Jesus was talking about them; on the other hand, he records Jesus' summary saying: 'I tell you that the kingdom of God will be taken away from you and given to a nation that will produce its fruit.' The parable is thus an indictment of the political and religious leadership of the Jewish nation for their mismanagement of 'the vineyard', but also a warning that the people whom they represent will come under divine judgement. The parable could be read as a warning to only the current leaders of the Jews that they would be displaced, rather than as a warning of judgement on the nation of Israel as a whole. But it is clear from Jesus' teaching elsewhere that Jerusalem and the Jewish nation as a whole face judgement, and that, although the opposition to Jesus in the nation is not universal (see the disciples!), the whole nation is implicated in the actions of its leaders (*e.g.* Mt 23–24).

So what is this parable saying about the coming of the kingdom and about Israel? First, the parable suggests that the nation of Israel have a privileged position in God's plan. They are, for the moment at least, 'tenants' of God's vineyard, responsible for 'bearing fruit', *i.e.* for doing God's will and working out his purpose. The servants and finally the master's son are sent to them. We are reminded of Jesus' words about his mission being 'only to the lost sheep of the house of Israel' and of his instructions to his disciples to go only to Israel (Mt 10:6; 15:24). The implication is that Jesus saw the message of the kingdom as particularly for Israel, something that is confirmed by his reference to the Jews as 'the sons of the kingdom' (NIV: 'subjects of the kingdom') in Matthew 8:12.

The context of that last saying in Matthew 8:10–12 may help clarify the point. Jesus says, commenting on the Gentile centurion,

> I tell you the truth, I have not found anyone in Israel with such great faith. I say to you that many will come from the east and the west, and will take their places at the feast with Abraham, Isaac and Jacob in the kingdom of heaven. But the subjects of the kingdom will be thrown outside, into the darkness . . .

We notice here that the kingdom of heaven is described as feasting with Abraham, Isaac and Jacob. This reminds us that the kingdom Jesus proclaimed was (and is) the fulfilment of the plan of God for the world through his ancient people, Israel. Jesus saw himself as the promised Messiah of Israel and as the Son of Man, whose task it was to bring God's promised salvation to his people and through his people to the world. It was no accident that he chose twelve apostles and spoke of them judging the twelve tribes of Israel (Mt 19:28). He did not see himself as abandoning God's plan as revealed in the Old Testament (or as digging up the vineyard!), but as bringing that plan to fruition. So Jesus saw the Jewish nation as God's chosen people and the Jews as 'the sons of the kingdom'. He believed that 'salvation is from the Jews' (Jn 4:22); the Jewish nation was called by God to bring his revolution to the world.

But, although the parable speaks of the Jews' privileged position, it speaks also, secondly, of judgement on the Jewish nation for failing to fulfil their part in God's plan. It speaks of a history of failure to produce the appropriate fruit, culminating in their refusal to 'hear the word of the kingdom' and in their rejection and murder of the 'son of the owner'. The consequence of rejecting God's Messiah and Jesus' message of the kingdom is judgement. They have rejected their calling as the saved people of God; they have refused to act as 'sons of the kingdom' and to be the instrument of God's salvation to the world. The dire consequence of this is that God will take away their privileged position, and the 'vineyard' will be given to others. It is not said who the 'others' are, but from Jesus' saying about the twelve apostles ruling the twelve tribes as well as from the parable of the great feast (which we will look at next) it is clear that the 'other nation' is the community of Jesus' followers, comprising Jews and (in due course) Gentiles – like the centurion who demonstrated faith in Jesus. Paradoxically the 'sons of the kingdom' will find themselves shut out, because they have shut out the Messiah.

Thus Jesus' coming does not represent the abandonment of God's plan for Israel, but its fulfilment; nor does it mean the condemnation of all Jews; on the contrary, Jesus and his disciples are Jews themselves. But it does mean judgement on the Jews who reject the Messiah – such 'sons of the kingdom' will be thrown out and others will be gathered in – and judgement on the Jewish nation, with the 'kingdom' being given to 'another nation'. It is the international fellowship of those who believe in the Messiah who are now the Israel of God and the heirs of Abraham (*cf.* Gal 3; 6:16).

There is a close parallel to this understanding of Jesus and the Jewish nation in Paul's letters, notably in Romans 9–11, where Paul agonises over the problem of Jewish unbelief. In Romans 11 he gives his own parable of the olive tree. He explains that, although the Jews are the natural branches of the olive tree, the majority have been broken off because of their unbelief, and the Gentiles are the branches of a wild olive tree that have been grafted in because of their faith. He explains that through this mysterious process God is working out his plan of mercy for the whole world and for the salvation of 'all Israel'. He urges his readers not to follow the Jews' example of unbelief; the new tenants (to use the terms of Jesus' parable) are to bear fruit faithfully.

The parable of the tenants comes in the synoptic gospels shortly after Jesus' dramatic entry into the temple and his violent ejection of the corrupt money-changers and merchants (Mk 11:15–18; Mt 21:12–16; Lk 19:45–46), and it may be seen in part as a comment on that incident: Jesus is the one who comes to the temple with the authority of God and finds it wanting. He says: 'Is it not written: "My house will be called a house of prayer for all nations"? But you have made it "a den of robbers"' (Mk 11:17). The Jews have not lived up to their calling, and in turning over the tables of the money-changers Jesus is speaking of God's judgement on them, *i.e.*, in terms of the parable, of the taking away of the vineyard from the tenants.

Jesus is also specifically warning that the presence of God will no longer be in the Jerusalem temple, which will indeed be overthrown. What and where will be the new temple? Jesus gives only hints of this, perhaps in his reference to himself as the 'cornerstone', in his remark about being 'greater than the temple' (Mt 12:6), in his references to the temple being destroyed and then raised in three days (Jn 2:19–21; Mt 26:61), and in his words to the Samaritan woman about the time coming when worship will be in neither Jerusalem nor Samaria, but in Spirit and truth (Jn 4:21–24). The hints point to the new temple being in the risen Jesus himself as the Messiah and in the community of his followers.

This is precisely the understanding that is made explicit in Paul's writings. He speaks of the church as the body of Christ and the temple of the Holy Spirit, and he significantly brings together the thoughts of the temple and the cornerstone in Ephesians 2:19–22 (see also 1 Cor 3:16; 6:19; 2 Cor 6:16):

> You are ... members of God's household, built on the foundation of the apostles and prophets, with Christ Jesus himself as the chief cornerstone. In him the whole building is joined together and rises to become a holy temple in the Lord ... a dwelling in which God lives by his Spirit.

Jesus' followers are thus the new tenants of the vineyard and the new temple of God, and are expected to bear fruit, to be a holy dwelling-place for God's Spirit and to take the revolution to 'all nations'.

To conclude, the parable of the tenants helps us to fit more of the revolution jigsaw together. We saw in chapter 4 that the revolution of God does not come overnight, but through the sowing of the word. We saw in chapter 5 how Jesus spoke of a time when he would be absent from his disciples; during this time Jerusalem would suffer disastrous desolation and the Gentiles would be evangelised, and after it Jesus would return. The parable of the tenants helps us to put these things together and also to make sense of Jesus' perhaps rather perplexing words about his mission and that of the twelve as being only to Israel. Why this exclusivism, and how does it relate to the prophecy of the destruction of Jerusalem? The answer is that Jesus saw Israel as God's chosen tenants, with a responsibility to produce fruits for their master and 'for all nations'. Jesus brought them the 'word of the kingdom' – God's final demand and final offer. They, however, failed to produce the fruits and failed finally and supremely by rejecting the 'son of the owner'. As a result they forfeited their tenancy, Jerusalem and the temple were doomed to destruction, and the responsibility of taking the gospel to all nations was given to the community of Jesus' followers.

### The great feast and the wedding garment
(Mt 22:1–14; *cf.* Lk 14:16–24)

The thought of the divine revolution being rejected by those who should have welcomed it and so being given to others comes out strongly in the parable of the great feast. This parable occurs in two different forms in Matthew and Luke, and it is not easy to be sure how their versions relate to each other. Did Jesus tell the same story in various different forms? Or is Matthew's parable actually several similar stories merged and mixed up together, one perhaps about a king inviting dignitaries from neighbouring countries to his son's wedding, another about a man giving a feast for friends and neighbours (as in Luke), another about an improperly dressed guest at a wedding? This could explain some of the surprising turns in Matthew's narrative.

However Matthew's and Luke's parables relate to each other, the story-line in the two parables is basically the same. The story is of a rich man going to trouble and expense to prepare a great banquet, and then of the originally invited guests crying off. The host, in face of this insult, sends his servants out into the streets to invite anyone they can find to the feast.

The general sense of the parable is plain. As we saw in chapter 3, the day of God's salvation is described in the Old Testament as 'a feast of rich food for all peoples' (Isa 25:6). In proclaiming the coming of the kingdom Jesus announced the beginning of that great feast. It was great good news, but the reception he received from the leaders of the nation was an insulting shrug, and in the event it is the 'outsiders' who were in fact gathered into God's feast by Jesus.

*Matthew's parable* (Mt 22:1–14)

**The invitation**
In Matthew's form of the parable the story is specifically about a king giving a wedding banquet for his son's marriage. Already we have seen in the parable of the bridegroom (Mk 2:19–20) how Jesus compared his ministry to a wedding feast and himself to the bridegroom; this parable significantly adds to that picture in speaking of a royal wedding for the king's son. There could hardly be a more important feast than a royal wedding, and to decline an invitation to such a feast would be almost unthinkable. To do so on grounds of routine business commitments would be doubly insulting, and to beat up and kill the king's servants, as the story describes, would be, literally and very seriously, to add injury to insult. Not surprisingly the king of the story takes drastic action against the ungrateful guests, sending out his troops to destroy them and their city.

The parable refers, like that of the tenants, to the Jewish

leaders' rejection of Jesus and the gospel of the kingdom. In this case the 'son' is not one of the king's messengers, but he is the one whose wedding is being celebrated. The implied reference is to Jesus again, and it is most significant that the kingdom of God is all to do with Jesus as God's Son. We are reminded of Revelation 19, with its vision of God's reign and of the 'wedding of the Lamb'. The lamb in Revelation is Jesus, and the comment is made 'Blessed are those who are invited to the wedding supper of the Lamb!' (Rev 19:9).

Jesus' parable portrays the Jewish leaders' rejection of this invitation. Their refusal of the most important invitation of all time is portrayed as an inexcusable insult to the author of the invitation (*i.e.* God himself). The parable is a warning of judgement on those leaders – they will be killed – and on 'their city' – it will be burnt with fire. The reference is evidently to the events of AD 66–70, when in the aftermath of a Jewish rebellion against their rule the Roman imperialists invaded Palestine and after a prolonged and horrible war captured and destroyed Jerusalem. It was the traumatic end of an epoch for the Jews.

As for the command to the servants to go on to the streets and to invite to the wedding 'whoever you find', the reference must be both to the tax-collectors, prostitutes and sinners who responded to the message of the kingdom in Jesus' lifetime (Mt 21:31), but also, by implication, to the biggest group of outsiders of all (*i.e.* the Gentiles). The point is similar to that made in the parable of the wicked tenants about the kingdom being given to 'others', and we will not repeat our discussion of that point (see pp. 125–33).

### The wedding garment

Matthew's parable goes on to describe the royal host seeing a guest not wearing 'wedding clothes'. Whereas the other guests are wearing best clothes appropriate for the occasion, this man sticks out because he is wearing his plain and everyday clothes. He is speechless when asked how he got into the wedding in such unsuitable garb, and he is unceremoniously thrown out. His failure to dress properly for the occasion is as insulting to his host as was the rudeness of the first guests.

This story of the wedding garment may originally have been a separate parable from that of the wedding feast, in which case scholarly discussions about how the guests just invited off the streets could be expected to be well dressed – were wedding clothes handed out at the door? – are quite misplaced. In any case, the other guests in the story are properly dressed, and the man has no excuse to offer when he is challenged.

As for the meaning of the parable of the wedding garment, it is best taken as one of many warnings in Matthew's gospel about hypocrisy and the need for the disciple to live in true righteousness: thus in Matthew 5:20 Jesus says forthrightly: 'Unless your righteousness exceeds that of the scribes and Pharisees, you shall not enter the kingdom of heaven,' and in Matthew 7:21–23 he says: 'Not everyone who says to me, "Lord, Lord," will enter the kingdom of heaven, but only he who does the will of my Father . . .' Jesus brought judgement on the religious Jews who rejected him, and he welcomed sinners, but those sinners were to be a new revolutionary people, with higher – not lower – standards than the 'pre-revolutionary' standards of Judaism. Jesus looked for an inner righteousness, not outward religiosity (see Mt 5:17–48). Paul expresses much the same thought in his comments on Christian 'clothing':

> You were taught, with regard to your former way of life, to put off your old self, which is being corrupted by its deceitful desires; to be made new in the attitude of your minds; and to put on the new self, created to be like God in true righteousness and holiness. (Eph 4:22–24; *cf.* Col 3:9–10)

We shall return to the question of living out the revolution in chapter 8.

### Luke's parable (Lk 14:16–24)

Luke's parable of the feast is, like Matthew's, a kingdom parable. It is Jesus' reply to a leading remark by someone who was a guest with him at a meal: 'Blessed is the man who will eat at the feast in the kingdom of God.' Jesus responds to this remark by telling a story about a feast.

The story in Luke is in some ways simpler than Matthew's, with none of what we might call the 'political' ingredients of Matthew's parable – the king's people being killed, the army, the city being destroyed. It is a straightforward parable about a feast – about the first lot of people who were invited making excuses (Luke has a fuller description of the excuses than Matthew), and about the invitation then being taken to two unlikely groups of people: first to 'the poor and maimed and blind and lame' of the town, and then to people from the roads and lanes of the countryside.

The differences between Matthew's and Luke's parables probably reflect the different focus of their parables. Matthew's is about Jesus, Israel and the nation, whereas Luke's is about Jesus, the rich and the poor. It is a comment on the fact that the well-heeled of Palestine in general tended to reject Jesus, but the poor and the marginalised of society welcomed him. Matthew's parable hints that the rejection of Jesus by Israel's leaders was for materialistic reasons; Luke's parable brings the point to the forefront, and is a warning to the rich.

The explanation of the failure of the rich to respond to Jesus comes out in their excuses for not coming to the feast: 'I have bought a field', 'I have bought five yoke of oxen', 'I have married a wife'. It has been suggested that the excuses are obviously spurious and therefore deliberately insulting. (Who buys five yoke of oxen and tests them after buying them? Why should marrying a wife prevent the man from attending the feast?) But even on a more charitable view, the excuses are not impressive from guests who had previously accepted invitations to the feast and who should have been expecting the second call, when the meal was prepared. It was evidently a custom to invite guests to such a meal, to prepare the food on the basis of people's acceptances, and then (as would be necessary in days before watches and precise time-keeping) to send word again when the meal was ready.

In describing the invitees' excuses Jesus is diagnosing the generally negative reaction of the wealthy of his society to his ministry. Whether consciously or unconsciously, they were rejecting the invitation to join the kingdom of God because of preoccupation with family and business commitments. It is the thorns and thistles of the parable of the sower again; in modern terms it is the stock market, family life and house maintenance (among other things) that keep people from the kingdom. Through his parable Jesus explains this reaction, but also exposes its insulting character and its fatal consequences. The rich will find themselves shut out, and others will take their place. The invitation goes to the 'poor and maimed and blind and lame' of the town, probably a picture of the destitute beggars of the town, and then to people on the country roads. The reference is to Jesus' ministry to the disadvantaged of Palestine, and then also to the church's mission to Gentiles.

The parable is thus an explanation of what has been called the 'bias to the poor' in Jesus' ministry. Jesus was not biased in the sense that he called some and not others to join the revolution. (One might wrongly deduce from the parable that his priority was to the rich; but the parable is limited in precisely that respect.) But although Jesus called rich and poor alike, and included among his disciples people from a relatively comfortable economic background, like the tax-collector Matthew, it was generally true that his ministry was welcomed more by the poor and marginalised of society than by the well-to-do. The parable explains this bias: the rich were too committed to their pleasurable and profitable way of life to want to join Jesus' revolution; they excluded themselves from the feast.

The revolution of God was especially good news to the poor and those conscious of their need, because they had little to lose and everything to gain; it was less good news to the rich – bad news indeed as they perceived it – because they too had everything to gain, but they also had something to lose in the present (as we shall see more in later parables). In Luke's form of the Sermon on the Mount Jesus says explicitly: 'Blessed are you who are poor, for yours is the kingdom of God,' and: 'Woe to you who are rich' (Lk 6:20, 24). To read this as meaning that poverty in itself is a qualification for entry into the kingdom would be out of keeping with Jesus' teaching as a whole. Jesus' parable of the feast helps clarify the meaning, as do James' words in his epistle: 'Has not God chosen those who are poor in the eyes of the world to be rich in faith and to inherit the kingdom he promised those who love him?' (Jas 2:5). It is not poverty as such that qualifies people for the kingdom, but it is often the materially or socially poor who are also 'poor in spirit' (Mt 5:3), and who commit themselves to Jesus' revolution. The materially and socially wealthy, however, reject the revolution. James echoes Jesus' warning to such people: 'Listen, you rich people, weep and wail because of the misery that is coming upon you' (Jas 5:1).

## The rich fool (Lk 12:13–21)

The parable of the rich fool takes up the thought of Jesus' ministry being a challenge to the rich establishment; it is a potent reminder of the folly of living for this world's possessions. The parable was provoked by a man coming to Jesus and asking him to 'tell my brother to divide the inheritance with me'. At the time it was quite common to go to a rabbi for a legal ruling, and in this case it sounds as though a younger brother is trying to enforce his legal right to part of his deceased father's property, whereas the elder brother wants to keep the family inheritance undivided and jointly managed. Jesus, however, refuses to arbitrate. Instead he warns his petitioner of 'all kinds of greed' (the Greek word used could be translated 'grasping ambition'), and he proceeds to tell a parable making clear the unimportance (in absolute terms) of the sort of property wrangle he has been asked to arbitrate.

The man in the story is a landowner for whom everything in his business goes right, so much so that he has no room in his stores and warehouses to put all his grain. He is the ancient equivalent of the industrialist who captures the market with a winning product and makes a mint for himself. Faced with the happy problem of what to do with his surplus, the man in the parable does not seem to think of giving it away; on the contrary, to judge from the parable, he thinks only in the first person singular – 'What shall I do? I will do this and that' – not of others. His solution to his problem is in the event a simple one: it is to pull down his old warehouses and build bigger ones in which to store his bumper grain harvest and all 'his good things'. He then looks forward to living off his wealth – eating, drinking and enjoying himself for many years.

The man's mistake is that he has thought only of himself, and he has not reckoned with God, who says: 'You fool! This very night your life will be demanded of you. Then who will get what you have prepared for yourself?' The answer to the question is that the man himself will not: his plans have been cancelled at a stroke by God; he has lost everything because he invested selfishly in possessions rather than with God. He is a fool, not in a weak sense, but in the terribly serious and dangerous sense that the word often has in the Bible (see Ps 14:1). Jesus' parable concludes: 'This is how it will be with anyone who stores up things for himself but is not rich towards God.'

The parable of the rich fool illustrates the 'deceitfulness' of riches of which the parable of the sower spoke. Their deceitfulness lies in their tendency to give people an illusory sense of security, to fill people's thoughts and horizons, and to stifle any interest in the revolution of God. In Luke the parable of the rich fool is followed by the passage where Jesus warns the disciples against worrying over food, drink and clothing, and urges instead the seeking of God's kingdom, this being the ultimate and lasting reality proclaimed and brought by Jesus. Living for the revolution is the antithesis of living selfishly and just for the here and now; it involves being rich towards God, investing in God's bank.

What that means in practice will become clearer as we look at other parables. However, we may immediately say that the parable does not imply that material things are wrong in themselves, but only when they become the focus and goal of life. The parable is a critique of 'all kinds of greed', because, as Paul says in Ephesians 5:5, using the same Greek word, greed is idolatry. An interesting parallel to

the parable in Paul's writings is in 1 Corinthians 7:29–31,
where Paul is discussing marriage and singleness. He will
have nothing to do with the supposedly spiritual asceticism
of the Corinthians who deny the goodness of sex and
marriage, but he does warn against a wrong attachment to
this present world:

> What I mean, brothers, is that the time is short. From now on
> those who have wives should live as if they had none; those who
> mourn, as if they did not; those who are happy, as if they were
> not; those who buy something, as if it were not theirs to keep;
> those who use the things of the world, as if not engrossed in
> them. For this world in its present form is passing away.

Paul does not mean that this-worldly things are not to be
used and enjoyed, as is clear from what he says elsewhere;
what he does mean is that we should not follow the rich
fool, whose priorities and investment were in the world that
is passing away, not in the new world of God's revolution.

One final point: it may be tempting to read the parable of
the fool and also the parable of the rich man and Lazarus
(which we shall look at next) as though they were simply
about getting into heaven or hell rather than about the
coming kingdom of God. But to read them that way is to
ignore the context of the parables in the gospels, since that
context is Jesus' kingdom preaching; it is also to contrast
'going to heaven' and 'getting into the kingdom' in a way
that does not do justice to the New Testament. For Jesus
and the New Testament writers the righteous dead are
destined for the coming kingdom of God just as much as the
righteous who live until the coming of the Lord. The coming
kingdom is a kingdom where the righteous dead are raised
and the living are transformed and glorified (e.g. Mt 22:23–
33; 1 Thess 4:13–18, etc.). The main difference between those
who live until the coming of the kingdom and those who die
before its coming is that the decisive moment when their
spiritual account is closed is the Lord's coming for the
former, but the moment of death for the latter.

Jesus' parables of the kingdom, as one might expect, cover
both eventualities: thus parables like that of the thief in the

night speak of the unpredictable coming of the day of the
Lord, and parables like that of the rich fool speak of the
unpredictable coming of death. But in both cases the issues
are the same: coming judgement, and getting into the
kingdom or not; and in both cases the warning is the same: it
is necessary to prepare for the kingdom by living out the
revolution of God now. The rich fool, like those in the
modern world whose creed is practical atheism, conspicuously
failed to do so. Jesus' parable is a challenge to such myopia,
exposing its folly and demanding quite different priorities.

### The rich man and Lazarus (Lk 16:19–31)

The parable of the rich man and Lazarus is also about a rich
man in life and death. We are not told this time how the man
got his wealth; in a similar Jewish story, which Jesus' hearers
may have known, the rich man is a tax-collector. What
matters in Jesus' parable, however, is not how the man
became rich, but simply that he was such and that he lived
accordingly. He wore expensive clothing: his outer garments
were of wool, dyed in imported purple dye, and his under-
garments of fine linen, probably also imported. He got his
clothes from the equivalent of a fashion designer, not from
the department store. And he lived as affluently as he
dressed: the Greek words literally translated mean something
like 'enjoying himself brilliantly'. He lived for pleasure – his
own pleasure.

The only blot on the horizon, though it does not appear to
have bothered him, was a poor man 'lying' at his gate; the
Greek word literally means someone 'thrown' down on the
ground, suggesting that he was a cripple of some sort. We
are not told that he was a beggar, but we may infer this: he
was badly diseased, with open sores on his body; and it is
said that he longed to be satisfied with the scraps of food
that fell from the rich man's table – probably the pieces of
bread or bone that the rich man threw away during the meal,
and that were snapped up by the dogs of the household.
Before the age of the welfare state, the diseased and disabled

of society were a burden on others and were often left sitting or lying at the roadside and in public places, asking for charity from passers-by. This was no doubt such a person; the revolting description of the dogs licking his sores suggests that he may have been severely disabled and so unable to protect himself. When the parable speaks of dogs here, we should not imagine the sort of well-groomed and affectionate pedigree dog that appears on modern TV advertisements for dog food, but rather the semi-wild dogs which roamed the villages and towns eating rubbish and fending for themselves. The only other thing we are told about the man is his name, Lazarus. Nowhere else in Jesus' parables are any of the actors in the stories named, and it may well be significant that Lazarus means 'God helps'. The rich man did not help.

After introducing the two contrasting neighbours, the parable moves from this life to the next. Lazarus and the rich man die, and their lots are dramatically reversed. Lazarus is 'carried by the angels to Abraham's side'. The poor man who had been so neglected in life and who, to judge from the parable's silence on the matter, was not even given a decent burial of any sort, is taken up by God's angels to be with his people in heaven. Abraham is, of course, the father of the people of Israel, and to be taken to his side (literally into his bosom or lap) suggests joining him at the heavenly feast, in other words in the coming kingdom (cf. Mt 8:11; Lk 13:28–29).

The rich man does receive a burial, no doubt a splendid one. But this is the last good thing to come his way, since he is then seen in agony. From his position of torment he can see Abraham 'in the far distance', and Lazarus with him, and he shouts out across the distance to 'Father Abraham'. As a Jew, he hopes he can claim a relationship to Abraham, and yet he knows he can only ask for mercy. He asks that Lazarus be sent to dip his finger in water and to cool his tongue, because 'I am in agony in this flame'. The excruciating combination of burning heat and desperate thirst is one of the most fearful things in a hot climate. The rich man is experiencing that in an acute form. There is probably deliberate irony in the rich man pleading for just a little

kindness from Lazarus, when he had not shown that to
Lazarus in his distress. It is possible that we are meant to
think of him still looking on Lazarus as an inferior and a
nobody, hence his suggestion that he be sent to help him in
his agony; but this is uncertain.

The man's request is in vain. Abraham addresses him as
'son', but tells him to recall the past when he did very well
for himself and Lazarus did so badly. Now Lazarus is
'comforted, but you are in agony'. The words are not simply
a statement of fact, but by implication are an explanation of
why the rich man's request cannot be granted; he had chosen
to 'receive his good things' during his lifetime and had given
no comfort to the suffering Lazarus. His present agony is the
just consequence of this. Abraham goes on to comment that
there is a great chasm fixed between Lazarus' heaven and the
rich man's hell to prevent any travel between them. The
rocky hills of Palestine are cut with deep gorges and ravines;
the chasm of the parable is such a ravine, only a totally
impassable one. The rich man is hoping for the impossible.

The picture of Lazarus in bliss and of the rich man in
torment with a chasm between them is a vivid one. But it
should be understood as pictorial rather than as anything
like a literal description of heaven and hell. In the Jewish
thought of Jesus' time there were all sorts of ideas about the
after-life and about the 'geography' of heaven and hell: it was,
for example, commonly believed that there were a number of
heavens: Paul thus speaks of the 'third' heaven in 2 Corinthians 12:2 (not that Paul shows any interest in speculating
about the heavenly realms). Scholars have tried to explain
Jesus' parable in the context of such Jewish thinking, and
have argued, for example, that we should probably not think
of the rich man and Lazarus as having reached their
respective eternal destinations, but as being in some sort of
intermediate state. This view has certain attractions, not least
because the picture in the parable of a world split down the
middle and containing people in ecstasy and people in
torment conversing with each other seems very different
from the Bible's vision of God's world being finally and
wonderfully restored and united under God's perfect rule

and with evil finally destroyed. However, even to try to explain the parable in terms of Jewish speculative thinking about the geography and chronology of the after-life is probably a mistake. Jesus shows no interest in such speculation, in this parable or elsewhere. The parable was not intended as a map of the after-life, though it has often been used or misused in that way, but was meant to make some very clear points about getting into the coming feast of the kingdom of God, or rather about the dangers of not getting in, and about the fearfulness and irrevocability of judgement.

But the story has not ended. The rich man goes on to ask Abraham to send Lazarus to his five brothers to warn them. This may seem a surprising turn in the narrative: are we now seeing a better side to the rich man's character? Is he beginning to reform and to think about the needs of others? Probably not. The rich man had no doubt been well-disposed to his brothers all along; it was they with whom he had lived in luxurious comfort. So his request does not indicate any new generosity. What it may indicate is bitter resentment on the rich man's part about what has happened to him: in suggesting that Lazarus be sent to his brothers, is he implying that he is suffering unfairly and without due warning? Certainly his request re-emphasises the direness of his situation.

If his request is a plea of ignorance, it is firmly rejected. Abraham refuses to send Lazarus to the brothers, saying: 'They have Moses and the Prophets. Let them listen to them.' The point being made here is a straightforward and obvious one: the Old Testament (which is what is meant by 'Moses and the Prophets') is full of instruction about caring for the poor and of warning about neglecting the poor. For example, in Deuteronomy 15:7–8 God says through Moses: 'If there is a poor man among your brothers in any of the towns of the land that the Lord your God is giving you, do not be hard-hearted or tight-fisted towards your poor brother. Rather be open-handed and freely lend him whatever he needs.' As for the prophets, the book of Amos is a sustained warning of God's judgement on the rich who live in luxury and 'trample on the heads of the poor' (Amos

2:7). Isaiah 58:6–7 is another very explicit passage: 'Is not this the kind of fasting I have chosen . . . to share your food with the hungry and to provide the poor wanderer with shelter – when you see the naked, to clothe him, and not to turn away from your own flesh and blood?' In the parable the rich man and his brothers had no excuse; they had these Scriptures, which they chose to ignore.

The rich man is not happy with this reply, and argues that someone like Lazarus returning from the dead would have a much greater effect than the Old Testament. He is, of course, speaking from his own past experience: the Old Testament did him no good, and he lived complacently oblivious of future judgement. He reasons that, had there been visible proof of the world to come in the form of a dead person rising from the dead, he would have done otherwise.

But Abraham rejects this logic. He comments: 'If they do not listen to Moses and the Prophets, they will not be convinced even if someone rises from the dead.' The final comment of a parable is often particularly important, and that is probably the case here. Abraham does not accept that the problem of the rich man and his brothers was lack of evidence; their problem lay in their own unwillingness to hear the word of God. Those who live in open and blatant defiance of the law of God are not going to change their ways given some extra and special revelation, even if that revelation is someone rising from the dead – and it is hard to think of anything apparently so convincing as a resurrection of someone you have known.

The point that people are capable of disbelief in face of what seems the most convincing evidence is one we are familiar with in the modern world; we all tend to explain things away (and not always wrongly!). It is a point that Jesus makes elsewhere in his teaching in connection with his own ministry. Matthew 12:38–40 is a particularly interesting parallel to the parable we are thinking about: the Pharisees and the teachers of the law ask to see a miraculous sign. Jesus sees the request as symptomatic of the adulterous wickedness of his contemporaries – they are asking not out of openness but out of disbelief – and goes on to say that only 'the sign of the prophet Jonah' will be given, 'For as Jonah was three days and three nights in the belly of a huge fish, so the Son of Man will be three days and three nights in the heart of the earth.' The request for a sign is viewed negatively as a sign of unbelief, as in the parable of the rich man and Lazarus, and again there is a reference to resurrection as a sign. This time it is a sign that will be given, but there is no suggestion that it will answer the doubts of unbelievers; on the contrary, the passage goes on to speak of the present generation facing judgement for their unbelief and failure to repent. John's gospel also expounds the same theme: Jesus does many signs, but the Jews characteristically do not believe; their failure to believe in Jesus is part and parcel of their failure to believe in Moses and the Scriptures (*e.g.* Jn 5:39–40, 45–47; 10:38).

The truth of the point made about the sign of the resurrection was of course demonstrated in practice, since Jesus' own resurrection was a stupendous event, demonstrating Jesus' Lordship, which should have convinced people. As Acts 1:3 puts it: 'He gave many convincing proofs that he was alive.' But many people still did not believe.

Did Jesus, then, have his own resurrection in mind in the parable of the rich man and Lazarus? There is little doubt that in recording the parable Luke will have seen this significance in it, and it is probable that Jesus himself intended it that way (we have noticed the similar teaching in Mt 12:38–40). Some scholars are reluctant to allow that Jesus foresaw even his own death, let alone his own resurrection. But there is no good reason to doubt that Jesus saw his mission as one of suffering leading to victory, in fulfilment of the Old Testament, and it is quite likely that Jesus spoke in the parable of one rising from the dead with this in mind.

Whether he did or not, we can now see why the parable of the rich man and Lazarus ends with an emphasis on the rich man and his brothers being unpersuaded even by someone rising from the dead. It does so because Jesus' parable is directed not to the rich in general, but in particular to the rich whose complacency was unaffected by the sign of his ministry. It is a parable arising specifically out of the context of Jesus' proclamation of the kingdom of God, with all its accompanying signs, warning rich people who count Abraham as their father that they will not get into the kingdom if they refuse to respond to the call to join the revolution with its commitment to the poor.

One further and final point is worth making. The parable ends not with a reference to people in general being unconvinced by someone rising from the dead, but to people in particular who do not 'listen to Moses and the Prophets': it is they who 'will not be convinced even if someone rises from the dead'. This is probably not an accidental combination of ideas: we have already seen that in Matthew 12 Jesus' resurrection is described in terms of the prophet Jonah's experience in the fish, and that in John's gospel the unbelief of Jesus' opponents is linked to their failure to listen to Moses and the Old Testament Scriptures. The same sort of link is made strongly in Luke's gospel, and in particular in his account of Jesus' resurrection; thus in talking to the two gloomy men going to Emmaus the risen Jesus says:

'How foolish you are, and how slow of heart to believe all that the prophets have spoken! Did not the Christ have to suffer these things and then enter his glory?' And beginning with Moses and all the Prophets, he explained to them what was said in all the Scriptures concerning himself. (Lk 24:25–27)

Jesus then says something similar to all the disciples in the upper room, as they continue to struggle with unbelief: 'This is what I told you while I was still with you: Everything must be fulfilled that is written about me in the Law of Moses, the Prophets and the Psalms' (Lk 24:44). The point is clear: Jesus' resurrection is the fulfilment of Old Testament prophecy, not therefore a freak event that is impossible to believe, but actually something to be expected by those who know their Old Testament and who understand its teaching about the kingdom of God coming through and out of the suffering of God's servant.

Given this emphasis in Jesus' teaching, how is our understanding of the parable furthered? We observed that the rich man and his brothers are culpable in the parable, because 'they have Moses and the Prophets', and we suggested that this referred to the Old Testament's teaching about caring for the poor. It may, however, be something wider than this. If the parable is essentially about Jesus' ministry and people's response to that, then the implication may well be that anyone listening attentively to Moses and the prophets should recognise Jesus and his revolution: Jesus' revolution is the fulfilment of the Old Testament, both in its ethical demands (*e.g.* in its commitment to and good news for people like Lazarus) and in the accompanying signs (*e.g.* in the resurrection). For the rich who rejected Jesus, the parable may thus be seen as an indictment of them for their failure to obey the Scriptures: had they listened to Moses and the prophets, they would have recognised Jesus' teaching on the poor as the fulfilment of the law and his signs and coming resurrection as the fulfilment of the prophets. As it is, they stand, and will stand, condemned by their own Scriptures.

The immediate context of the parable in Luke's gospel favours this understanding, since it contains first a saying about the era of the 'kingdom of God' having superseded the era of the 'Law and the Prophets', but then a saying about nothing being dropped from the law, and then Jesus' categorical prohibition of divorce (Lk 16:16–18). Commentators have found it difficult to explain these sayings; however, the probable sense is that the new era of the kingdom brought by Jesus does not mean the abandonment of the moral standards of the Old Testament, but rather their 'fulfilment' (to borrow a word from the very similar passage in Matthew, which speaks of Jesus' higher righteousness, *i.e.* Mt 5:17–48). Jesus' saying on divorce illustrates this higher righteousness, and the parable of the rich man and Lazarus continues the theme of Jesus fulfilling the law and the prophets.

To sum up: the parable of the rich man and Lazarus is anything but a one-point parable. In fact it speaks about three central aspects of Jesus' ministry: (1) the revolution of God is the fulfilment of 'the Law and the Prophets'; (2) the revolution is good news to poor people like Lazarus, and it involves practical mercy on the part of the rich; (3) the revolution is accompanied by thoroughly convincing signs (especially Jesus' resurrection). In its Lukan context the parable makes several different, though related, points: first, it is a terrible warning to the rich about the danger of neglecting the poor; second, it is a warning against the sort of sign-seeking that is really an excuse for disobedience; third, it is an affirmation of the law and the prophets, which express the will of God and are also the context of Jesus' revolution: fourth, and fundamentally, it is a parable about the kingdom of God which Jesus announced, and is an indictment of those who ignore the Old Testament teaching and so reject Jesus' revolution with its demands and signs.

# 8 REVOLUTIONARY NEIGHBOUR RELATIONS

The revolution that Jesus proclaimed was, as we have seen, good news of God's love to the needy and bad news of God's judgement to the comfortable and complacent. But what did joining the Jesus revolution mean in practice? We have already had many hints of this, for example in the parable of the sower with its picture of fruitful crops, in the parables about the end with their call for faithful service to the absent master, and in the parables on wealth with their warnings about a selfish this-worldly lifestyle. But a number of other parables spell out more of what is involved.

Several of Jesus' parables make it clear that joining the revolution means active commitment to the exciting work of the revolution. It means, in other words, living out and spreading the love and healing work that characterised Jesus' ministry.

Both Matthew and Luke have parables illustrating this. Thus we have seen that Luke's parable of the lost sheep is a comment on Jesus' ministry to sinners; Matthew's equivalent parable is about the church's responsibility to its erring members (Mt 18:12–14). Jesus' disciples, who have been found by Jesus the shepherd, are themselves to be good shepherds.

## The unmerciful servant (Mt 18:23–35)

The same chapter in Matthew contains the parable of the unmerciful servant. The story describes a king calling his servants to account and being confronted with one servant who owed him ten thousand talents – a huge amount, millions of pounds. Debt was a major problem in first-century Palestine, not, of course, because of excessive consumer credit, as in some modern Western countries, but because the poor of Palestine, like the poor of Africa or India today, lived on the edge of starvation and ruin and often had to resort to the mercies of the money-lender when things did not work out. But the man in the parable is no ordinary debtor whose crops failed: the size of his debt suggests that he is a state official, not one of the king's household slaves. Perhaps we should imagine a provincial governor or someone with equivalent power and responsibility. In any case the intention is to suggest an unthinkably large debt, such as could probably never be repaid.

The king orders that the man, his wife and children and all that he has be sold to meet the debt. Slavery was widespread in the ancient world – not so much in Palestine as elsewhere, but the story probably intends to portray a Gentile ruler – and it was often debt that drove people into bondage. The man in the story, on hearing his master's perfectly just verdict, falls down before him, bowing before the king, and pleads for time to repay his debt.

The king's response is extraordinary: 'his heart went out to' the man, and he does not just give him extra time; he forgives him all his debt, at great cost to himself of course. We are reminded of the parable of the prodigal son. The parable portrays the undeserved and immense love of God brought by Jesus.

But the story goes on to describe the servant who had been forgiven so much meeting a fellow servant who owed him just a hundred denarii, just a hundred days' wages, an amount that could easily be repaid. His treatment of his fellow debtor is brutal: he grabs him, holds him in a stranglehold and demands his money back. The man falls to his knees and asks for time to pay. But, although the request is the same, the answer is quite different. The first servant refuses to listen and has his fellow debtor thrown into prison until he pays. We should not think of a modern Western prison for long-term prisoners, but probably of a very unpleasant and insanitary lock-up, where the prisoner would be chained or in the stocks, getting rough treatment, and where he would be held until his family or friends came up with the money.

This shocking turn of affairs is not allowed to stand. The king is informed of what has happened, and his previous compassion is now replaced with anger. The unforgiving servant is himself arrested and handed over to 'torturers' until he pays off all of his original debt – an impossibility, we presume. Torture was forbidden in Jewish law, but was used by people like Herod the Great and was a favoured way of persuading people to pay their debts. The king's comment to the man sums things up: 'Was it not necessary for you to have mercy on your fellow servant, just as I had mercy on you?'

The parable brilliantly weaves together several key strands in Jesus' ethical teaching: first, the starting-point of everything is the immense, undeserved love and forgiveness of God; then, second, the only proper response to that is love for others, a love reflecting and spreading the divine love. It is the essence of Christian discipleship not just to love your neighbour in the way you would like to be treated, but also in the way you have been treated by God. The revolution is to snowball. The classic statement of this principle is Jesus' saying to his disciples: 'Love each other as I have loved you' (Jn 15:12), and it is vividly illustrated in the story in John 13 of Jesus washing the disciples' feet and then calling them to follow his example. Those who receive God's revolutionary love are to share it with others. Third, there is such a thing as judgement, which is not to determine whether people deserve divine forgiveness – a total impossibility – but whether they have rightly received the undeserved gift of forgiveness and the gift of the kingdom by identifying themselves with the revolution of love.

The focus of the parable itself and of its context in Matthew's gospel is specifically on forgiveness, not on love in general. It is introduced by Peter's question to Jesus about how often he should forgive his brother. Jesus rejects the suggestion that seven times might be appropriate, and says instead seventy-seven times. There is here a deliberate reminiscence of Genesis 4:24, where Lamech comments on the revenge he has taken on an enemy: 'If Cain is avenged seven times, then Lamech seventy-seven times.' Both in this verse and in the teaching of Jesus the phrase 'seventy-seven times' is meant to suggest an unlimited number of times; but whereas Lamech looked for unlimited vengeance, Jesus taught unlimited forgiveness. Jesus' day was no different from our own in that life in families and in society was regularly soured by feuds and personal animosities. Jesus brought a revolution of forgiveness. He expressed God's forgiveness to sinners himself, and he commanded his followers not just to receive but also to show such forgiveness. This is the sense of the words 'Forgive us our "debts" as we forgive our debtors' in the Lord's Prayer (Mt 6:12): we ask God for his forgiveness and pledge ourselves to give such forgiveness to others.

### The good Samaritan (Lk 10:25–37)

Several of Luke's parables illustrate the same point. Luke is, as we have seen, especially interested in Jesus' ministry to the down and out. The kingdom is pre-eminently good news to the poor, the lost and the outcast. But it is not just Jesus' prerogative to live in this way. It is also the calling of others. They too are to show mercy to the undeserving and the lost. The point is clear if we recall that Luke's two most famous parables are that of the prodigal son and that of the good Samaritan, the one commenting on Jesus' ministry to the outsider, the other commending such ministry to others.

The parable of the Samaritan is a comment by Jesus on the Old Testament command to 'love your neighbour as yourself', given in response to the question of a Jewish theologian about the meaning of 'neighbour'. The Jews had different views as to who was and who was not covered by the word 'neighbour'. It certainly did not include everyone; Gentiles at least were not reckoned in.

In his parable Jesus describes a man going down the road from Jerusalem to Jericho. Today there is a fine modern road sweeping down from the hills of Jerusalem into the great Rift Valley, where Jericho is situated. But when reading Jesus' parable we have to remember that the roads in Jesus' Palestine were very rudimentary and rough – the famous Roman road system had not yet been extended to Palestine – and that travel on foot was slow and also dangerous, because of brigands. It was desirable and common to travel in groups. The Jerusalem to Jericho road, although it was quite a busy route, was particularly hazardous. In about seventeen miles it descended steeply (from a height of 2,500 feet above sea-level to 770 feet below) through desolate and craggy limestone hills – ideal terrain for bandits. Jesus' hearers will have been familiar with the scene, and the description of the man being set upon, brutally beaten and left half-dead will have made uncomfortable sense. It was what everyone feared about the road in Jesus' day, and indeed what pilgrims and others have often feared since. (In the twelfth century the Crusader Order of Templars was founded to protect pilgrims travelling that way; in the nineteenth century pilgrims were given an escort of Turkish soldiers for the journey.)

The scene is thus set, and Jesus' story continues with first a priest and then a Levite coming to the place where the man was. The priests were the clergy responsible for the worship and sacrifices of the temple in Jerusalem, and the Levites assisted them in these and other temple duties, for example in providing music for the worship and in maintaining security in the temple buildings. Both priests and Levites were quite literally a class apart in Jewish society, and they were expected to observe high standards of ritual purity for their sacred ministry. Many of them lived in the fertile Jericho region (famous for its date plantations, and a delightfully warm place to stay in winter), and there will have been a lot of toing and froing on the Jerusalem to Jericho road as they came on and off duty.

The priest and the Levite of Jesus' story saw the wounded man by the roadside, but kept away from him and passed on their way. It is not difficult to imagine why: to have stopped would have been troublesome, perhaps useless (if the man died, as he looked like doing), and extremely risky, since the man was irrefutable evidence that there were dangerous robbers around. Whatever the reasons – and it has been suggested that the priest at least might have had good religious grounds for not approaching someone who might be dead or foreign, and therefore unclean – they did nothing to help the man who had been mugged.

But, Jesus continues, a Samaritan came next. The Samaritans were possibly the Jews' least favourite people: they lived in central Palestine between Jewish Judea in the South and Jewish Galilee in the North, but they were regarded by the Jews as semi-foreign, being the descendants of the people settled in Palestine by the Assyrians in the eighth century BC (2 Kings 17:24–41), and as semi-pagan, although in New Testament times they seem to have been more Jewish than anything else. The animosity between the two peoples went back into Old Testament times, but increased subsequently, notably when the Samaritans built their own temple on Mount Gerizim. Jewish objections to an alternative temple can be imagined, and, when they had opportunity and sufficient military power, the Jews attacked Samaria – this was in 128 BC – mercilessly destroying the temple and the city and trying to force the Samaritans back into line with themselves. The Roman takeover of Palestine brought some relief to the Samaritans, and led to Jewish settlers in Samaria being dispossessed.

There was thus a legacy of long-standing mutual hatred between the two peoples in New Testament times, and within the New Testament period itself there were violent clashes between Jews and Samaritans. This meant that the direct route from Galilee to Judea through Samaria was a rather risky one, which people often avoided by going the much longer way round across the river Jordan and back. One incident symptomatic of the situation was in AD 6 or thereabouts, when some Samaritans got into the Jerusalem temple at night during the Passover period and scattered human bones there, thus making the temple unclean. The tensions between Jews and Samaritans are clear from the New Testament itself, for example from Jesus' conversation with the Samaritan woman in John 4 and also in Luke 9:51–56, where Jesus as a Jew going to Jerusalem is refused a welcome in a Samaritan village and his infuriated disciples suggest taking retaliatory action.

Given this background, it is easy to appreciate the controversial nature of Jesus' introduction of a Samaritan into his parable. His hearers, as they listened to his story, may well have expected Jesus to follow his description of the failure of the priest and the Levite to help with a description of an ordinary Jew helping the poor man and so putting the clergy to shame; such an anti-clerical parable could well have been appealing. But a Samaritan was different and extremely uncomfortable.

And Jesus goes out of his way to emphasise the Samaritan's kindness. Although he was on a journey – quite likely a long journey, since he was away from Samaria – he did not veer away from the robbers' victim when he saw him, but 'his heart went out to him'; the same word is used here as of the father in the parable of the prodigal son and of the king in the parable of the unmerciful servant. His compassion was expressed in practical action; he bound the man's wounds, after pouring in some of his own oil and wine – his equivalent of ointment and disinfectant; he put him on his donkey, which he had quite probably been riding himself; he brought him to an inn and took personal care of him; and then, with extreme generosity, he gave the innkeeper two denarii, asking him to care for the man and promising to pay anything more that might be needed on his next visit. Inns were often rough-and-ready places, little more than a walled-off area with an open space in the centre for travellers' animals and porticoes round the sides under which visitors would sleep on the ground. It has been estimated that the Samaritan's two denarii would have paid for twenty-four nights at an inn; it was certainly a generous provision, and he promised more if need be. All this done by a hated Samaritan for a Jew!

According to Luke the parable was given by Jesus in reply to the theologian asking about the meaning of the command

to 'Love your neighbour as yourself.' He was looking for a
definition of 'neighbour' that might limit its scope, perhaps
to fellow Jews. Jesus' story does not directly answer his
question. But his parable quite deliberately features two
unquestionably 'holy' people, the priest and the Levite, and
one distinctly unholy person, the Samaritan, whose claim to
being a neighbour must have been in doubt in the questioner's
mind. And then at the end Jesus asks him which of the three
characters in the parable he considers to have been neighbour
to the man who was mugged; the theologian is bound to
answer a question put that way as he does: 'The one who
showed mercy on him.' Significantly he does not say 'the
Samaritan', but by his answer he has indirectly admitted that
there can be no limitation on the meaning of 'neighbour'
such as he looked for.

Jesus, however, is not primarily offering a definition of
'neighbour' in his parable, but more a definition of 'loving
one's neighbour'. He is making clear, as Matthew puts it
twice in his gospel, that 'I [God] require mercy, not sacrifice'
(Mt 9:13; 12:7) – not sacrifice as represented by the priest
and Levite, but generous mercy that reaches out, such as the
Samaritan exemplified.

The parable probably implies a criticism of the temple
authorities for their failure to 'produce the fruit' expected of
them (see chapter 7). But it is also and primarily a parable
about the kingdom of God which Jesus proclaimed. Even
before asking Jesus for a definition of 'neighbour', the
theologian asked Jesus: 'What must I do to inherit eternal
life?', in other words: 'How can I enter the coming kingdom
of God?' Jesus' final recorded words to him are: 'Go and do
likewise': eternal life, life in the revolution of God, involves
living like the good Samaritan.

Exactly this point is made also in the Sermon on the
Mount, where Jesus says: 'You have heard that it was said,
"Love your neighbour and hate your enemy." But I tell you:
Love your enemies and pray for those who persecute you,
that you may be sons of your Father in heaven' (Mt 5:43–
45). Here again Jesus contrasts an interpretation of 'love
your neighbour' that excluded some people – no doubt

Gentiles and very probably Samaritans – with the higher standards of the revolution of God.

Jesus' call to love the Samaritan and the enemy was indeed revolutionary in the context of his day. This has been emphasised in a recent book by a Canadian scholar, Marcus Borg, called *Conflict, Holiness and Politics in the Teaching of Jesus*. He points out that it was characteristic of the Judaism of the time to emphasise religious and social separation from all sorts of 'unclean' people, including sinners, Gentiles, Samaritans, tax-collectors, and also lepers. Such separation was not only something religious, but was seen as important in preserving the Jewish national and cultural identity in a threatening time of political and cultural imperialism. It is not difficult to think of modern equivalents. Jesus, however, was a revolutionary in that he advocated an outgoing holiness of healing and bridge-building rather than a defensive holiness of withdrawal.

This was not simply a humanitarian policy. Nor was it a pragmatic policy of compromise on Jesus' part, though Jewish religious and nationalistic isolationism was, of course, to prove disastrous in the war of AD 66–70. Nor was it a betrayal of the Jewish heritage, though that is what Jesus' opponents said. On the contrary, it was a reflection, more than anything else, of Jesus' belief that the revolution of God had come, fulfilling the promises and hopes of the Old Testament for reconciliation and renewal.

The kingdom of God was the fulfilment of a passage like Ezekiel 37:15–28, where the prophet is told to take two sticks, one representing the Old Testament kingdom of Judah and the other representing the kingdom of Samaria, and to 'join them together into one stick'. This action is prophetic of God's reunification of his people:

> There will be one king over all of them and they will never again be two nations or be divided into two kingdoms . . . I will save them from all their sinful backsliding, and I will cleanse them . . . My servant David will be king over them, and they will all have one shepherd . . . I will make a covenant of peace with them; it will be an everlasting covenant . . . My dwelling-place will be with them; I will be their God, and they will be my people. (vv. 22–24, 26–27)

Jesus proclaimed the day of fulfilment, the coming of this divine revolution, through a parable like that of the good Samaritan and also through his ministry to people, sinners and Samaritans. The point is well illustrated in the story of his meeting with the Samaritan woman in John 4. The meeting is startling evidence of the revolutionary nature of his ministry, since the woman was (1) a Samaritan, with whom Jews would not normally deal (see v. 9), (2) a woman, with whom a man would not normally carry on a public conversation (see v. 27), and (3) a thoroughly immoral person, with whom a religious leader would not be expected to associate (vv. 17–18). The reason for Jesus' revolutionary behaviour was not because he was unconventional by temperament or an anarchist, but because he was the announcer and bringer of the healing revolution of God. Thus he speaks to the Samaritan woman of the time coming – and having come – when the old division between Jews and Samaritans, one group worshipping in Jerusalem and one in Samaria, will be broken down and all will worship in Spirit and truth; he speaks too of himself as the awaited Messiah (vv. 21–26). The age of the Messiah is a new age when the old barriers and divisions are done away with. (It is not hard to see the implications of this teaching for our modern divisions of caste, class and race.)

This understanding of the kingdom and of Jesus' mission is echoed in many other places in the New Testament. We noted earlier Jesus' words about his work as the good shepherd (Jn 10), bringing sheep from inside and outside the fold into one flock, and his prayer in which he asks 'that all of them may be one, Father, just as you are in me and I am in you. May they also be in us so that the world may believe ...' (Jn 17:21). The vision is of God's people united with God and with each other in love: this will be a demonstration of God's reality, a proof of the revolution. Paul has the same vision: he speaks of Christ's work as being one of bringing reconciliation to us 'when we were God's enemies' (Rom 5:10), and more broadly in his letter to the Ephesians of God's plan for the world being 'to bring all things in heaven and on earth together under one head' (Eph 1:10). He goes on in Ephesians to speak of Christ having 'destroyed the barrier, the dividing wall of hostility' between Jew and Gentile (Eph 2:14); he may have had in mind the barrier in the Jerusalem temple which carried notices warning Gentiles not to pass further into the temple on pain of death. The barrier was symbolic of a deep division, which is destroyed in the revolution of God which Jesus brought. Paul sees the church as a prototype of God's plan for world reconciliation; the church is to manifest unity and to call other people into the experience of God's reconciliation (2 Cor 5:16–21). The revolution of God means the bringing back of all God's world into peace. The parable of the good Samaritan is the imperative of this revolution.

As we saw in chapter 1, commentators in previous centuries often interpreted the parable of the good Samaritan in terms of Christ and his redemptive ministry to sinners. Modern commentators, almost with one accord, dismiss that interpretation, and they are probably right to do so. But there is at least one important grain of truth in it: the actions of the Samaritan in the parable are, as we have seen, similar to the actions of the father in the parable of the prodigal son; both feel compassion for one in need, whom they might be expected to treat as their enemy, and both are extraordinarily generous. The similarity is not a coincidence, but is because Jesus both exemplified the undeserved love of God himself, including of course to Samaritans, and also called others to the same revolutionary lifestyle. He lived the revolution himself, and invited others to join it.

### The unjust steward (Lk 16:1–13); also laying up treasure in heaven, and places at table (Mt 6:19–21; Lk 12:32–34; Lk 14:7–14)

Jesus' care for the needy and the outcast was not simply a matter of attitude or feeling, but was something practical and down-to-earth. His mixing with sinners, Samaritans, tax-collectors and others, his healing of the sick and supremely his death on the cross were concrete demonstrations of his love. The parable of the unjust or dishonest steward shows that he looked for similarly tangible compassion on the part of his followers.

The parable takes us back again to the world of big business. It is the story of a rich man whose affairs were run for him by a manager. The manager, or steward, typically had great authority to do business on behalf of his master, to negotiate, make contracts, and so on. His was a powerful and responsible position, and a lucrative one.

So when the manager of Jesus' story was given his notice, for allegedly wasting his master's goods, the charge was a serious one and his predicament was a serious one. He was, to put it bluntly, facing ruin. He would be unlikely to get a comparable job; there were not all that many such jobs around, and in any case who would employ someone who had been dismissed as he had? The outlook was bleak; the man could not see himself surviving as a manual labourer. He was probably not a young man, and the change from a comfortable white-collar job to the rigours of a twelve-hour day labouring job would be too much; nor did he have the face to start begging. So the question, 'What am I to do?' was extremely urgent, the more so if he had a wife and children dependent on him and accustomed to a good standard of living.

The answer that came to him was that he must quickly win himself some influential friends, so that 'when I lose my job as steward [lit. am transferred from my stewardship] they may receive me into their homes'. His strategy was to summon each of his master's debtors, and to get them to alter the documents relating to their debts in a way that was greatly to their advantage. The first owed a hundred baths of oil, approximately nine hundred gallons (reckoned to have been the annual yield of 146 olive trees), and he was told to write fifty instead; a fifty per cent reduction was some discount, worth perhaps five hundred denarii (a denarius being a labourer's daily wage). The second man owed a hundred cors of wheat, approximately 550 hundredweight, and was told to substitute eighty – a lower discount, but reckoned again to be worth about five hundred denarii.

It is reasonably clear what is going on in the story. The manager has been told by his master to hand over his steward's papers and accounts, which will have included all sorts of documents relating to business deals he had concluded. Instead of handing them over as they are, the manager takes out the documents relating to debts owed to his master – probably promissory notes signed by the debtors concerned – and replaces them with the redrafted – and now considerably less valuable! – notes. The manager had the authority to make the original contracts, and, until he relinquished his job, he had the power to modify or replace them. Whether, having received his notice, he had the right to do this is less certain; the parable makes it clear that he acted hurriedly: he could not delay handing over his papers and his position for long.

The story ends with the comment that 'the master praised the dishonest manager because he had acted sensibly'. This sentence has caused all sorts of problems to commentators. Essentially the problem is: How could the master possibly praise the manager who was so obviously a rogue and who had seriously defrauded him? Various answers have been given to that question.

The first explanation suggested is that his action was not dishonest at all, but, if anything, the opposite: either, it is said, he was forgoing his own commission on the deal – so using what was properly his own quite legitimately and to good effect – or he was cancelling out that part of the debt which was interest on the loan, and so bringing his master into line with the Old Testament prohibitions on the charging of interest (*e.g.* Lev 25:36). There are various problems with such ideas: for example, it is doubtful if the manager's own commission would have been included in the statement of the amount owed to the master. Also, the overall impression given in the parable is that the manager was a bad lot; it was the accusation that he had wasted his master's goods that led to his dismissal, and, although this could have been an unfair slander, the later reference to him as 'the dishonest manager' probably tells against this.

A second explanation has been proposed by Kenneth

Bailey: he does not doubt the man's dishonesty, but suggests that the effect of the manager's action was to put the master into a corner: the relieved debtors will have been so full of gratitude and praise for the master for his unexpected generosity that the master had either to risk great bitterness by disowning the manager's action, or to take the credit for himself and, whatever he really felt privately, to praise the manager for his action. He took the second course of action. This is a highly ingenious interpretation, but it involves more reading between the lines than is probably necessary.

A third view is that the sentence about 'the master' praising the manager is not in fact part of the parable at all, but is Jesus' own comment on the story. Jesus is the 'master' (literally 'lord' in Greek) who praises the manager. This view (which has much to be said for it, *cf.* Lk 18:6) eliminates the difficulty of having the master praising his disastrous servant, but it means instead that it is Jesus who is found to be praising a rogue!

This has, of course, been many Christians' major worry about the parable as a whole – namely that it seems to be setting forward sharp practice in business as an example to be followed; it is because of this concern that those views which offer an honest explanation of the manager's conduct have been appealing to many. However, the worry is misplaced. We have seen in other parables how Jesus has been uninhibited in using dubious characters, such as a thief, to illustrate features of the kingdom, not in any way condoning the morality of the people concerned, but using some characteristic of their operations to make a point (*e.g.* the unexpectedness of the thief). So this parable is not a commendation of dishonest stewardship, but of shrewd fore-thought and preparation for a future crisis. The application of the parable in Luke 16:8 is unambiguous in this respect.

The third view may well be correct. But even if the master of Luke 16:8 is the master of the parable, the point about the focus of the parable being on the shrewdness of the manager remains. It may be that the master deplored the morality of the manager's action and still praised his shrewdness; but the parable only tells us the latter point, since that is what the story is all about.

The story is explained and applied in the verses that immediately follow it. Verse 8, as we have seen, comments on the manager's shrewdness, and goes on: 'for the sons of this age are more shrewd than the sons of light towards their own kind'. There is a clear recognition here that the unjust steward is a worldly man, not a 'son of light' whose moral example is to be followed; but still he and his ilk can teach something to the people of God. We may compare in modern society the dedicated revolutionary, who may be utterly misguided in the cause for which he gives his life, and yet still be a powerful challenge to the Christian in his commitment. In this particular case the point is that worldly non-Christian people are often more shrewd and sensible in their own affairs than are the people of God in the things of God.

The meaning of this is made clearer in the following verse: 'And I say to you, make yourselves friends through the mammon of unrighteousness, so that when it fails they may receive you into the eternal tents.' This verse is not as difficult to understand as it first looks: in terms of the parable it is saying that the disciples of Jesus should follow the example of shrewdness set by the dishonest manager, who prepared for his coming redundancy by ingratiating himself with people financially. What does that mean? It may be helpful to take the different phrases in the verse one at a time.

(1) The disciples too are to use 'the mammon of unrighteousness': this expression means 'worldly wealth' (not ill-gotten gains!). The word 'mammon' is an Aramaic word meaning wealth, and the phrase 'of unrighteousness' makes it clear that the sort of wealth being referred to is the wealth of this unrighteous world. The parable urges the disciple to make use of worldly wealth.

(2) Why? 'So that when it fails ...' The manager was going to lose his job; that was his crisis. Jesus' hearers face a similar crisis, when earthly mammon will fail. The point is similar to that made in the parables about servants awaiting their master's return and also in parables like the rich fool.

Whether at death or at the Lord's coming, people's present way of life is going to come to an end, and they will be faced with the reality of the kingdom of God where life will be transformed and money redundant. In this crisis situation the disciples are not to be like the rich fool, who failed to reckon with the failure of his wealth, but like the manager who used his wealth to prepare for the future.

(3) Specifically they are to use it 'so that they may receive you into the eternal tents', or, as we might translate it, 'into the dwellings of the age to come'. The disciples are not to live for this world and its wealth, which will fail, but for the age to come, in other words for the coming kingdom of God. The dwellings of the age to come are, in terms of the parable of the rich man and Lazarus, the place where Abraham is with the people of God, and Jesus' followers are to use their money so as to be received there.

(4) How can that be done? The answer is that 'they are to make friends' by means of money. The meaning of this is suggested, negatively at least, by the parable of the rich man and Lazarus: the rich man found himself excluded from the heavenly dwellings because of his callous neglect of the poor beggar. He conspicuously failed to use his money to 'make friends' of Lazarus. Jesus in the parable of the manager teaches that his followers are to use their money generously with eternity in view.

(5) The phrase 'so that they may receive you' may suggest the picture of those whom we befriend in this life welcoming us in the next: Lazarus might have welcomed the rich man to Abraham's fellowship, but as it was he could not even take him a drop of water across the chasm. But it may simply be part of the story that we should not press too much. The general point about 'being received' in heaven is clear.

So the parable of the unjust steward speaks of the need to prepare for the future crisis of judgement by practical generosity in the present. The point is reinforced and clarified in other sayings of Jesus: the well-known sayings about laying up treasure in heaven where neither thief nor moth destroy come in both Matthew and Luke in the context of teaching about money and about the kingdom (Mt 6:19–

21; Lk 12:32–34), and the point is simple: that we should invest our money in God's kingdom, not in this temporary and insecure world with its moths, rust and limited span.

The Lukan version of these sayings is particularly explicit that such investment means, 'Sell your possessions and give to the poor' (Lk 12:33); this is the sort of 'making friends' Jesus advocates. This is the work of the kingdom, of Jesus' revolution.

The point is made even clearer in Luke 14. This chapter contains the parable of the great feast, which, as we have already seen, describes a man's sumptuous banquet being spurned by those first invited, and then being opened up to 'the poor, the crippled, the blind and the lame' (Lk 14:21). That parable is descriptive of Jesus' own ministry. But in the same chapter Jesus gives instruction to others about how they should behave (Lk 14:7–14). Noticing how guests at the feast he was attending were vying for the most honourable places near the host, Jesus first gives some good advice about how to behave at feasts. His advice is: 'Take the lowest place, so that when your host comes, he will say to you, "Friend, move up to a better place." Then you will be honoured in the presence of all your fellow guests.' Luke quite rightly realises that this advice is a 'parable': Jesus is not giving hints on etiquette at feasts, but is explaining that the way into the kingdom of God is by humbling oneself (we recall the parable of the Pharisee and the tax-collector).

But Jesus goes on next to give advice to those on the giving end of a 'luncheon or dinner'. His advice is:

Do not invite your friends, your brothers or relatives, or your rich neighbours; if you do, they may invite you back and so you will be repaid. But . . . invite the poor, the crippled, the lame, the blind, and you will be blessed. Although they cannot repay you, you will be repaid at the resurrection of the righteous.

Once again we are dealing not with practical tips on social etiquette but with a parable about the kingdom. It is no accident that the words 'the poor, the crippled, the lame, the blind' occur in this parable and that of the great feast: Jesus here is saying in a vivid, pictorial way that others should

follow his example of sacrificial ministry to the needy. This is
laying up treasure in heaven, and making friends for the time
when money fails. Despite the parable, Jesus is not saying
that it is bad to be kind to friends and family; that would be
quite out of keeping with his teaching elsewhere. He is,
however, warning that there is a type of generosity which is
really only this-worldly self-interest: 'You scratch my back,
and I will scratch yours.' That will bring its rewards in this
life, but should not be confused with investing in God's
kingdom: that means living as Jesus did for those who
cannot repay the kindness.

Does this parable, and for that matter the parable of the
unjust manager, imply that the way into the kingdom is by
charitable good works? Any such impression is ruled out
when the three parables of Luke 14 are seen together. The
kingdom is a great feast generously offered by God as a gift
to the poor and others in need; and the appropriate response
and way in is 'to take the lowest place', *i.e.* by recognition of
one's need. But then the consequence in terms of behaviour
is to live out the revolutionary love of God by continuing
Jesus' practical ministry to the needy.

The parable of the unjust manager in Luke 16, to which
we must return, spoke particularly of the proper use of
'worldly wealth'. To some Christians down-to-earth talk
about money may sound materialistic and unspiritual: isn't it
our attitudes that matter, not our financial dealings? Jesus'
sayings about 'laying up treasure' suggest one answer to that:
'Where your treasure is, there will your heart be also.' Yes, it
is our attitudes that matter, but our attitudes and our
material things are not separable: how we invest our pounds
and pennies reflects and influences our attitudes.

Another answer is given in the sayings following the
parable of the unjust manager (*i.e.* Lk 16:10–13): they speak
about trustworthiness in something small being a measure of
trustworthiness in something great. We are reminded of the
parables of the steward and of the talents, where the faithful
steward and servants were rewarded with greater responsibility. But Jesus goes on to apply the principle
specifically to 'worldly' and 'spiritual' wealth: money is in

eternal terms a triviality, but the use of money is a measure of faithfulness and of a person's fitness for the greater wealth of the kingdom.

Jesus goes on to say: 'And if you have not been trustworthy with someone else's property, who will give you property of your own?' The picture is again very similar to that in the parables of the steward and the talents, where faithfulness in handling the master's affairs is rewarded with much greater responsibility and unfaithfulness with the loss of everything. In this context, the thought is that worldly wealth is a temporary trust and a test of faithfulness, whereas entry into the coming kingdom is permanent wealth.

What we have in these verses after Luke's parable of the unjust manager/steward is a significant statement about worldly wealth and its relationship to the kingdom of God. Jesus is not an ascetic who sees everything material as evil, nor a materialist who sees the material as everything; he sees money as something temporary, but still as something with value when properly used. It is interesting to compare Jesus' and Paul's teaching on marriage: marriage is good, and it matters very much how we use it; but it is something temporary and is not to become a distraction from what is eternal (see, *e.g.*, Mt 19:1–12; 22:23–33; 1 Cor 7, as mentioned in chapter 7).

Money is, emphatically, not to become a master: the final comment in Luke 16:10–13 is the saying about the impossibility of serving two masters, ending with the words: 'You cannot serve both God and Money.' Unrighteous mammon is to be used for God, not to become a substitute for God. Jesus knew, as well as we do in our world, that worldly wealth can easily become people's god. The rich fool and the rich man who neglected Lazarus found out the folly of this too late.

Jesus' teaching in these parables is then: 'Invest in the revolution of God,' by which he means literal investment. (Or should we perhaps say disinvestment, since it involves giving money away to others?) Just as the dedicated Marxist revolutionary is expected to commit himself and his finance to the cause, in the same way Jesus expects his followers to be practically and not just theoretically committed to the exciting world-changing mission that he inaugurated.

This is what actually happened in the early church in Jerusalem, where 'All the believers ... had everything in common. Selling their possessions and goods, they gave to anyone as he had need' (Acts 2:44-45). As a result of this literal obedience to Jesus' teaching 'there were no needy persons among them' (Acts 4:34). Modern commentators have sometimes criticised the early church for this so-called experiment in communism and said that it was a failure and not an example to follow. This may be a convenient argument for those who do not want to follow the early church's example, but is quite unacceptable for anyone who takes the New Testament and Jesus' teaching as his or her guide. Jesus said bluntly: 'Any of you who does not give up everything he has cannot be my disciple,' and he said to his disciples in general – not just to the rich young ruler – 'Sell your possessions and give to the poor' (Lk 14:33; 12:33). The early Christians of Jerusalem took Jesus' words seriously, under the guidance and inspiration of the Holy Spirit, as Luke makes clear in his description of their common life.

Such sharing was not simply humanitarian, nor was it a means of attracting the poor into the church (though it may properly have had that effect). It was, as we have seen, part of the revolution of God – a demonstration of that revolution in action, because the revolution of God is something that brings unity and equality, not just between Jew and Samaritan, but also between rich and poor, and not just on a spiritual level, but also on a social and material level. The Greek word *koinonia* is often translated 'fellowship' and understood as some sort of spiritual camaraderie. But the word literally means 'sharing', and the New Testament does not recognise our modern distinction between the spiritual, the social and the material. Fellowship is practical sharing.

This is made clear by Paul in Romans 15:27, where he speaks of sharing (the *koinonia* word) in spiritual and material things, and also in 2 Corinthians 8 and 9, where he urges the Corinthians to give generously to the Jerusalem church. The Corinthian church does not seem to have had the same pattern of community life as the early Jerusalem church, but Paul urges on them the same principle of sharing. He comments:

> Our desire is not that others might be relieved while you are hard pressed, but that there might be equality. At the present time your plenty will supply what they need, so that in turn their plenty will supply what you need. Then there will be equality, as it is written: 'He who gathered much did not have too much, and he who gathered little did not have too little.' (2 Cor 8:13–15)

In the same context Paul speaks of Jesus himself as the model of such giving: 'You know the grace of our Lord Jesus Christ, that though he was rich, yet for your sakes he became poor, so that you through his poverty might become rich' (2 Cor 8:9).

The revolution of God is not anti-material or even anti-riches, but God's purpose is that all share in the riches, and the call of Jesus is that those who are now rich should give to others. The parable of the unforgiving servant was about bridging divides of hatred and hurt through forgiveness; the parable of the good Samaritan was about bridging divides of nationality and class by love; the parable of the unjust steward is about bridging divisions of wealth and poverty by generosity: this is the way of the coming revolution.

## Other sayings from the Sermon on the Mount

So much of Jesus' teaching is pictorial or 'parabolic' that it is hard to know where to stop in describing and discussing it, but it may be worth mentioning in passing a few other examples from the Sermon on the Mount of Jesus' teaching about living out the divine revolution. The Sermon has been described as 'the manifesto of the kingdom', and it is full of striking images.

*Salt and light, and the city on a hill* (Mt 5:13–16; *cf.* Mk 9:49–50; Lk 14:34–35)

In the Sermon Jesus describes his disciples as the salt of the

earth and the light of the world, and urges them to function
as such: just as salt gives flavour and is also a preservative –
something particularly important in ancient society before
the invention of refrigeration – and just as a lamp brings
light to a dark house, so Jesus calls on his disciples to live the
revolution out in the world, so that others may see and be
brought into the revolution (Mt 5:13–16; compare also pp.
48–50 above and also Lk 11:33–36; Mt 6:22–23 emphasising
singleminded commitment).

It is not explained in the Sermon exactly what being salt
and light means in practice, except in so far as there is a
reference to 'good deeds', such as will lead people to glorify
God. But there is no doubt that what is meant is living out
the revolutionary teaching of the Sermon on the Mount
which is to follow. It is interesting that in Mark's gospel
there is a parallel saying of Jesus about salt, and there an
explanatory comment is added: 'Have salt in yourselves, and
be at peace with each other' (Mk 9:50). The saltiness of the
kingdom is harmony and reconciliation, as we have already
seen in this chapter; Jesus puts it this way in John 13:35: 'By
this all men will know that you are my disciples, if you love
one another.' Paul speaks of the Christian's conversation
being 'always full of grace, seasoned with salt' (Col 4:6): the
thought is a similar one.

We notice two further things about the light saying. The
first is the interesting parallel in John's gospel, where Jesus
speaks of himself as 'the light of the world' (Jn 8:12). The call
in the Sermon on the Mount to the disciples to be the 'light
of the world' is another example of a call to the disciples
to be and do what Jesus himself was and did.

The second is the probable Old Testament background to
the saying. The Old Testament describes God's coming
salvation or revolution as the coming of light into darkness.
Isaiah 9 is the most obvious passage: it speaks of Galilee and
then says: 'The people walking in darkness have seen a great
light; on those living in the land of the shadow of death a
light has dawned.' It then goes on to speak of the child to be
born who will be called 'Wonderful Counsellor, Mighty
God, Everlasting Father, Prince of Peace' and who will reign

on David's throne (Isa 9:1–7). Another striking passage is Isaiah 60, where Zion is addressed:

Arise, shine, for your light has come, and the glory of the Lord rises upon you. See, darkness covers the earth and thick darkness is over the peoples, but the Lord rises upon you and his glory appears over you. Nations will come to your light, and kings to the brightness of your dawn. (Isa 60:1–3)

Passages such as these are important background to Jesus' description of himself and his disciples as 'the light of the world', since the coming of the kingdom is the fulfilment of Old Testament promise. The Old Testament background may also explain the reference in Matthew 5:14 to the disciples as a 'city on a hill that cannot be hid': the thought may be that of the shining Mount Zion (*i.e.* Jerusalem) of Isaiah 60, to which the nations come. This is the destiny and calling of those in the revolution.

## Going to court (Mt 5:25–26; Lk 12:57–59)

After the sayings about salt and light, Jesus goes on to illustrate more concretely the standards of God's revolution and to show how much higher they are than simply the letter of the Old Testament law. There is, first, the saying about settling matters with an adversary before he takes you to court. This has a parallel in Luke's gospel. The saying may look at first sight like a piece of practical wisdom, not a parable about the kingdom of God. But the context tells against this. The context in both Matthew and Luke is teaching about the coming kingdom, and Jesus is urging his hearers to reconciliation before they come to the divine court. The immediate context of the saying in Matthew is Jesus' discussion of the commandment: 'You shall not kill.' Jesus says that you must not even hate or insult your brother, and that if you have wronged him you must put things right. This is the other side of the coin to the parable of the unmerciful servant: this time it is not the one sinned against who is to forgive, but the person who offends who is to put things right while there is time, and before the final judgement of God comes.

## Cutting off eye and hand (Mt 5:29–30; Mk 9:43–48)

Jesus goes on in the Sermon to speak about adultery and divorce, another obvious area where people offend and hurt each other. Jesus' standards are as high in this area as in every other: he has nothing to do with the liberal ideas of many of his contemporaries about divorce and remarriage, and he even condemns the adulterous look and thought. This is not the harsh morality of a social conservative who does not understand human nature, but is the standard of the revolution of God: the revolution is the coming of God's rule and perfection into the world, and Jesus' followers are to live by its perfect standards (Mt 5:48). It is characteristic of Jesus that he looks not just – nor indeed primarily – for outward purity, but for inward purity, since he sees the heart as the root of human corruption (see Mt 15:17–20; Mk 7:14–23).

The parable Jesus uses in this context is his advice to gouge out the eye through which temptation comes and to chop off the hand that sins. This is not the harsh regulation of an authoritarian cleric, but again a vivid picture expressing the need for radical commitment to God's revolution. Mark has the saying, not in the context of teaching about marriage and divorce, but in a more general context. The meaning is the same: Jesus calls people to a total commitment that is ruthless with those things in their lives that stand in the way of God's revolution and that lead to hell instead of heaven.

## The plank and the speck (Mt 7:3–5; Lk 6:41–42)

Later in the Sermon Jesus illustrates his instruction to 'Judge not' (Mt 7:1) with the humorous and vivid picture of the man with a plank in his eye trying to get a speck of dust out of his neighbour's eye. Jesus is not here saying anything about the role of judges in the law-courts, but about the sort of fault-finding and malicious gossip which is so prominent a feature of normal life, but which has no place in the revolution.

## Dogs and pigs (Mt 7:6)

In the same context Jesus goes on to yet another vivid

saying: 'Do not give dogs what is sacred; do not throw your pearls to pigs. If you do, they may trample them under their feet, and then turn and tear you to pieces.' The meaning of this pictorial saying has perplexed commentators no end.

In the first place, the picture is not quite clear: throwing pearls to pigs is intelligible (even if not advisable), but what is 'giving dogs what is holy'? One ingenious idea is that the original Aramaic spoke of giving gold rings to dogs (since in Aramaic the words for 'holy' and 'ring' are similar); this would make a nice parallel to pigs and pearls. An alternative view is that the reference is to food offered in sacrifices. Either way the picture is of giving something valuable but wholly inappropriate to dogs and pigs and reaping the consequences, the good things being trampled under foot and the ungrateful beasts turning to attack their would-be benefactors.

But what is the meaning of the saying? Dogs and pigs were usually and traditionally dirty and unpleasant, as people who have lived in poor countries where dogs and pigs scavenge in filthy rubbish may appreciate. The Jews used both terms to describe heathen Gentiles; Jesus himself used such language provocatively to test the faith of the Gentile woman who came seeking his help, though his own view of Gentiles was the opposite of insulting (Mt 15:26; Mk 7:27). Given this background, the probability is that Jesus is speaking of offering the 'holy food' or the pearls of the kingdom to unreceptive and hostile unbelievers. He has warned against 'judging', but he makes it clear that his followers will need discrimination in proclaiming the revolution. As he said when sending them out on mission, they are to be 'as shrewd as snakes and as innocent as doves', and there will be times when it is necessary to leave a place and to shake the dust off their feet as a symbolic warning of God's judgement on the resistant (Mt 10:14–16).

*Wolves in sheep's clothing; good and bad trees; blind guides* (Mt 7:15–20; Lk 6:43–45; Mt 12:33–35; 15:14; Lk 6:39)

Another warning parable in the Sermon on the Mount is the warning against false prophets as 'wolves in sheep's clothing'.

From a distance a wolf can look like a sheep. Jesus in another of his semi-humorous sayings pictures a wolf dressed up as a sheep. His point is deadly serious: the false prophet is one who looks like one of the flock, but is actually a deadly destructive enemy. The revolution of Jesus is, as we have seen, a revolution with an opposition, and Jesus warns of fierce opposition from those who appear to be its supporters. Paul makes the same point in 2 Corinthians 11:14, where he speaks of false apostles and comments: 'And no wonder, for Satan himself masquerades as an angel of light.'

How is the false prophet to be recognised? Jesus uses yet another picture to explain this, when he says: 'By their fruit you will recognise them.' He goes on to speak of trees producing good and bad fruit, and it is clear that the test of the false prophet is his or her life: is he or she simply saying 'Lord, Lord' or actually doing the will of God and living out the revolution?

In a similar passage in Matthew 12:33–35, where Jesus speaks of fruit indicating the quality of trees, he comments that the test of what is in a person's heart is what comes out of his mouth – Jesus compares the person bringing things out of his cellar into the light of day. He says this when discussing his opponents' accusation that he casts out demons by the prince of demons. At first sight the two sayings may seem to be in tension with each other, the one saying that a person's words betray him, the other that a person's words may be deceptive. But there is no contradiction: the fact is that there are two sorts of opposition to Jesus and his revolution – the overt opposition of those who make no claim to be his followers and the covert opposition of those who claim to be committed to the revolution, but whose lives betray them.

Jesus' saying about 'the blind leading the blind' (Lk 6:39; Mt 15:14) may be mentioned here. It is a warning about those who claim to know the way to the kingdom of God, but who are actually blind guides of the blind, and whose advice will lead to disaster. Jesus had in mind his religious opponents, who were in the business of shutting the kingdom of God in people's faces, making people children of hell rather than of heaven (Mt 23:13–16).

*Conclusion*

The theme that comes out most strongly in the sayings that we have looked at from the Sermon on the Mount is that the revolution of God is to be lived out in relationships – no hatred, immorality, or fault-finding. Joining the revolution is a bit like being in a foreign country and boarding a plane of one's own national airline to return home: already in the plane the language and customs of the home country are used. So the revolution of God as brought by Jesus means beginning to experience the life of the future kingdom and being called to live by its standards, though still *en route*. The standards of the kingdom of God are perfection, naturally. Jesus knows that his disciples will fail; so he teaches them to ask for forgiveness in the Lord's Prayer. But he still calls them to be light and salt in the world. He also, as we shall see in chapter 9, promises them the Father's help and the Holy Spirit's presence, which is what makes the apparently impossible excitingly possible (see Mt 19:26).

# 9 LIVING WITH THE GOD OF REVOLUTION

In the previous chapter we looked at Jesus' teaching on neighbour relations. But in summing up the law and will of God Jesus put the command to 'Love the Lord your God with all your heart and with all your soul and with all your mind' before love of neighbour (Mt 22:35–40). What did he mean by 'loving God' in practice?

The parable of the sheep and goats suggests that for Jesus love of God is expressed, perhaps more than in any other way, through practical down-to-earth love of my needy neighbour. Not that Jesus reduced the love of God to love of neighbour in the way that some modern theologians have tended to do: he deliberately put love of God first in his definition of the will of God, because the kingdom of God is what it says – i.e. to do with God as king and ruler. Perhaps the greatest weakness with the expression 'revolution of God' as a paraphrase of 'kingdom of God' is that it does not by itself convey the sense of God as ruler in the revolutionary society. Indeed modern political revolutions are usually democratic, in theory if not in practice, whereas the revolution of God, as Jesus understood it, is liberation through the restoration of monarchy – the divine monarchy; and living in the revolution is living for the king. So, although for Jesus love of God is expressed primarily through love of my neighbour, God is the source and focus of the kingdom. He is the Father whose love brings people into the kingdom, and he is the king whose kingdom is being restored and who is served by his followers as and when they love one another.

But a few of Jesus' parables speak not of serving God

through others, but more directly of the believer's personal relationship with God – as Father and as Lord and Master.

### The friend at midnight (Lk 11:5–8); also the father and his children's requests (Lk 11:11–13; Mt 7:9–11)

We have already seen that Jesus was revolutionary himself, not only in his love for the needy, but also in the intimacy of his relationship with God. The Jews of his day were typically very reserved in their speaking of God, recognising the holiness of his name and of his person. Jesus had an equally high view of God, but he was at the same time conscious of his close relationship to God, constantly speaking of him as Father and causing offence to his Jewish critics by doing so. John's gospel says explicitly what the other gospels imply: 'For this reason the Jews tried all the harder to kill him; not only was he breaking the Sabbath, but he was even calling God his own Father, making himself equal with God' (Jn 5:18).

This closeness to God was not something intended for Jesus only, but was to be a characteristic of life in the kingdom. The Old Testament in speaking of the day of the Lord looked forward to renewed fellowship between God and his people. For example, in the great passage about the new covenant in Jeremiah 31:34 the promise is: 'No longer will a man teach his neighbour, or a man his brother, saying, "Know the Lord," because they will all know me, from the least of them to the greatest.' Jesus taught his followers that they could have such intimacy.

Thus he taught them to call God 'Abba', as he did himself. 'Abba' was probably the opening word of the Lord's Prayer – see Luke 11:2 – and Paul in his letters to the Galatians and the Romans speaks of Christians having the Spirit of Jesus and being sons of God: 'Because you are sons, God sent the Spirit of his Son into our hearts, the Spirit who calls out, "*Abba*, Father"' (Gal 4:6; see also Rom 8:15). It is striking that in writing those letters in Greek to Greek-speaking readers Paul uses the Aramaic word 'Abba' to describe the Christian's cry. This was because that way of speaking of

God was something distinctive of Jesus, and revolutionary, which the Christians remembered and treasured. The Christian life is family life.

Jesus' relationship with his Father was expressed practically in prayer, and this was something about which Jesus taught his followers, for example in the parables and sayings on prayer in Luke 11:5–13.

The parable of the friend at midnight is about a man waking up his neighbour in the middle of the night to request some bread for an unexpected visitor. Visitors were liable to arrive unannounced because, of course, there was no telephone or public postal service. And they might well arrive late at night: journeys were slow, and, although it was desirable to arrive at one's destination by dusk, that was not always possible. Indeed in the heat of summer, travel at night was sometimes necessary, at least in the lowlands of Palestine.

When a visitor came, it was essential etiquette that a meal should be provided. In any case the traveller would probably be hungry after a long journey. In the story the host has run out of bread; his wife will no doubt be baking a new batch in the morning. But they know that friends of theirs still have bread – village life then was much more a shared, public life than life in modern cities, and it would be quite normal to know which neighbours had baked recently – and the man goes to ask for 'three loaves', enough for a meal and perhaps some to spare.

The man does not get a very warm reception from the friend, who is already in bed with the family. It is bad enough for those of us who live in sizeable modern houses to be woken up in the middle of the night. But in this case we need to imagine a small, dark, one-room house, with a raised area at the back: the door will be left open in the day-time, but at night a cumbersome wooden bar is fixed across the door, the animals are at the front of the house, and the family sleep side-by-side on mats on the floor, perhaps under one covering, in the back raised part. It was a considerable nuisance to be asked to get up and find some bread.

But, despite the nuisance, Jesus concludes the parable thus: 'I tell you, though he will not get up and give him the bread because he is his friend, yet because of the man's boldness he will get up and give him as much as he needs.' The word translated 'though' here may better be translated 'even if', and the word 'boldness' is literally 'shamelessness'. Although there is some doubt about the exact sense of this word, the overall force of Jesus' comment is clear: even if the neighbour's appeal to the sleeping father as 'friend' falls on deaf ears, the man will still do what is asked, not out of friendship, but because of his neighbour's nerve and audacity in asking. He may well have in mind what the other neighbours will say if he does nothing; they would be sure to hear! He has got to help his friend, whether he likes it or not.

The point of the parable is spelt out by Luke in the sayings about asking, seeking and knocking that follow; these sayings are found also in Matthew, though not with the preceding parable. The point is quite simply that as the man who dared to ask his friend got his request, so those who through prayer ask, seek and knock will be heard by God.

But is not the reluctant giving of the neighbour in the parable rather an unfortunate picture of divine generosity in response to prayer? Would it not have been better if the neighbour had responded because of the depth of his friendship, rather than because he could not help it? The answer to this is that the parable is not one that works by saying: 'God is or acts like this . . .', but rather by saying: 'If people are or act like this, how much more will God . . .?' In this case the argument is: If a friend who is not really much of a friend (at least in the middle of the night!) will give you the bread you ask for, how much more will God your loving Father give you the things you need if you have the sense to ask him?

That this is the meaning is shown by the sayings about a father that follow in Luke, and which are explicitly of the 'how much more' variety. Jesus observes that if a human father is asked by his son for a fish or an egg, he will not give him a snake or a scorpion instead. It has been suggested that Jesus paired 'fish' with 'snake' and 'egg' with 'scorpion' because of their superficial resemblances: there is one type of fish in Galilee that is particularly snake-like, and a rolled-up scorpion is said to look like an egg! But the main point is that whereas fish and egg are good and nutritious, the snake and scorpion are two of the greatest dangers to children in a country like Palestine. Human fathers 'know how to give good gifts' to their children, even though by comparison with God's goodness they are evil. 'How much more,' Jesus concludes, 'will your Father in heaven give the Holy Spirit to those who ask him!'

An equivalent saying of Jesus in Matthew is slightly different in two respects: Jesus speaks this time not of egg and scorpion, but of bread and stone – a small bread roll looks a bit like a stone. And Jesus' promise is worded slightly differently: 'How much more will your Father in heaven give good gifts to those who ask him!' Whether the differences between the good and bad items as listed by Matthew and Luke reflect Jesus' choice of different images on different occasions, or whether Jesus gave three examples, with Matthew and Luke choosing different pairs, is not important. The point in both gospels is the same: Jesus encourages his followers to pray, in the assurance that God will answer prayer (so the parable of the friend at midnight), and will answer by giving what they need and ask for. God is the good Father who loves his children, and it is the privilege of those who are in the revolution to live as his children, to bring their requests to him, and to receive his answers.

This general point about the importance and value of praying to the heavenly Father is quite clear. But is it possible to be any more specific about the nature of the promise being made? Is Jesus giving his followers a blank cheque: 'Ask whatever you wish, and it will be given you' (Jesus' words in Jn 15:7)? Such an interpretation is completely excluded by the context of the words in all the gospels, as well as by what we know of Jesus' teaching as a whole. Thus the apparently blank cheque of John 15:7 is in the context of teaching about 'remaining' in Jesus and bearing fruit: it is a promise of power in doing the will of Jesus or living out the revolution.

So far as Luke is concerned, there are two clues about the force of the parable of the friend at midnight. The first is

that it ends with the sentence: 'I tell you . . . he will give him
everything he needs.' The second is that it is a parable about
bread which follows the Lord's Prayer, with its petition for
'daily bread'. Putting two and two together, we deduce that
the parable is a promise (to those who are seeking the Lord's
kingdom: 'Your kingdom come') that the Lord will hear his
children's prayer for their needs to be met. We are reminded
of Jesus' words in the Sermon on the Mount urging the
disciples not to be anxious about food, drink and clothing.
Jesus compares the birds, whose food God provides, and the
flowers of the field, whose magnificent clothing God supplies,
and he comments: 'your heavenly Father knows that you
*need all these things*' – note the similarity of the phrase to
what we find in the parable of the friend at midnight – 'but
seek first the kingdom and its righteousness, and all these
things will be added to you' (Mt 6:32–33; Lk 12:29–31). The
promise in this passage and in the parable is that God will
give daily bread and whatever else they need to those who
join the revolution and who ask God to provide.

The parable is followed in Luke by the sayings about the
father who gives his children good things, which are explained
as follows: 'How much more will your heavenly Father give
the Holy Spirit to those who ask him!' The promise this time
is of spiritual, rather than physical, provision, and it is not
fanciful to see this promise also in the context of the Lord's
Prayer, since Jesus taught his disciples to pray not just for
bread, but also for forgiveness and deliverance from temptation and evil. How does such spiritual provision come?
Answer: through the Holy Spirit. So Jesus in the Lord's
Prayer teaches his disciples to pray for their physical and
spiritual needs, and through the parables about prayer he
promises that these prayers will be answered.

Matthew's saying about the father giving gifts to his
children is probably to be understood similarly. The promise
in this case is that 'Your Father who is in heaven will give
good things to those who ask him.' The promise of 'good
things' is a lot more general than the promise of the Holy
Spirit in Luke, and in the context of the Sermon on the
Mount following the Lord's Prayer it very probably includes

material and not just spiritual provision. So, in Luke's gospel
the parable of the friend speaks of material provision and the
saying about the father of spiritual provision; in Matthew
the saying about the father covers both points. This is an
interesting example of gospels diverging in wording, but
agreeing in overall sense.

The conclusion is, then, that the promise of answered
prayer is not a blank cheque guaranteeing that God will
answer every prayer for a miracle, let alone prayers for the
satisfaction of personal whims or desires. What it is is a
promise that in calling people to join the revolution of God,
with all its sacrifices and demands, Jesus is not calling people
to a lonely and impossible struggle, but into a relationship
with a Father who listens to his children, cares about their
needs and loves to give them good things. It is an invitation
to act on his promise and to ask him to provide materially
and spiritually for the life of revolution.

Paul's words in Philippians 4:13, 'I can do everything
through him who gives me strength', are a good commentary
on the promise of Jesus. Paul did not mean that he never
suffered disappointment or difficulty – he makes it very clear
that he did – but that he experienced Christ's contentment
and sufficiency even in the difficult times. As he puts it
elsewhere, he learned in practice that 'My grace is sufficient
for you' (2 Cor 12:9).

Before finally leaving these parables on prayer, it may be
worth commenting a little more on the difference between
the wording of Jesus' promise in Matthew and Luke. As we
saw, the promise is of 'good things' in Matthew and of the
'Holy Spirit' in Luke. It is uncertain how this difference is to
be explained; it may be that Jesus said 'good things' and that
Luke put 'Holy Spirit' in order to clarify the meaning. But if
he did so, he did not introduce anything alien to Jesus'
teaching. On the contrary, the Holy Spirit is central to Jesus'
understanding of God's revolution.

Not that Jesus speaks all that much about the Spirit,
except in his farewell discourses to his disciples in John 13–
16. However, even from the little he does say it is clear how
important the Holy Spirit is in the context of his teaching

about the kingdom. The Holy Spirit is, to put it simply, the power behind the revolution. At his baptism Jesus himself was filled with the Holy Spirit for his mission, and it is by the power of the Holy Spirit that he goes on to do his revolutionary work (see his words in Mt 12:28: 'If I drive out demons by the Spirit of God, then the kingdom of God has come upon you'). Jesus explicitly identified himself with the one spoken of in Isaiah 61: 'The Spirit of the Sovereign Lord is on me, because the Lord has anointed me to preach good news to the poor' (Isa 61:1; Lk 4:18–21). Jesus promises the same indwelling presence of God to his followers: they too will receive power to live out the revolution (see Mt 10:20; Acts 1:8). The Old Testament looked forward not just to the coming of one Spirit-filled Messiah, but also to a general pouring out of God's Spirit (see Joel 2:28–32 and also the new covenant passage in Jer 31:31–34, which speaks of the law of God being written on people's hearts). The coming of the revolution of God in Jesus sees the fulfilment of both these prophecies.

Paul in his letters develops the thought of the Holy Spirit as the Spirit of the revolution: the Holy Spirit is the Spirit of Jesus who leads the Christian to cry 'Abba'; he is also the one who makes possible the higher righteousness of the revolution, working in the hearts of believers and enabling them to 'fulfil' the law and will of God (see Rom 8; 2 Cor 3, *etc.*).

## The unjust judge (Lk 18:1–8)

Jesus' parable of the unjust judge is similar to that of the friend at midnight, in construction, wording and meaning. It is the story of someone 'bothering' someone else – the identical phrase is used – and of them getting their way from someone who is ill-disposed towards them.

In this case it is a widow bothering a judge. Widows were a traditionally vulnerable group in Palestinian society. Girls were regularly married at the age of thirteen or fourteen, and so a widow could be quite young, with no grown-up children to care for her. For such a wife to lose her husband was to

lose her position and status in society, and also her natural
male protector. It is no accident that in the Old Testament
widows and fatherless children are mentioned together (see
Exod 22:22; Deut 10:18; Isa 1:17). Whether young or old,
widows were often easy game for the ruthless exploiter, and
Jesus speaks in Mark 12:40 of teachers of the law who
should have been the first to care for the weak 'devouring
widows' houses' – presumably a reference to economic
exploitation of some kind.

We may imagine the widow of Jesus' parable having
some financial problem, perhaps with a debtor who would
not pay his debt or a relative who would not give her a
part of the inheritance. She brings the problem to a 'judge'.
There does not seem to have been one uniform judicial
system in Palestine, but when Jesus speaks of the widow
coming to a 'judge', we should probably imagine some
prominent local citizen, perhaps having links with the Herod
family, who had authority to decide disputed cases. In Jesus'
story the judge in question is one who 'neither fears God
nor respects people': he is in short a bad example of his
type, literally an 'unjust judge' (Lk 18:6). He is the sort of
person who will listen to money (which the widow did not
have) rather than to considerations of morality or even to
public opinion.

The story has him living up to expectation, and refusing
for some time to help the widow. But in due course he
relents, not because he is a reformed character – not at all –
but 'because this widow is a bother to me' and 'so that she
does not keep on coming to me forever and wearing me out'.
The word translated 'wearing me out' is literally 'giving me a
black eye', and the judge could be saying, ironically, that, if
he does not do something soon, it could in due course come
to blows. More likely the thought is of the woman battering
the judge by her dogged unwillingness to give up, or just
possibly of her blackening his public image. The general
point is clear: the powerful judge, for all his corrupt laziness,
is forced to act by a poor impotent widow.

The conclusion is again a 'how much more . . .' conclusion.
It can be conveniently set out as follows:

| if an unrighteous judge | how much more | God in his righteousness |
|---|---|---|
| faced with the persistent cry of a widow in whom he has no interest | | faced with the persistent cry of his elect |
| responds eventually and vindicates her | | will respond and vindicate them quickly |

And the point of the whole comparison is not just to give reassurance of answered prayer, but is to encourage persistent prayer. So verse 1: 'He told a parable to them to show the necessity of always praying and not giving up.'

The overall thrust of the parable is quite clear. But it is not presented in Luke's gospel as a parable about prayer in general. It comes immediately after a long section of teaching about the second coming, and it is applied quite specifically to the promise of the Lord's coming in verses 7 and 8: 'Will not God bring about justice for his chosen ones, who cry to him day and night? And he is patient over them. I tell you, he will see that they get justice, and quickly. However, when the Son of Man comes, will he find faith on the earth?' The parable about the judge who unwillingly and slowly vindicates the persistent widow is thus taken as a promise of God's willing and speedy vindication of his praying people at the coming of the Son of Man.

There is one particularly difficult phrase in verse 7, the phrase we translated 'And he is patient over them.' The difficulty is twofold. First, there is a question over the meaning of the word translated 'be patient', which could alternatively be translated 'be slow'. Second, there is a question about the punctuation of the whole sentence: the difficult phrase seems almost to interrupt the flow of the sentence. Various suggestions have been made as to how the phrase fits in: thus the verse has been understood as either 'Will not God bring about justice for his chosen ones ... even though he is slow with them?' or 'Will not God bring about justice . . .? Will he be slow with them?'

Perhaps the simplest way of construing it is as 'Will not God bring about justice for his chosen ones ... being patient with them?' There may be an implied contrast between God's

patience and the impatience of the judge in the story; or
perhaps more likely the thought is similar to that found in 2
Peter 3:9, which speaks of the Lord's coming and says: 'The
Lord is not slow in keeping his promise, as some understand
slowness. He is *patient*' – the same Greek word – 'with you,
not wanting anyone to perish, but everyone to come to
repentance.' On this interpretation the phrase in the parable
describes the Lord's 'patience' before the second coming
(patience which the believers are called to share in Jas 5:7–8).
It is the same thought as is found in the parable of the seed
growing secretly in Mark 4:26–29, where the master seems
frustratingly inactive between sowing and harvest, though in
fact the seed of the kingdom is growing. It is the same
thought also in Revelation 6:9–11, where the martyrs of God
ask: '"How long, Sovereign Lord, holy and true, until you
judge the inhabitants of the earth and avenge our blood?"
Then ... they were told to wait a little longer, until the
number of their fellow-servants and brothers ... was completed.'

If this is the sense of the phrase in the parable, then we
have two contrasting ideas about the coming of the Lord,
side by side: the predominant emphasis is that the Lord is
coming surely and quickly, and yet alongside this is a
reference to the Lord's patience. Some would see in this
tension a contradiction between the original idea of Jesus
(about a near end) and the later idea of the church (about
a delayed end). But it is preferable to recognise two
complementary emphases in Jesus' own teaching: on the
one hand, the revolution is under way and coming; on the
other hand, the revolution is coming through a process of
growth, involving the preaching of the word and with
people being given time to repent. This double emphasis is
characteristic of the whole of Jesus' teaching and of the
New Testament: consequently the call is, on the one hand,
to be alert and patient, and, on the other hand, to proclaim
the good news.

Whatever the meaning of the phrase about the Lord's
patience, the parable as a whole is a call to persistent prayer,
and particularly to prayer for the Lord's coming. It is an

assurance that such prayer will be answered. Whereas the parable of the friend at midnight and the sayings about the father giving gifts to his children were a promise that the second half of the Lord's Prayer would be answered, the parable of the unjust judge is in effect a promise that the first half of the Lord's Prayer, with its petition for the coming of God's kingdom, will be heard and answered. The temptation is to give up hope (as the experience of the church, ancient and modern, attests); so the parable is introduced by Luke as an encouragement to constant prayer and 'not to give up'. We may appropriately compare the Lord's promise at the end of the book of Revelation, 'Yes, I am coming soon,' and note the author's prayerful response: 'Amen. Come, Lord Jesus' (Rev 22:20).

The parable of the wise and foolish girls emphasised the need for perseverance in awaiting the Lord (see chapter 5); the parable of the unjust judge explains that that perseverance includes perseverance in prayer (see also Lk 21:36). Living out the kingdom of God means living in fellowship with God as Father and king, looking to him both for present needs and for the completion of his royal revolution.  The kingdom is his business, and he may be trusted to provide for his servants and to bring the revolution. But his servants are not simply to presume on his goodness or to be passive spectators of God's action. They are to be actively involved in the work of the kingdom through earnest and persistent prayer.

Prayer is commonly understood in the modern world as a psychologically therapeutic exercise, benefiting the worshipper but having little other effect. Accordingly we do not make it a priority. The New Testament, however, sees prayer as a powerful God-given instrument, effecting God's purposes in the world. This is clear, for example, from Paul's emphasis on the need to 'pray continually' and to 'keep on praying', and from the way he requests his friends to pray for the success of his work (e.g. 1 Thess 5:25; Eph 6:18–20; Col 4:2–4; cf. Jas 5:16–18). Paul is only following Jesus in this. Jesus made prayer a priority himself, believing that God chooses to do his work in response to prayer (e.g. Mk 1:35; 9:29). He explained to his disciples that they should ask, seek and knock – persistently – in order to receive, find and see doors opened.

Prayer is an expression of human weakness, but also a weapon of divine power. The thought of God's power being displayed in and through human weakness is an important theme in Paul's letters (*e.g.* 2 Cor 12:9–10): prayer is the expression of our powerlessness and of our dependence on God, and at the same time the most powerful means we have of collaborating in God's work. God does not bring the kingdom independently of his people, but through his people as they trust him and express that trust in prayer. Prayer is thus a top priority in the revolution of God.

## The humble servant (Lk 17:7–10)

If the parable of the friend at midnight and the sayings on the father and his children spoke of God as the Father who provides, and the parable of the unjust judge spoke of God as the judge who vindicates, the last parable that we shall look at in this chapter, that of the humble, obedient servant, portrays God as master or lord.

This parable, which only Luke records, pictures a man who has a small-holding and just one servant to help him on the farm and in the house. The servant works out in the field in the morning, and then, probably in mid-afternoon, comes in. When he does so, the master does not tell him to sit down and put his feet up, but expects him to get on with preparing and serving the evening meal before he has time to himself. In doing what is required, Jesus explains, the servant is not doing anything creditworthy, deserving the master's thanks; he is simply fulfilling his duty. Jesus goes on to say that his disciples' attitude to their Christian service should be similar.

The background to the parable is the ancient institution of slavery, which we have discussed already (*e.g.* in chapter 5). The slave was someone who because of debt or for some other reason had been sold and become the property of his (or her) master, with few rights of his own (though in the

Old Testament Jewish slaves were protected). A slave could do any number of tasks, skilled or unskilled (*e.g.* teaching the children, cooking, labouring, *etc.*). In our parable the slave works both in the field and in the house.

Masters were often benevolent to their slaves, and, although conditions of employment were harder and hours of employment longer in the ancient world than in modern industrialised countries, there is no need to think of the master in our parable as being particularly harsh or callous in his expectations. He had paid for his slave (perhaps when the man was in debt), and he has a right to expect him to work.

The basic point of Jesus' story could just as well be made in modern terms: the garage mechanic or the school teacher who finds a job and is paid to work a forty-hour week is not doing something marvellous, deserving special thanks, when he does so; he is simply doing his proper duty to his employer. That is not to say that common courtesy and saying 'thank you' are unimportant. The point is that the worker doing a job for which he is paid cannot boast of having done his employer a favour such that his employer is in his debt. He has merely done what he should have done.

In the same way, Jesus says that his followers should say: 'We are useless slaves; we have only done what we ought to do.' To describe themselves as 'useless' or 'unprofitable' may sound excessive; but it is to be understood as an expression of humility rather than as a strict statement of fact, and the point being made is that Jesus' followers, who have been brought into the kingdom by God's great mercy, can take no credit for the work they do for the revolution. It is the work of the Lord of the revolution who took them into his service in his own kindness and generosity. A modern analogy might be the situation of a rich benefactor building a hospital at his own expense: the credit for the building goes to him, not to the labourers whom he employs and pays. So, Jesus says, the disciples cannot claim credit for their work for the kingdom; they are slaves sent by their master.

Of course, it is clear from other parts of Jesus' teaching that the Lord does treat his slaves as his children, not just as

servants (see the parable of the prodigal son and Jn 15:15). It
is also true that the Lord rewards his faithful servants, and
that, far from treating them callously, he will himself sit
them down at table and serve them (see Lk 12:37 and
chapter 5). But this is all his generosity: it is because of him
that they can work in the kingdom in the first place, and,
although he chooses to reward them for their service, they
can never claim credit for their work. Their attitude can only
be that of humble, grateful servants. We might imagine the
prodigal son after his return home being congratulated for
working well for his father; he would rightly give all the
credit to his father for welcoming him home and allowing
him to work again.

Related ideas come out in Paul's letters – not surprisingly
as his teaching derives so often from Jesus – either directly or
indirectly. When thinking of what God had done for him,
Paul characteristically speaks of sonship and freedom from
slavery; when thinking of his own responsibility to Christ
and of his ministry, he speaks of himself as a 'slave' of Christ
and as one who is under obligation to the Lord who
redeemed him and who can claim no 'pay' for fulfilling his
calling (see Rom 1:1, 14; 1 Cor 9:15–19; Phil 1:1). Paul and
also Peter speak of the Christian as one 'bought with a price'
and the price being 'the precious blood of Christ' (1 Cor
6:19–20; 7:22–23; 1 Pet 1:18–19). It is because such a price has
been paid that the Christian can live a new life in the Spirit
and also can claim no credit for doing so. Paul frequently
speaks of the gospel excluding human boasting, and he
emphasises the point because of the human tendency to
boast. But there is only room for humble gratitude in the
revolution of God, since it is all his work. As his servants
brought into the revolution we can (and should) work for the
revolution of God from morning till night; but we will never
deserve credit, being (in the words of the hymn) 'debtors to
mercy alone'.

# 10 CALL TO DECISION

Jesus was not in the entertainment business, but was a revolutionary for God who challenged people to join the revolution. 'Repent and believe the good news', he said (Mk 1:15); or, as we may paraphrase it, 'Turn round, and commit yourself to the message of God's revolution.' Very many of the parables that we have already discussed contain this note of urgent challenge, and in this chapter we look at a few more.

## Roads and doors (Mt 7:13–14; Lk 13:23–27)

The Sermon on the Mount, as we have seen, has been described as the manifesto of the kingdom of God, and it concludes, after the revolutionary standards of the kingdom have been expounded, with a pointed challenge to decision, or rather a series of pointed challenges.

First there is the picture of the two gates and the two ways in Matthew 7:13–14 and the challenge to 'enter by the narrow gate'. The idea of two ways is a familiar one in the Old Testament. For example, in Jeremiah 21:8 the Lord offers people a choice: 'See, I am setting before you the way of life and the way of death.' Jesus in offering a similar choice speaks of the gate to life being narrow and the road to life being 'hard', and he contrasts this with the broad gate and wide road that lead to destruction. The picture is clear enough: in Jesus' Palestine there were well-trodden main roads between the major centres of population, like the 'King's Highway' going North–South through the Jordan valley; such roads were primitive by modern standards, and even by Roman standards, but nevertheless were major, well-used routes. There were also many rough-and-ready tracks criss-crossing the countryside, on which two loaded animals would sometimes have difficulty in passing. As for gates, cities like Jerusalem had magnificent and impressive main gates through which you could literally drive a coach and horses; but there were also many small gates, not fit for much more than pedestrian use.

Jesus speaks of the gate to God's revolution as narrow. In the context of the Sermon on the Mount the thought is probably of the revolutionary high standards of which Jesus spoke: 'Unless your righteousness surpasses that of the Pharisees and the teachers of the law, you will certainly not enter the kingdom of heaven' (Mt 5:20). We are again reminded of Jesus' meeting with the rich young man who was unprepared for the call to join the revolution of Jesus, giving up all his possessions, and of Jesus' comment that 'it is easier for a camel to go through the eye of a needle than for a rich man to enter the kingdom of God'. Jesus' humorous and yet serious comment makes it clear that the gate is indeed narrow and only passable with the help of God (see Mt 19:23–30; Mk 10:23–31; Lk 18:24–30).

Jesus speaks also of the way to life being 'hard'. The Greek word means literally something like 'pressurised', and the picture is probably of an uncomfortably narrow path where passing is difficult. But the Greek word is used also of suffering or oppression, and is related to the word used in the parable of the sower when Jesus speaks of people receiving the word of the kingdom but giving up because of 'suffering and persecution'. Jesus is thus probably alluding to the fact that the way of revolution is a way of conflict, suffering and pressure.

This is something Jesus is very honest about elsewhere in his teaching, unlike some modern preachers. For example, when he told people that discipleship involves 'taking up the cross' (e.g. in Mt 16:24), he was using a horribly contemporary picture of the cost involved in joining the revolution. When sending the disciples out on mission Jesus warned them of opposition, persecution and betrayal (see Mt

10). It would be wrong to paint a wholly black picture: he also promised the help of the Holy Spirit in times of crisis, as well as final reward. But Paul accurately conveys Jesus' meaning when he says: 'We must go through many hardships to enter the kingdom of God' (Acts 14:22).

The opposite of the narrow gate and the hard way is the broad gate and way. This is the comfortable road which the rich young man eventually opted for, when he left Jesus without taking up the challenge to discipleship. Some early copies of Matthew refer only to the broad and easy way, not to a broad gate. It is doubtful if this is the original wording that Matthew wrote, but if it is, it may be significant: there is no need to go through any gate to get on this road; it is the road everyone is on, unless they deliberately opt out.

Jesus' parable does not simply contrast the gates and the ways, but also the differing destinations. Like so many of his parables, it speaks of reversal: just as the tiny mustard seed becomes a tree (see chapter 4), so the narrow door and way lead to life, whereas the super-highway for all its attractiveness and popularity ends in a total and fearful cul-de-sac, *i.e.* destruction. We saw earlier how Jeremiah spoke to the people of 'life' and 'death': he spoke in a context of political crisis and meant life and death in a literal sense. Jesus in the context of his teaching about the kingdom meant 'life' in the sense of entry into the final kingdom of God and 'destruction' in the sense of exclusion from the kingdom. In the terms of the parable of the rich man and Lazarus, it is the difference between feasting with Abraham and the people of God on the one hand, or being in agony and irrevocably separated from the feast on the other. (We may note, in passing, that the word 'destruction' suggests something terminal rather than ongoing and everlasting agony. But see our earlier discussion in chapter 7.)

Jesus' advice to people to go the narrow way to life is not the advice of an uninvolved spectator. It is in fact a call to the disciples to 'follow me' – to follow Jesus on the way of revolution. He lived out the narrow standards of the Sermon on the Mount, and incidentally demonstrated how different such narrowness is from a dry and loveless narrow-minded-

ness. He also suffered and went the way of the cross. And he
broke through to life – to the resurrection life of the
kingdom of God. The book of Hebrews describes Jesus as
the 'pioneer' of the faith, and Paul describes Jesus as the
'firstfruits' of resurrection life (Heb 2:10; 12:2; 1 Cor 15:20).
His resurrection was the prototype of the final transformed
life of the revolution of God. He opened up the way to this
life and invited people to follow him to it via the narrow
way.

Paul understood this well. For example, in Romans 8 he
speaks of believers being 'co-heirs' with Christ and of sharing
in his sufferings 'in order that we may also share in his
glory' (Rom 8:17). He goes on in the same chapter to speak
of Christians longing for the 'redemption of our bodies' and
of all creation waiting for liberation (Rom 8:22–23), in other
words for the day of God's revolution.

Luke too has a parable of a narrow door that is difficult to
enter (Lk 13:23–27). In his case the picture seems to be of a
door to a house where a banquet is being held, which will at
some point be shut. The language reminds us of Matthew's
parable of the wise and foolish girls and also of the passage
at the end of the Sermon on the Mount in Matthew's gospel
(Mt 7:21–23), where Jesus warns that saying 'Lord, Lord'
will not save anyone. It may be that Luke has combined
several of these sayings of Jesus. In any case the point is
clear, namely that it will one day be too late for people to
get into the kingdom. It will do no good on that day for
people to claim acquaintance with Jesus – 'We ate and drank
with you, and you taught in our streets' – if they have
failed to identify with his narrow revolution of righteousness.
They will find themselves shut out and disowned by the
master of the house as 'evildoers' – literally 'workers of
unrighteousness'.

In the similar passage at the end of the Sermon on the
Mount Jesus warns that calling him 'Lord, Lord' and even
claiming to have done wonderful spiritual works in his name
will do no good if unaccompanied by obedience to the 'will
of my Father who is in heaven'. The terrible and final verdict
will be 'Away from me, you workers of lawlessness' (Mt

7:21–23). The point is simple: failure to live out the way of
God's revolution – with its higher righteousness and law of
love – is fatal. We may compare Paul's warnings about
baptism without obedience being a recipe for disaster – the
earliest baptismal creed was probably 'Jesus is Lord' – and
about spiritual gifts without revolutionary love being useless
(1 Cor 10:1–11; 13:2). Joining the revolution is not just a
matter of words of allegiance, but of following Jesus in
serious, costly commitment.

### Good and bad trees; the fig tree (Mt 7:16–20; Lk 13:6–9)

The parable of the two gates and ways is followed in
Matthew's version of the Sermon on the Mount by the
warnings against false prophets who are wolves in sheep's
clothing and like trees bearing bad fruit (Mt 7:15–20). The
thought is related to what has gone before: having spoken of
the narrowness of the way to life, Jesus now warns of those
who offer plausible and attractive alternatives, claiming and
even appearing to be prophets with Christian credentials. In
fact these dangerous counter-revolutionaries do not live the
life of God's revolution themselves, and they are in the
business of misleading others.

Having considered these sayings already (in chapter 8) we
will not spend more time on them here. But we may note the
two points Jesus makes when speaking of good and bad
trees. First, he explains that the test of a tree is its
fruitfulness. Thus referring to the main traditional fruits of
Palestine, he asks: 'Do people pick grapes from thornbushes
[or brambles] and figs from thistles?' The answer is obviously no: the fruit is evidence of what species the tree is.
Fruit is also the test of the quality of a particular tree, as
Jesus goes on to say: a good tree produces good fruit and
a bad tree bad fruit. The point is a straightforward one:
the test of discipleship and of whether someone belongs to
the revolution or not is his life, not the label he or she
wears. The second point Jesus makes about trees is that a
tree that fails to produce good fruit is cut down and

burnt. The reference is to the destruction which is the end of the broad road.

If these tree sayings in Matthew are in the first instance a warning against being deceived by others, Jesus' parable of the fig tree in Luke 13:6–9 speaks of the dangers of self-deception. (Though that thought is probably not absent from the Matthew saying.) Fig trees were all over the Palestinian landscape, and once established (in about three years) good trees would produce fruit for as much as ten months of the year. Jesus' parable describes the owner of a fig tree coming for three years to look for fruit and finding none. We may assume that the tree was at least six years old by this stage. The owner threatens to have it dug up, but his servant who looked after the vineyard requested one more year to dig round the tree and to fertilise it with manure.

The context of the parable in Luke describes people coming to Jesus with a report about two recent disasters in Jerusalem: one was apparently a massacre of some Galilean pilgrims by Pilate in the temple; we don't know the circumstances of this, but we know from the Jewish historian Josephus how Pilate had several violent confrontations with his Jewish subjects, usually caused by his insensitivity to their religious feelings (*e.g.* when he appropriated temple money for the building of an aqueduct). The other incident was the collapse of a tower, probably in the old city wall of Jerusalem, which left eighteen people dead. Jesus' reaction on this news was to observe that those who had died in these recent disasters were no worse sinners than other Galileans and residents of Jerusalem and to warn his hearers: 'Unless you repent, you too will all perish.' The parable of the fig tree then follows, and its meaning in the context is self-evident: it is a warning to Jesus' hearers of the judgement that will come on them if they fail to respond to his call to repent.

The parable has the master in dialogue with the man who looks after the vineyard, and it is the servant who suggests a one-year postponement of the decision to cut the tree down. It is possible that the thought is of Jesus' ministry representing the last chance for the vineyard: just as the man promises to

dig round the tree and to fertilise it, so Jesus brings a last
and very good opportunity for people to repent.

The thought may be of the people of Israel in particular
being given a last chance, as in the parable of the tenants in
the vineyard. The fact that the fig tree is described as planted
in a vineyard could support this interpretation, since, as we
have seen, the vineyard has strong associations with Israel
(see chapters 6 and 7). If this is the sense, then this spoken
parable of Jesus is very similar to his acted parable of cursing
the fig tree (Mt 21:18–22; Mk 11:12–25). That story is closely
connected (notably in Mark's gospel) to Jesus' symbolic
cleansing of the temple: Jesus acts out two parables of judgement – in the temple and with the fig tree.

But, although Luke's parable could be such a warning to
Israel as a nation, the preceding discussion of the individuals
who died in Jerusalem and the warning that 'unless you
repent, you too will all perish' probably favours a broader
interpretation: Jesus urgently tells all his hearers to seize the
chance he has brought, or to face destruction.

## The true vine (John 15:1–8)

The other passage in the gospels which emphasises fruit-
bearing and warns of judgement is the famous chapter in
John's gospel about Jesus as the true vine. It begins with one
of Jesus' great 'I am' sayings which are so distinctive in
John's gospel: 'I am the true vine'. Jesus goes on: 'My Father
is the farmer', and then some verses later, 'You are the
branches' (v.5).

Two things are notable about this listing of the cast of the
parable. First, Jesus' identification of himself as the true vine
is striking, since the vine was the traditional symbol of Israel
as a nation, being used as such in numerous Old Testament
passages and also on Jewish coinage, for example on that
used during the war of AD 66–70. Second, it is notable that
he speaks of his disciples as 'branches' of him as the true
vine. These two things make sense together, and confirm
what we saw when we examined Jesus' use of the title 'Son of

Man', namely that Jesus saw himself as the focus and representative of the new Israel and as the one through whom others could be members of the revolutionary people of God (see chapter 4). One Old Testament passage that is of particular interest is Psalm 80, since the psalmist speaks of Israel as a vine planted by God (also as his 'son'; so literally, Ps 80:15), and he prays both for the restoration of the vine and also for 'the man at your right hand, the son of man you have raised up for yourself' (Ps 80:8–19). The man in the psalm is undoubtedly the king under whom the people will be restored; so we have in Psalm 80 a remarkable combination of ideas that are important for Jesus: the vine, son of God, king and son of man. It is quite possible that the psalm is the background to Jesus' teaching in John 15: he sees the psalmist's prayer being fulfilled in himself – he is the King, 'Son of Man' and Son of God in whom the vine of Israel is being restored.

But the focus of John 15 is, as we have said, on fruit-bearing. Jesus speaks of a farmer tending a vine, cutting out non-fruiting branches – branches that would eventually be burnt – and pruning others to make them more fruitful. This was apparently normal practice: the non-fruiting branches would be cut out in the winter, perhaps in February or March, and then side shoots would be pinched out during the summer in order to ensure maximum growth of fruit on the main branches.

Jesus describes such viticulture as an exhortation to the disciples to 'bear fruit' and as a warning that the alternative is to be thrown away, to wither and to be burnt. The way to bear fruit is, as the passage stresses, for the branch to continue to remain firmly attached to the vine, or in other words to 'remain in me'. The expression is a significant one: Jesus is not just the messenger of God who tells people how to enter the revolution and get eternal life; rather he is himself the embodiment of the revolution, and it is by being joined to him and keeping in living contact with him that people participate in the revolution. This makes sense in the light of what we saw about Jesus as king and Son of Man: Jesus is God's promised Messiah and shepherd, who gathers

the people of God together as one flock. It is one of the
distinctive things about John's gospel that he makes it very
explicit that eternal life, the life of God's promised revolution,
is to be found in and through Jesus. That is implied in the
other gospels and is sometimes explicit, as in Jesus' great
invitation to the weary and burdened to come to him and
find rest (Mt 11:28); but it is John who says it most directly
and with most emphasis.

But what does it involve in practice to remain in Jesus?
The probable answer to that is suggested in a number of
tell-tale references in John 15 to the 'word' or 'words' or
'commands' of Jesus. For example, 'You are already clean
because of the word I have spoken to you' (v.3); 'If you
remain in me and my words remain in you, ask whatever you
wish, and it will be given you' (v.7). The way to remain in
touch with Jesus and his life and so to bear fruit is to hear
and obey the words of Jesus, and in particular his command
that sums up everything: 'Love each other as I have loved
you' (Jn 15:12).

The passage has much in common with other parables we
have looked at. Like the parable of the sower it speaks of the
creative word of Jesus and of the responsibility to hear and
to bear fruit. Like the parable of the wheat and weeds it
speaks of Jesus as the initiator of the fruit-producing work –
he is the sower of the good seed and the true vine – and of
the gathering for fiery judgement of those who fail to bear
fruit, *i.e.* the workers of 'lawlessness' in Matthew's parable
and those not doing Jesus' commands in John. Like the
parable of the good Samaritan and others it speaks of
obedience being expressed in love.


### The two houses (Mt 7:24–27; Lk 6:47–49)

We return to the Sermon on the Mount and to its concluding
challenge in the parable of the two houses. Matthew and
Luke both have the parable, in slightly differing forms, but
with the same main points. The parable contrasts two men
building a house, one who built his house founded solidly on

rock, the other who built on 'sand' or 'soil'. In due course winter storms came: the picture is of torrential rain, wind, and dried-up stream beds filling up and overflowing their banks. The house on the rock stood up to the flood waters and the onslaught of the elements; the house on the sand collapsed and 'it fell with a great crash'.

Storms are often pictures of divine judgement in the Old Testament, not surprisingly since there is hardly anything to match the terrifying power of a storm, even for those of us who live in more moderate climates and stronger houses than did the people of Palestine in biblical times. For example, in Ezekiel 13:13–14 God warns: 'In my wrath I will unleash a violent wind, and in my anger hailstones and torrents of rain will fall with destructive fury. I will tear down the wall ...' (see also Isa 28:17–18). This is the sort of picture Jesus is using at the end of the Sermon on the Mount, as he speaks of the coming day of God's judgement.

As we have seen, judgement is a prominent theme in Jesus' teaching, not least in the Sermon on the Mount. The Sermon is not simply, or even primarily, ethical advice from a great teacher; it is all about the kingdom of God and how to enter it, and the concluding parable of the two houses speaks of the day of decision. The man in the parable who builds his house on the rock is the person who is prepared for judgement day and who will enter the kingdom; the man building on the sand is unprepared, and his end is a devastating crash. The contrast between the 'wise' and the 'foolish' reminds us of the parable of the wise and foolish girls, but also of the 'wise' or prudent steward who laid up treasure 'in heaven' and of the rich 'fool' who had nothing when his soul was required of him (see Mt 25:1–13; Lk 12:13–21; 16:1–15 and our previous discussion).

The parable of the two houses explains that the deciding factor on that day will quite simply be people's response to Jesus' word. The contrast is between those who 'hear these words of mine and do them' and those who hear and do not do them. This is a natural enough emphasis at the end of the Sermon on the Mount, but it is, of course, the emphasis throughout Jesus' teaching. He has brought the 'word of the kingdom', and for all its apparent weakness and insignificance (emphasised in the parables of growth) it is in fact the key to entry into the kingdom, the solid rock on which to build. As John's gospel puts it, Jesus has 'the words of life' and judgement depends on response to him and his words (Jn 6:68; 5:24, *etc.*).

The implied claim is remarkable. It is one that caused offence in Jesus' lifetime, and continues to cause offence in our pluralistic society. And yet it is in keeping with what we have seen of Jesus' teaching elsewhere. It is almost true to say that Jesus himself is the kingdom or revolution of God in his own person and in his words and actions. On the one hand it is in and through Jesus that God is intervening to bring the revolution and to save his people; on the other hand it is in and through Jesus as representative Son of Man and Messiah (and, we may add, as the servant who suffers for others) that God's people are reformed and gathered together. Jesus is at one and the same time God with us and the firstfruits of the new humanity (Mt 1:23; 1 Cor 15:23). Entry into the revolution is thus through Jesus and in particular through receiving his word. This is building on the rock.

## The tower-builder and the king going to war (Lk 14:28–33)

The parables that we have looked at so far in this chapter have been parables of challenge and warning, emphasising the importance of hearing and obeying Jesus' call to revolution. Other parables speak of the need to weigh up the cost.

Thus another parable about building is the parable of the uncompleted tower (or farm-building, as the Greek word can mean) found in Luke 14:28–30. The picture is a familiar one in our modern world of concrete tower-blocks as well as in the ancient world. It is of a developer with a flamboyant building plan, who only gets part-way through the building before he goes bankrupt. He failed to calculate the expense of the undertaking and the extent of his resources accurately, and ends up a laughing-stock and with the work incomplete.

Even more serious is the position of the king facing a war against an enemy with numerically superior forces. He needs to consider very carefully if he can win before committing his troops. If it is clear that he cannot win, then he must sue for peace as quickly as possible, in order to avert what could be a massacre and humiliation.

Both parables emphasise the dangers of undertaking projects that are too costly – in terms of money or life – and the need for realistic forward planning. The point of the parables in Jesus' teaching is to emphasise the need for  intending followers of Jesus to weigh up the heavy cost of what they are undertaking.

What is the cost? Jesus has spoken in the immediately preceding context of the need for would-be followers of his to 'hate' father, mother, wife, children, brothers, sisters and 'even his own life' and to take up the cross. In speaking of 'hating' Jesus is, as so often, expressing himself in a startling way in order to make a point. He is not in fact advocating neglect of family responsibilities, as it might seem. On the contrary, he specifically criticised those Jewish leaders who allowed people to evade the fifth commandment to 'honour your father and your mother', and he described himself as 'fulfilling', not undermining, Old Testament law, as we have seen (see Mt 15:1–9; Mk 7:1–13; and Mt 5:17). What Jesus is doing, as is clear in Matthew's equivalent passage (Mt 10:37–38), is speaking of priorities and of the need for the revolution of God to take precedence over all other commitments, even family commitments. He expressed the same point in an equally startling way when a disciple came to him and said: 'Lord, first let me go and bury my father'; Jesus replied: 'Follow me, and let the dead bury their own dead' (Mt 8:21–22; Lk 9:59–60). In saying this Jesus was not being callous to a bereaved person, but speaking of priorities to someone whose father had probably not yet died but who was making his family an excuse for not following Jesus on the road of revolution. Jesus knew from his own experience that commitment to the revolution of God would cause family discord and that this was one of the costs involved (see Mt 10:34–36; Mk 3:20–35).

But the costs of discipleship are greater than this: Jesus speaks of 'hating' even one's own life and of taking up the cross, and then, after the parables of the builder and the king, he says bluntly: 'Any of you who does not give up everything he has cannot be my disciple' (Lk 14:33). We are reminded of the rich young man, who was called to sell all that he had and give to the poor. The revolution is not a spare-time activity or club that can be tacked on to a secular lifestyle; it involves 'hating' family, material possessions and one's own life and safety. In short, it demands total commitment such as Jesus himself exemplified. The revolution is something total in its glory and promise, but also in its present demands.

The message of the parables of the builder and the king is similar to that of Jesus' saying about the ploughman, who must give his full concentration to his task: 'No-one who puts his hand to the plough and looks back is fit for service in the kingdom of God' (Lk 9:62). Jesus calls his followers to count the cost, to follow in his footsteps, and not to be distracted or to look back.

## The treasure and the pearl (Mt 13:44–46)

Matthew's chapter of parables (Mt 13) contains two parables which we did not look at earlier, the parables of the treasure and the pearl. The other parables that we have looked at in this chapter have been sombre in some ways, warning of the dangers of not responding to Jesus' call to revolution but also of the cost of doing so. These parables put the question of cost back into the context of the good news of the kingdom, and are an appropriate point at which to conclude our survey.

The parable of the treasure has a link with other parables in Matthew 13 in that it refers to a man in a field. But this time he does not sow: he finds hidden treasure. It was quite normal in those days for poor people wanting to preserve valuables to wrap them in a cloth and to bury them in a secret place, and even the wealthy would do so in unsettled times. (I recall a friend of mine quite recently doing the same with some of the family silver, when going away from home!) From time to time, inevitably, the owner of the valuables would die without anyone else knowing of their whereabouts. It is easy to see how this could happen, particularly in a time of war when people were killed and land changed hands. Palestine was overrun by foreign invaders many times in its history.

In the parable of Jesus a man, perhaps a hired labourer, found such a cache, maybe a jar containing silver coins or jewels. His excitement can be imagined, and his strategy was simple: he reburied the treasure since he had no right to it while it was in someone else's land; he rushed off and with joy sold everything he had – evidently he was not a very rich man; hence his excitement at the find. And he bought the land.

The parable is specifically described as a kingdom parable and it illustrates several aspects of the kingdom or revolution of God proclaimed by Jesus. First, the parable portrays the kingdom as something exciting and valuable: finding it is finding treasure and a matter of tremendous joy. We are reminded of the very first parable we looked at, the parable of the bridegroom and the wedding guests, and also of the parables that compare the kingdom to a feast. The revolution of God is not something gloomy that impoverishes people; it is something that enriches immeasurably and brings great joy – joy in heaven and on earth.

Second, it may be significant that the treasure is something hidden, not visible to all, since this was true of the revolution of God in Jesus. Many people failed to recognise the revolution in Jesus. The disciples, on the other hand, were like the man finding the treasure: they recognised Jesus as bringing the revolution of God.

In what sense was the revolution hidden? Not in the sense that it was underground or invisible; there were amazing signs of its presence for those with eyes to see. Nor simply in the sense that the kingdom in Jesus' ministry did not come according to people's expectations, but only as an insignificant-looking seed (see the parables of growth). But rather in the sense that many people were blind to what was going on in Jesus. Jesus explained the disciples' insight as the gift of God – 'To you it has been given to know the mysteries of the kingdom of God' (Mt 13:11) – and he spoke of God having 'hidden these things' from the wise and learned (Mt 11:25). In saying this Jesus was not suggesting that those who failed to see the revolution were not at fault; on the contrary, he speaks often of their guilt. But he did mean to say that the disciples' understanding was because God through Jesus' ministry had opened their eyes to the truth; they take no more credit for their discovery of Jesus than the man who happened to light on the treasure in the field.

Third, and much more significantly, the parable speaks of the man finding the treasure selling everything he had to buy the field and the treasure. Here we are back with the thought of giving up everything for the sake of the kingdom. We are back with the rich young man who wanted to enter the kingdom and who was told to 'sell everything' and to follow Jesus. The parable of the treasure makes it clear that the call to the rich young man was not an individual call which, conveniently, does not apply to other intending disciples. In fact it is the only way to enter the kingdom. The kingdom is the treasure to give everything for.

By putting the 'selling everything' into the context of joy at obtaining hidden treasure, Jesus makes it brilliantly clear that joining the revolution, though demanding, is not something negative, but immensely positive. Yes, there is a cost to be reckoned with, but it is as nothing when seen in the context of obtaining the treasure. Paul makes a similar point in his letters, for example in Philippians 3:7–8, where he speaks of 'the surpassing greatness of knowing Christ Jesus my Lord, for whose sake I have lost all things' and in 2 Corinthians 4:17, where he describes present troubles as 'achieving for us an eternal glory that far outweighs them all'.

Precisely the same point is made in the companion parable of the pearl. Pearls were then, as now, highly valued (see Mt 7:6). Divers fished for them in the Red Sea, the Persian Gulf and the Indian Ocean, and they were used in necklaces and for decoration. The famous Egyptian princess Cleopatra is said to have had one pearl worth a hundred million sesterces (*i.e.* twenty-five million denarii, a denarius being a day's wage). Jesus' story is of a big-businessman who was actively looking for good pearls, and who one day found a pearl to beat all others, the sort of pearl that dealers dreamt of getting their hands on. In order to buy it he, like the man finding treasure, had to sell all that he had.

The parable of the pearl depicts a rich man's search being rewarded by a find almost beyond price; the parable of the treasure portrays a poor man lighting on treasure unexpectedly. It is doubtful if we should see any significance in these differences. The significance of both parables lies in the two obvious features that they have in common; first the idea of finding something tremendously valuable, and second the thought of selling up everything to get it. In announcing and bringing in himself the kingdom of God, Jesus brought to people, first, good news of great joy, good news of God's promised and liberating revolution; and second, an invitation and a challenge – an invitation to receive the treasure and a challenge to give up all for it. Of course, the kingdom is not something that can be bought; in that respect the two parables taken by themselves could be misleading and need to be complemented by others such as that of the prodigal son. But what these parables do make clear is that in calling people to follow him and to give up themselves, their money, and their old lives for the kingdom, Jesus was calling them to incalculable gain and great joy.

### Finally . . .

'What shall we say the kingdom of God is like . . .?' It is quite impossible to sum up the teaching of Jesus' parables adequately, but it may be helpful to look back and briefly recall some of the principal themes we have looked at in the course of this book.

Parables like that of the bridegroom and his guests or of the new wine and wineskins speak of the exciting and joyful 'day of the Lord' having broken into history powerfully in Jesus. The parable of the strong man shows that this divine revolution is an anti-Satan revolution, going to the root of the world's ills and to the heart of the human condition. God is in the business of bringing a new world through Jesus, not of tinkering with the old. (*See chapter 3.*)

But the new world does not come overnight, as parables like that of the sower explain. God's revolution is one of redeeming love, spread through the proclamation of the word, not one of immediate judgement. So the present is a time of ambiguity, with evil much in evidence; it is a time of small beginnings. But the promise is that one day the revolution will come in its fullness; evil will be destroyed, and the world and God's people will be gloriously transformed. (*See chapter 4.*)

The theme of the final judgement is taken up in parables such as the thief and the talents. They speak of Jesus, who inaugurated the revolution, going away and leaving his followers to carry on the work. The call is for faithfulness. The promise is that he will return to call people to account, to bring in the new world, and to reward his faithful servants with joy in his presence. (*See chapter 5.*)

Parables like the marvellous trio in Luke 15 (the lost sheep, coin and son) fill out our understanding of the revolution as a revolution of God's love, bringing healing and forgiveness to his divided and suffering world. Jesus demonstrated this divine purpose through his ministry to the ill, the outcast and the sinful, and supremely by giving his life for others. The revolution is good news to the poor and needy. (*See chapter 6.*)

But to the rich and the establishment the message of a coming world of justice, sharing and equality, and the call to join Jesus in his revolutionary work, was an uncomfortable threat. This other side of the coin is illustrated by parables such as that of the rich fool and that of the tenants of the vineyard. The parable of the tenants is particularly about the Jewish nation, whose leaders rejected Jesus' call to join the revolution and who brought God's judgement on themselves and the nation. (*See chapter 7.*)

The revolution of God means a new world of restored relationships, and through parables such as that of the unforgiving servant and the good Samaritan Jesus called his followers to begin to live out this revolutionary righteousness in the present. They were to be a cell of the revolution, overcoming barriers of hatred, race and wealth. Jesus looked for perfection (inward and not just outward), because the kingdom of God is the coming of God's perfection. (*See chapter 8.*)

But going hand in hand with that, and essential for it, are renewed relationships with God as Father and Lord, as Jesus makes clear in his parables about prayer such as the friend at midnight. The revolution is God's work, and he cares for his children, providing them with daily bread and the power of the Holy Spirit in the present, and promising to hear their prayer, 'Your kingdom come'. (*See chapter 9.*)

The parables of the two ways and the two houses make it clear that the revolution of God is no take-it-or-leave-it matter, because judgement is coming to everyone. Jesus leaves people under no illusion about the cost of joining the revolution in the present; but he calls them to count the cost realistically and to commit themselves joyfully and totally to the treasure that is beyond compare. (*See chapter 10.*)

 Jesus still calls today. He invites us to receive God's love, to side with his revolution, to join his campaign troops, to live out his revolutionary righteousness, to bring his peace to others, to await his return, and so to be his saved people in the new world of the revolution.

# APPENDICES

# APPENDIX 1
# THE AUTHENTICITY OF THE PARABLES

It is well known that scholars have widely, even wildly, differing theories and ideas about the gospels and about the teaching of Jesus recorded in them. To have discussed even the most important of these ideas in the main text of this book would have been expensive in space and distracting from the main purpose of the book. We have therefore kept the discussion of technical issues to a minimum in the text. But it is important now to explain briefly the critical positions that have been adopted in our exposition.

One of the most contentious issues in the scholarly world concerns the historical reliability of the gospels. Traditionally Christians have taken the gospels to be straightforward historical accounts of Jesus' life and teaching. But in the last two hundred years a very different view has come to prominence, with a significant number of scholars (and churchmen too) being sceptical about the historical value of the gospels and arguing that they are highly tendentious portraits of Jesus, which tell us more about the faith and outlook of the first Christians than about Jesus himself. Between the traditional view and the thoroughly sceptical view there is a whole spectrum of mediating positions.

To the layman this wide divergence of opinion may seem a reason for despair: the evidence must be thoroughly ambiguous, and we cannot but be agnostic on the issues. However, that conclusion is not inevitable. It is true that historical evidence can usually be read in a number of different ways; that applies to very recent history, such as that of the Second World War. It is also true that historical judgements can never be 'proved' in the way that scientific theories can be tested in the laboratory. But, although it is salutary to recognise the limitations of scholars and their theories, we should not too quickly conclude that scholarly disagreement means that the historical evidence is quite ambiguous and that we cannot come to any conclusions.

The position adopted in this book is that the gospels should be taken very seriously as historical accounts of Jesus' life and ministry. The writers of the gospels were not, of course, trained 'scientific' historians in a modern mould, nor were they disinterested reporters of the events they describe. On the contrary, they were very strongly committed advocates of 'the gospel of Jesus Christ the Son of God' (Mk 1:1); but the good news as they understood it was the historical person of Jesus, and, although they felt free to present and arrange the stories and sayings of Jesus in a way that would make sense to their particular readers, they saw their task as one of passing on and preserving the traditions of Jesus.

It is not possible to justify this understanding of the gospels here in detail. A complete justification would include discussion of the dating of the gospels, of the traditional ascription of the four gospels to Matthew, Mark, Luke and John (an ascription that should not be as readily dismissed as it is by some scholars), and of the evangelists' stated interest in giving an accurate account of things (*e.g.* Lk 1:1–4; Jn 19:35), of the gospels' bluntness in describing the faults of Jesus' followers and his own limitations, and so on.

But here, at the risk of over-simplification, two particular points may be brought out, both of interest for a study of the parables.

1. The stories and sayings of Jesus which we have recorded for us in the gospels go back to a very early date. Scholars· date the actual writing of our gospels between about AD 60 and AD 100 (with a few scholars wanting to go earlier and a few later). Still the most popular scholarly opinion is that Mark's gospel was the first to be written, probably between AD 60 and 70. That in itself is an important conclusion if it is justified: AD 70 is not all that long after Jesus' ministry, and it is still within the lifetime of eyewitnesses.

But even more important than this is the increasing recognition by scholars in recent years of the importance of 'oral tradition' in the early church. It is now recognised that the stories of the gospels were used and well known in the early church long before they ever came to be written down by Mark. There is evidence for this in the writings of the apostle Paul, for example in his first letter to the Corinthians, which was written about AD 55. Although Paul does not often directly quote from the teaching of Jesus, he frequently alludes to it, and he presupposes that the readers of his letters have heard and learnt the stories of Jesus (*e.g.* 1 Cor 7:10–11; 9:14; 11:23–26; 15:1–6).

There is also evidence of this in the gospels themselves, since in a number of passages it can be shown that all three synoptic evangelists are using a common source of information which antedates them all. A good example of this is in the parables and sayings at the end of Jesus' discourse about the future (Mk 13:33–37; Mt 24:37–25:46; Lk 21:34–36): despite the common assumption of scholars that Matthew and Luke were dependent on Mark in this passage, it is in fact probable that Matthew, Luke and Mark himself all drew on a pre-synoptic collection of parables, which is thus partly preserved in Matthew 24–25, partly in Luke 12:35–48, and partly in Mark 13. It is not possible to explain all the arguments for this here – some of the relevant evidence is mentioned briefly in chapter 5 – but even the amateur detective might guess that this was the case, given the curious pattern of agreements between Matthew 24–25, Mark 13 and Luke 12 and 21. It turns out that a tradition of Jesus' teaching (evidently a well-recognised one, since all three synoptists use it) lies *behind* our gospels. And there is some reason to think that Paul draws on this tradition in 1 Thessalonians 4 and 5, for example, where he speaks of the 'day of the Lord' coming like a thief, thus echoing Jesus' parable of the thief.

This sort of evidence indicates that the evangelists were heirs to a solid tradition, not inventors of tradition.

2. One of the most interesting and promising developments in recent scholarly study of Jesus and the gospels has been

the attempt to explain Jesus in terms of the life and religion of so-called 'Second Temple Judaism', *i.e.* the Judaism of New Testament times. And it is increasingly clear from such study that the gospels' portrait of Jesus is a historically credible one. The central features of Jesus' teaching, *e.g.* his teaching on the coming kingdom of God and his description of himself as Son of Man, make sense in that context: the Jewish people were looking for God's intervention; they were looking for the fulfilment of the book of Daniel with its promise of 'the kingdom' being given to the people of God, the people being portrayed in Daniel 7 as 'one like a son of man'. Themes such as the 'kingdom' and 'Son of Man' make sense in a first-century Palestinian context, much more so than in the later context of the Greek-speaking church.

It is not only the content of Jesus' teaching that fits a first-century Palestinian background. So does the form and language of his teaching: Jesus' sayings, though recorded in Greek in the gospels, have a decidedly Hebraic/Aramaic feel to them. The gospels' portraits of people like Herod the Great and Pilate also fit in well with what we know of these people, for example from the first-century Jewish historian Josephus: Herod in Josephus, as in the gospels, is an insanely jealous and murderous man, Pilate a rather weak and vulnerable figure, who ultimately lost his job because of his mishandling of a 'Messianic' movement.

Given such evidence as this, it is apparent that there is a strong prima-facie case for taking the gospels seriously as historical sources of the life and teaching of Jesus. That is not to say that there are no historical difficulties in the gospels. There are particular problems: for example, Luke (Lk 2:1–2) puts Jesus' birth at the time of the census held by Quirinius, governor of Syria, which our extra-biblical sources suggest was in AD 6, but this seems to contradict the testimony of both Matthew and Luke that Jesus was born in the time of Herod the Great, who died in 4 BC. There is also the more general problem of the divergences between the gospels, some of them trivial, like the number of blind men healed by Jesus on a particular occasion, some of them rather more serious, such as the apparent disagreement of the gospel writers as to whether Jesus died after or at the time of Passover.

But, although the problems are real, they are hardly sufficient to undermine the overall impression of the gospels' historical reliability. Indeed the fact of gospel divergences is something which could put in question the reliability of the gospels, but which may on closer analysis be seen to strengthen their claim to historicity, since in some cases at least the divergent accounts can be shown to be independent of each other and to be complementary rather than contradictory. The amateur detective is reminded of the testimonies of independent witnesses in a legal case, which appear at first to be contradictory, but which on closer examination turn out to be quite compatible.

The one other 'difficulty' in the gospels which has been influential in leading scholars to doubt their historicity is the prominence of the miraculous in their narratives; the stories seem frankly fantastic to many people brought up in a scientific and secular age. However, effectively to dismiss the gospels as unhistorical on such grounds is, on the one hand, to do injustice to the intelligence of the gospel writers and their contemporaries: the ancients were not all gullible, and the gospel writers are conscious of writing about quite extraordinary events. It is, on the other hand, to be too much influenced by the cultural secularism of the West, which for all its attractive power is in fact a highly unsatisfactory account of our wonderful and mysterious world as well as an ultimately sterile philosophy to live by. Although there is no virtue in easy credulity, there is even less in an approach to history which explains away or dismisses the mysterious and miraculous and which is not open to what, if the gospels are true, is the most dramatic and important history of all time. The gospels at least deserve to be given a serious historical hearing.

Our conclusion is that the radical scepticism of some critics is unjustified, and that the gospels can and should be taken seriously as historically valuable sources.

But what of the parables in particular? There has for some years been a strong consensus among scholars that, whatever other doubts we may have about the gospels, the parables themselves have a very strong claim to being authentic teaching of Jesus. In favour of this, there is, in the first place, good reason to believe that Jesus did preach in parables. All the gospels (and all the 'sources' that scholars have detected behind the gospels, including the so-called 'Q' tradition of sayings of Jesus that Matthew and Luke are often thought to have used alongside Mark) testify to this, and there is little reason to doubt the gospels' testimony that teaching in parables was a prominent feature of Jesus' teaching ministry (*cf.* Mk 4:33–34; Jn 16:25). In the second place, the parables which we have in the gospels have a strongly Palestinian flavour and atmosphere. This has been argued expertly by the German scholar Joachim Jeremias, and supported by many other scholars, such as Kenneth Bailey, drawing on his knowledge of modern Middle Eastern culture. (The exposition that we have offered in this book has drawn heavily on Jeremias and Bailey, and hopefully illustrated the value of their approach.) In the third place, there is coherence in the form and content of the parables which we find in the gospels, and their teaching fits in well with what we know of Jesus' preaching and message. This last argument for their authenticity is a somewhat uncertain one, since different scholars analyse Jesus' teaching in different ways and all explain Jesus' parables accordingly. However, it is in principle an entirely sound approach to argue from the coherence of the different types of Jesus' preaching.

In recent years there have been a few dissenting voices to the opinion that the parables are bedrock Jesus-tradition. These scholars have raised questions particularly about some of the parables found only in Matthew and Luke, seeing these as 'redactional' (*i.e.* as deriving from the evangelist) rather than as originating with Jesus. However, the argument that certain parables reflect the theological interests of the evangelist concerned rather than of Jesus is quite inconclusive: it is true that parables such as that of the prodigal son and of the good Samaritan reflect Lukan interests, and this no doubt helps explain why Luke has made a point of including them in his gospel; but they are also entirely compatible with Jesus' teaching as we find it in the gospels as a whole, and there is no probability that they are Lukan creations.

But if the consensus among scholars has for some time been that the parables go back to Jesus himself, that is not to say that scholars believe that the gospels preserve them in their original form or sense. Indeed it is Joachim Jeremias, who argues so strongly for their derivation from Jesus, who also argues that they have been radically modified by the evangelists and that we need to do some complex detective work in order to get back to the original meaning of Jesus. In other words: yes, the parables do go back to Jesus, but not the parables as we know them.

Why do Jeremias and many others believe this to be the case? There is more than one reason. A significant factor is that Jeremias accepted the now discredited view of Adolf Jülicher that Jesus' parables were simple single-point parables rather than more complex allegorical forms of speech: this inevitably led to the conclusion that, for example, the four-point interpretation of the parable of the sower given in the gospels (*e.g.* in Mt 13:18–23) is not original; Jeremias believed that this was shown also by a variety of other con- siderations.

But although Jülicher's view of the simplicity of parables may be discredited (see further below, pp. 227–29), a more substantial consideration raising questions about the re- liability of the parable tradition is the fact of divergence between Matthew, Mark and Luke in their narrating of the same parable. A simple example is the parable of the two houses which occurs at the end of the Sermon on the Mount in Matthew 7 and also in a comparable position in Luke 6. It has often been noted that, whereas Matthew (apparently) has the houses built directly on to rock and sand, Luke has the wise builder dig a foundation. Why the difference? Matthew, it is suggested, is reflecting Palestinian building conditions and practices; but Luke is thinking of a Graeco-Roman house and setting, where digging down was an essential part of building a house. Luke's version thus illustrates the point that the parables got modified in the course of transmission, and that we need to find our way back behind the present form of the parables to what Jesus originally said. Another parable that comes in two significantly different forms is that of the lost sheep, which is found in Matthew 18 and Luke 15 (see chapter 6). In this case Matthew's version is often regarded as secondary: he has applied a parable which was originally to do with Jesus' public ministry to the needs and problems of the church.

Analysing such evidence as this, Jeremias seeks to work out how the parables tended to be changed (*e.g.* from a Palestinian context to a Hellenistic one, from the public ministry of Jesus to meet the needs of the church, from a simple original meaning to a more elaborate allegorical interpretation), and so to enable us to work back from the present form of the parables to their supposed original form and meaning.

What is to be said about this approach to the parables? First, the variations between the different gospels' versions of particular parables do indicate that the evangelists (and presumably others in the early church) felt a measure of freedom in retelling Jesus' stories. Luke may have added the thought of the builder digging down to lay his foundation (though there is nothing very unPalestinian about doing that), but his changes, if they are such, do not significantly alter the point of the parable about building on the rock of Jesus' teaching.

Second, it is often assumed by scholars that parables which are similar but not identical in the different gospels are different versions of one parable of Jesus, whereas it is entirely possible, even probable, that Jesus himself used variations on a parabolic theme and that some of the gospel divergences are explicable in this way. This possibility must be taken particularly seriously when the parables concerned are found in quite different contexts in the different gospels. The Matthean and Lukan versions of the parable of the lost sheep are a good case in point: it could be that one or both of the evangelists has reapplied the original parable of Jesus; but it could well be that Jesus himself used this powerful image in different ways.

Third, Jeremias gives the impression that he has discovered 'laws of transmission' which enable us to get behind the present form of the parables to the supposed original meaning of Jesus; however, his 'laws' of transmission are simply a generalisation of his conclusions about particular parables (rather than anything more objective), and, if those conclusions are questioned, so are his generalisations. If indeed Luke's version of the parable of the lost sheep is original and Matthew's is not, then here is a case of a parable about Jesus' public ministry being applied to the church. But, if the two versions of the parable both go back to Jesus, or if Luke's version is judged to be as unoriginal as Matthew's (as some scholars argue), then Jeremias' 'principle' is put in question. Much the same is true of his principle of increased allegorisation: if his view that the parable of the sower was originally a one-point parable about the abundant eschatological harvest is true and the interpretation in the gospels is secondary, then we have here an example of church allegorisation. But, if the interpretation in the gospels has a strong claim to originality (as is the case; see our discussion of the parable, pp. 41–48), then the evidence for an allegorising tendency is reduced.

Given such observations as these, a considerable number of scholars have recently come to recognise that Jeremias' confidence in his ability to reconstruct the history of the parable-traditions is not well founded. And, although for some scholars this has been a depressing conclusion – at least in the sense that they conclude that there is no sure way to recover the intended meaning of the historical Jesus – it is possible to look at the matter differently, and to agree that many of Jeremias' premises are faulty, but to argue that this may have encouraging conclusions. For example, his assumption (and the assumption of many other scholars influenced by so-called 'form criticism') that the early church 'forgot' the original interpretation and context of the parables – *i.e.* the interpretation intended by Jesus in his context – and that the interpretative clues that we now find in the gospels are secondary is very much open to question: in fact it seems improbable that Jesus' parables were preserved as free-floating, uninterpreted traditions, and quite probable that the gospels have preserved an accurate recollection about the context and meaning of the parables as Jesus intended them. Jeremias has certainly done nothing to disprove this, and, if the generally positive view of the gospel tradition we proposed is justified, then it is at least a good working hypothesis.

Our working hypothesis is, then, that not only the parables, but also the interpretative clues about their meaning which the gospels give, have a strong prima-facie claim to be viewed as teaching of Jesus. Such a hypothesis does not preclude discussion of particular evidence that may contradict the hypothesis; it does mean that our method is 'inclusive' rather than 'exclusive', and that we will seek to make sense of the traditions in question as deriving from Jesus before concluding otherwise. Scholars discuss from time to time the issue of the 'burden of proof': we believe that with the gospels the burden of proof is on those who deny that the gospels are what they purport to be (*i.e.* records of Jesus' life and teaching); and we believe that a discerning use of an 'inclusive' methodology is historically sounder and likely to be more productive than a more sceptical approach. We hope that the use of such a methodology in this book is in itself evidence of its usefulness, since we believe there to be an impressive coherence about the contents and teaching of the parables when this approach is adopted. There is a coherence in things great, such as the major theological themes, and in things small, for example in the recurrent and perhaps surprising use of shady or criminal characters and their dealings to illustrate the kingdom of God, which confirms that they derive from one creative mind, and specifically from the mind of Jesus.

### A note on source and redaction criticism

It may be important to say something about my approach to questions of 'source' and 'redaction criticism', since this has an inevitable influence on my discussion of the parables.

Matthew, Mark and Luke are extraordinarily similar in certain respects, but very different in others. Explaining their convergence and divergence is not easy, and 'source critics' have given lifetimes seeking to solve the so-called 'synoptic problem'. The most widely accepted hypothesis in recent years has been that the convergences are because Matthew and Luke based their gospels on Mark, plus a hypothetical collection of Jesus' sayings, called 'Q' by scholars. I, along with a significant number of scholars, am unpersuaded of the validity of this 'two-source hypothesis'. I suspect that Mark may indeed have been the first of our Greek gospels to be written, but I am sure that Matthew and Luke also had extensive non-Markan sources – quite likely oral traditions, very often overlapping with Mark (not just 'Q') – and that these were probably as (or more) influential on Matthew and Luke as Mark. The whole 'synoptic problem' remains very much an open issue, though scholars once regarded it as finally solved beyond reasonable doubt! In line with this conclusion I have not depended heavily on any particular 'source hypothesis' in my explanation of the parables; I have assumed that in any passage any of the evangelists could have preserved original tradition independent of the other gospels.

My view of the synoptic problem also affects my attitude to redaction criticism. Redaction criticism is the study of the distinctive features and ideas of the different gospels, and is a valid and valuable method of studying the gospels. However, redaction critics who accept the two-source hypothesis tend to see the divergences of Matthew and Luke from Mark as a particularly important clue to their theological concerns. This is not unreasonable, and yet, if it is right that all the gospels were influenced heavily by oral tradition, then, even if Matthew and Luke did know Mark, their divergences from Mark and additions to Mark may often be a reflection of the oral tradition and not necessarily of more than usual significance for an understanding of the evangelists' theology. An insufficient appreciation of this point has led scholars to underestimate the likelihood of Matthew and Luke having independent access to Jesus' teaching and to overestimate the theological distinctiveness and creativity of the evangelists.

This view inevitably affects my approach to the parables in this book. I do note differences between the gospels, but I do not feel obliged to use the heavily redaction-critical approach of someone like John Drury, who in his recent *The Parables in the Gospels* looks at the parables of each gospel in separate chapters of his book and deliberately renounces any attempt to reconstruct Jesus' teaching. I consider that the evangelists were strongly committed to preserving a common tradition of Jesus' teaching (see above, pp. 213–17), and that differing versions of the parables may legitimately and profitably be used in an attempt to understand Jesus' meaning. Whether the differences reflect independent use of the oral tradition or are because one evangelist has interpreted the tradition for the sake of his readers, or both, the divergences tend, if anything, to enhance rather than impede our understanding. I hope that my study of the parables shows the validity and fruitfulness of the approach I have adopted. (I have not used the 'Gospel of Thomas' in this book, as it is doubtful whether it contains a significant amount of historical tradition about Jesus independent of the canonical gospels, and it is not certain in any case whether it would add much to our understanding of the parables we have discussed.)

# APPENDIX 2
# THE INTERPRETATION OF PARABLES

## *What is a parable?*

'Parable' is a word that we commonly use, especially in the context of discussing Jesus' teaching, though more broadly also in discussions of literature. But it is a word that many of us would find hard to define. The traditional definition 'an earthly story with a heavenly meaning' had some virtues, but it does not obviously describe everything that the word 'parable' can cover, and it could be misleading: some parables are not stories, and many parables have a distinctly 'earthly' meaning and application. So what is a parable? In particular, what is a parable in the New Testament?

The root meaning of the Greek word *parabole* suggests putting things side by side, and broadly speaking a parable is just that: a putting together of ideas from different spheres in such a way that the one idea illuminates the other. However, it is generally agreed that for an understanding of the New Testament 'parable' we must look not to the meaning of the Greek word or to Greek rhetorical definitions of parable but to the Hebrew and Aramaic words *mashal/mathla*.

Those words have a very broad spectrum of meaning. Thus the standard Hebrew lexicon of Brown, Driver and Briggs gives the following meanings (p. 605 of the 1962 edition):

(1) a proverbial saying: *e.g.* 1 Sam 10:12, 'It became a saying: "Is Saul also among the prophets?"'';
(2) a 'byword': *e.g.* Ps 44:14, 'You have made us a byword among the nations';
(3) a prophetic figurative discourse: *e.g.* Isa 14:4, 'You will take up this taunt against the king of Babylon . . .';

(4) a similitude, or parable: *e.g.* Ezek 17:2–3, 'Son of man, set forth an allegory and tell the house of Israel a parable. Say to them, "This is what the Sovereign Lord says: A great eagle with powerful wings, long feathers and full plumage of varied colours, came to Lebanon . . ."';
(5) poems of various kinds: *e.g.* Ps 78:2, 'I will open my mouth in parables, I will utter hidden things, things from of old – what we have heard and known, what our fathers have told us';
(6) sentence of ethical wisdom: *e.g.* the Old Testament book of 'Proverbs'.

So the term has a range of meaning, covering riddles, fables, proverbs, stories and so on.

But how is the word used in the New Testament? It is in fact used only twice in the New Testament apart from in the synoptic gospels, namely in Hebrews 9:9, which speaks of the sanctuary in the tabernacle being closed, 'which is symbolic for the present age', and in Hebrews 11:19, which speaks of Abraham 'figuratively' (literally, in a parable) receiving Isaac back to life. In both these verses from Hebrews the word suggests something figurative, pictorial, symbolic, with perhaps the idea of a comparison between one reality (the Old Testament reality) and the other greater reality, which has come with Christ.

In the gospels the word is used broadly, not just of classic stories like the parable of the sower. It is used

(1) of enigmatic/pictorial sayings: *e.g.* in Mk 3:23, of Satan casting out Satan; in Mk 3:27, of the strong man being bound; in Mk 7:15, 'Nothing outside a man can make him "unclean" by going into him. Rather, it is what comes out of a man that makes him "unclean"'; or in Lk 4:23, 'You will quote this parable to me, "Physician, heal yourself . . ."';
(2) of explicit similes: *e.g.* those beginning, 'The kingdom of heaven is like . . .' (Mt 13:31, '. . . a mustard seed'; Mt 13:44, '. . . treasure'; Mt 13:45, '. . . a merchant'; Mt 13:47, '. . . a net');
(3) of stories: *e.g.* Mk 4:2–9, the parable of the sower.

We could perhaps sum up by saying that a *parabole* in the gospels is characteristically a pictorial story or saying.

John's gospel does not use the Greek term *parabole*, but has another word, *paroimia*, three times. It is used in John

10:6 of the shepherd and the sheep and the thief; and then in
16:25,29, 'I have been speaking in figures', 'Now you are
speaking clearly and without figures of speech.' (The same
word is used in 2 Pet 2:22: 'Of them the proverbs are true:
"A dog returns to its vomit," and, "A sow that is washed
goes back to her wallowing in the mud."') Both John's and
the synoptic evidence suggest that characteristically a parable
is something other than plain speaking. Parables are indirect,
sometimes teasing sayings.

But can we analyse the so-called 'parables' of Jesus more?
A Jülicher, a German scholar who is regularly thought of as
the father of modern parable studies and whose major book
on the parables, *Die Gleichnisreden Jesu*, was first published
in 1888, distinguished three types of parable in Jesus' teaching:

(1) comparisons, or similes, such as 'The kingdom of heaven is
like . . .'; these are sayings that compare the kingdom with a
well-known event or phenomenon, such as the growth of a plant.
(2) 'parables' proper, or stories, such as the parable of the sower
or that of the prodigal son; these he saw as extended similes.
(3) example stories, which are not similes comparing one thing to
something else, but which describe an example to follow or not
to follow, *e.g.* the parable of the good Samaritan, with its
conclusion 'Go and do likewise.'

He also believed that in the gospels as we now have them
there are 'allegories', though he did not consider that these
went back to Jesus. An allegory according to this understanding is a story in code, a story that appears to be talking
about one thing and is in fact talking about another. For
example in Judges 9:8 we read that 'One day the trees went
out to anoint a king for themselves,' and we know that this is
not a realistic story, but a story in code. Such allegory
usually has many points of comparison, and is intelligible
only to those who know the code. Jülicher saw such allegory
as quite different from and inferior to Jesus' genuine
parables, as they characteristically had a simple point and
were readily understandable. However, there are allegories of
the sort Jülicher disliked within the gospels, the most
obvious example being the parable of the wheat and the

weeds, where the code is explained to the disciples of Jesus (*cf.* Mt 13:37–43, 'The one who sowed the good seed is the Son of Man. The field is the world ... *etc.*'). Jülicher maintained that such allegory derived not from Jesus, but from the later Christian church.

Jülicher's analysis of the parables commanded wide respect for a long time. But in recent discussion it has been criticised from all sort of angles, so much so that G B Caird in his important book *The Language and Imagery of the Bible* can speak of Jülicher's 'house of cards'. What objections have been raised against Jülicher's analysis?

In the first place, the view that Jesus never used allegory is seen to be arbitrary and improbable. Jesus was a Jew steeped in the Old Testament, and both in the Old Testament and later Jewish writings allegory is an important rhetorical/literary form. Scholars such as Christian A Bugge and Paul Fiebig, writing soon after Jülicher, noted this, and their argument has been strongly supported by various recent scholars.

Second, Jülicher made a sharp distinction between parable and allegory, comparing it to the difference between simile and metaphor. But, although it is true that the level and type of correspondence between picture and reality are different in different parables/allegories, it is doubtful whether the distinctions are anything like as clear-cut as Jülicher supposed, and even more doubtful whether allegory and metaphor are inferior to a parable and simile. (How is the simile 'He is like a pig' superior to the metaphor 'He is a pig'?) Scholars will no doubt continue to define terms such as 'allegory' and 'parable' in different ways; but that the matter is much more complex and open than Jülicher recognised is clear from the fact that Hans-Josef Klauck, in one of the most important German works on parables in recent years, can write of allegory as a basic and poetic procedure and of parable and fable as belonging to the category of allegory (*e.g.* p. 354), and from the fact that a Swiss author, Hans Weder, can entitle his standard work 'The parables of Jesus as metaphors'. Jülicher may be turning in his grave at his successors; but there is little doubt that he underestimated the value and power of metaphor and allegory, and under-estimated also the variety and richness of Jesus' teaching methods.

Third, an examination of the parables themselves makes it very difficult to believe that all the parables are (or were originally) simple one-point parables. Many, if not most, have more than one point, and many have what Jülicher would have seen as 'allegorical' features. Thus a parable like that of the vineyard draws on a stock image (the vineyard as Israel) and contains a complex of ideas about God (the owner of the vineyard), the servants (the prophets), and the son. To try and make that parable, and others too, into simple similes is to do violence to the form of the stories and to underestimate Jesus' versatility as a story-teller, and to deny them to Jesus because of their relative complexity is arbitrary. What Jülicher was reacting against – and not without some reason – was the anachronistic allegorical interpretation of the parables by many Christian interpreters (see pp. 230–31); but he threw out the proverbial baby with the bathwater when he dismissed the whole idea of the parables as allegories along with the mistaken allegorical interpretations of Christian interpreters.

Can we then do better than Jülicher in defining Jesus' parables? Perhaps as useful a categorisation as any is G B Caird's, who distinguishes the following types of gospel parable:

(1) simple simile: e.g. 'the kingdom . . . is like leaven' (Mt 13:33);
(2) simple metaphor: e.g. 'don't throw your pearls before swine' (Mt 7:6);
(3) simile story: e.g. 'the kingdom . . . is like a landowner who went out early . . .' (Mt 20:1–16);
(4) metaphorical story: e.g. the prodigal son (Lk 15:11–32);
(5) example story: e.g. the good Samaritan (Lk 10:25–37).

## How are parables to be interpreted?

In our discussion of the authenticity and form of the parables, we have already touched on the question of the interpretation of parables, referring to the work of such influential scholars as Adolf Jülicher and Joachim Jeremias. It is neither possible nor necessary to survey the history of the interpretation of parables here. Those interested will find it discussed in numerous more technical books on the parables, and should refer particularly to Warren S Kissinger's *The Parables of Jesus: A History of Interpretation and Bibliography* (1979), and for the most recent period to Craig Blomberg's *Interpreting the Parables* (1989). What may be helpful, however, is to make a few observations about some aspects of the history.

## Allegorising interpretation

Until the modern period probably the dominant method of interpreting the parables was to treat them as detailed allegories. Perhaps the most famous example of such interpretation is that of the parable of the good Samaritan by Augustine (bishop of Hippo in North Africa from AD 396 to 430). He explained the parable of the good Samaritan as follows (in his *Quaestiones Evangeliorum* 2). The man going down from Jerusalem to Jericho is Adam, going down from the city of heavenly peace to the world; the robbers who assault him are the devil and his angels; they attack him and leave him half-dead in sin, and the priest and the Levite, who represent the Old Testament law and the prophets, pass him by on the other side; the good Samaritan is, naturally, Christ himself, who takes 'man' into the inn of the church (with its innkeeper the apostle Paul), pays two denarii to the innkeeper, being the two commands to love God and one's neighbour, and promises to return. Such interpretation of the parables was commonplace until the last one hundred years or so, and is still to be found in some places today.

Although he was not the first or the only person to question this approach, the man who is particularly associated with its decline and fall was Adolf Jülicher (1888). He rejected allegorical interpretation of the parables, and insisted that the parables of Jesus had a single point. Jesus' parables were not, according to Jülicher, complex theological allegories, but were designed to teach simple moral truths. Jülicher's reaction to the interpretation of parables by people such as Augustine was an over-reaction, albeit an understandable one. What was wrong with their interpretation was not primarily that they interpreted allegorically, but that they interpreted inappropriately and anachronistically, reading into Jesus' parables ideas which Jesus himself did not intend. However, Jülicher's view became dominant in the scholarly interpretation of the parables, and most of us have been brought up on the 'one main point' theory of parable interpretation.

Very recently, however, this scholarly consensus has begun to crumble, with scholars of widely differing theological traditions, including M Boucher, J Drury, G. B. Caird, and C Blomberg, raising serious questions about it and arguing that Jülicher's exclusion of allegory in interpreting the parables was hardly less arbitrary than the over-fervent allegorising that he reacted against. John Drury goes so far as to argue that the parables are esoteric stories in code, akin to the highly symbolic visions of Jewish apocalyptic (*e.g.* in the book of Daniel) rather than, as is so often supposed, stories taken from real life to illustrate spiritual truths. This almost certainly represents too radical a reaction to the Jülicher/Jeremias tradition of parable interpretation. Despite the arbitrariness of Jülicher's one-point principle and the inadequacies of some of Jeremias' interpretation, there is a very strong case for seeing the parables as stories reflecting and drawn from real life in Palestine, albeit with features that have symbolic significance in the context of Jewish thought (*e.g.* the vineyard of Mk 12:1–11) and some surprising relatively 'unrealistic' twists, which may be a clue to the parable's meaning (*e.g.* the equal pay given to the labourers in Mt 20:1–16). The interpreter needs to be sensitive to such features in the parables and to the overall shape of the parable he or she is interpreting, but not be excessively bound by assumptions about parables having one or many points.

## Eschatological interpretation

Whereas Jülicher's theory about the simplicity of parables was the scholarly orthodoxy for many years, his view that they taught simple moral truths (*e.g.* the parable of the talents teaches that effort will be rewarded) was seen to be hardly less anachronistic than some of the earlier allegorical interpretation. Jülicher was interpreting Jesus and the parables in terms of contemporary nineteenth-century liberalism. Over against this scholars such as J Weiss and A Schweitzer argued forcefully and correctly that Jesus was not a preacher of general moral truths, but of the breaking-in of God's promised kingdom – of the 'end-times'. The parables are, therefore, to be understood 'eschatologically' – in the context of Jesus' proclamation of the end-times. This perspective was reflected in the influential writings of C H Dodd, a British scholar (in his *Parables of the Kingdom*, 1935), and by Joachim Jeremias (in his *Parables of Jesus*, 1954). Although they had slightly differing perceptions of Jesus' message – with Dodd arguing that Jesus taught that the eschatological kingdom had come in his ministry, and Jeremias that he taught that the kingdom was in the process of coming – they agreed that Jesus' parables must be interpreted in terms of his teaching about the coming of the end-times in his ministry.

There have been some voices that have questioned this, for example David Flusser in his recent book comparing Jesus' parables with the parables of the Jewish rabbis; but despite these questions and despite the embarrassment that some modern scholars feel about seeing Jesus as a prophet who expected a near end, it is difficult to avoid the conclusion that one of the things that marked Jesus' ministry and distinguished it from that of some of the rabbis was the sense of eschatological urgency that permeated his outlook. It is in our view quite right to interpret the parables in this context, and we have tried to do so in our discussion.

## Historical and other approaches

Jeremias' eschatological reading of Jesus' parables was part and parcel of his strongly historical approach to their interpretation. He saw the interpreter's task as to explain the parables in the context of Jesus' own historical situation and purpose, and his work was a sustained attempt to do just that. His historical interpretation entailed two closely related things: on the one hand, trying to get back behind the present gospel texts to the underlying teaching of Jesus (on the assumption that the present gospel picture of Jesus is to a significant extent coloured by the situation and interests of the post-Easter church), and on the other hand seeking to make sense of that teaching in the context of the life, history and customs of first-century Palestine.

Since the time of Jeremias there has been something of a move away from his purely historical approach, towards a variety of other approaches. In the first place there has been a general trend in the scholarly study of the Bible away from the quest for the historical sources of biblical texts and traditions – the so-called 'diachronic' approach to texts – and towards the so-called 'synchronic' approach which focuses on the biblical texts in the form and context in which we now encounter them. This trend has manifested itself in the decline of interest in 'source' and 'form criticism', both of which are attempts to trace the history of the biblical traditions, and in the rise of 'redaction criticism', being the attempt to analyse the thrust and emphasis of the biblical texts as we have them. Such an approach to the parables is exemplified particularly in John Drury's book, which is deliberately entitled *The Parables in the Gospels*, not 'The Parables of Jesus'. In it he explains the parables of each gospel in separate chapters, explicitly renouncing any attempt to explain Jesus' intended meaning, since he regards this as inaccessible to us.

The trend has also manifested itself in the application of modern literary approaches to the Bible. Whereas redaction criticism often builds on source- and form-critical conclusions, this sort of approach typically takes the biblical stories as they now stand in their present form and context and seeks to make sense of them as stories in their own right. The critic examines the structure and dynamics of the stories, bringing to bear on them the insights and techniques of modern literary and rhetorical criticism (*e.g.* the insights of so-called 'structuralism'). An example of such work on the parables is that of the American Dan Via, who divides the parables into 'comic' and 'tragic' parables (using those terms in a technical literary-critical sense) and seeks to interpret them in such categories.

As well as a move away from historical reconstruction to the study of present texts, another recent trend has been to emphasise the existential and contemporary interpretation of the parables. This trend is exemplified, for example, in the so-called 'new hermeneutic' of scholars such as E Fuchs, E Linnemann and (again) D Via. They have argued that the parables were never intended to be packages of information but to be instruments of confrontation, and that the task of the interpreter is not to analyse the meaning of the parables, but rather to enable the modern reader to be confronted by the parables in the way that the ancient reader was and to experience the same 'language event'. The parable of the good Samaritan is a good example of a parable that will have confronted Jesus' Jewish hearers with a powerful and uncomfortable challenge, and the task of the modern interpreter is not to explain the parable, but to help people to experience it.

One of the roots of the new hermeneutic is the philosophy which sees language not as something propositional which we interpret and analyse, but rather as something powerfully creative that interprets us. Another somewhat similar perception lies behind the understanding of parables as works of art which are to be appreciated as such and which cannot be adequately described in propositional form.

Such an appreciation of parables as art is nothing new. What is relatively new is the corollary drawn from this by some modern scholars, namely that parables, like paintings or pieces of music, have a life and validity of their own irrespective of the original artist's meaning and intention. This view leads to the conclusion that there is no such thing as 'the correct interpretation' of a particular parable, and that it is as valid to interpret the parable of the good Samaritan in terms of psychoanalytic theory, or of existentialist or Marxist philosophy, as in any other way. Parables are thus 'polyvalent', a point which scholars see as supported by the fact that within the gospels the parables are interpreted differently by the different evangelists.

There are a number of positive things to say about these recent trends in interpretation. First, the concern that the parables should be heard to speak today and not simply be the objects of historical study is welcome. Second, the recognition of the parable as an artistic, literary or rhetorical form is important. Parables are not doctrinal statements, but pictures with particular dynamics which need to be understood. It is not true to say that parables cannot be explained in propositional form: such explanation is possible and often useful in helping us to feel the rhetorical force of a parable. But explanatory propositions are not a substitute for the parable itself, and the interpreter's task is to help people to feel and experience the parable rather than simply to understand what it is saying. Third, the modern focus on interpreting the parables in their present form and context is a good emphasis: such an approach is much less speculative than much 'source' and 'form' critical study of the gospels, and for the Christian it is the present biblical text (not its reconstructed antecedents) that is canonical Scripture.

However, there are also three more negative things to say about the modern trends. First, the view that the parables are works of art which have a life of their own and which can be understood in any number of ways independent of their original meaning must be rejected. The authority of the parables lies for the Christian in the fact that they are parables deriving from Jesus, not in their value as works of art, and the Christian interpreter must start from Jesus' intended meaning. It is true that some scholars believe Jesus' meaning to be inaccessible to us. If that were the case, the gospels as the earliest interpretations of Jesus available to us must still be the starting-point and the controlling factor in any interpretation that has a claim to being distinctively Christian.

Second, some scholars have a tendency to concentrate on the interpretation of the gospel texts in their present literary context to the exclusion of considerations of their history and historical context. But this is an unsatisfactory way to read almost any text. The gospels are first-century texts about a first-century person, and it is absurd to read them without reference to that context. Also, although it is indeed better to give priority in interpretation to the texts as we have them than to speculative reconstruction of what lies behind them, it is foolish to neglect anything that can be learnt about the sources and history of a particular story or saying, since this may facilitate understanding.

But, third, the assumption implicit or explicit in many of the modern approaches is one of pessimism about the feasibility of historical interpretation. After all, if Jeremias' ambitious and brilliant historical reconstruction of Jesus' parables was in the last analysis unsuccessful, as many agree, then what hope is there for such an approach to the gospels? Obviously the evidence is insufficient to go on. Some people would see the problem as lying not just in lack of evidence, but more fundamentally in our own human limitations: the fact is that we all read historical texts in the distorting light of our own contexts, and it is thus impossible for us to get back into the mind, not just of Jesus, but even, some would say, of the evangelists. In view of such historical doubts, some would say that the best we can do is to interpret the parables in the gospels as we have them without trying to penetrate to the mind of Jesus. Others would doubt if even that is really possible.

In response to this sort of historical pessimism, two things can be said. First, on the whole question of historical method, it is true that we cannot and will not achieve a perfectly accurate historical understanding of Jesus' or the evangelists' teaching (or of anything else historical). However, we can achieve an approximate understanding, and, especially if we recognise the influence of our context on our reading of the parables, an increasing understanding. Second, I do not believe that the real flaws in Jeremias' work should lead us to conclude that we have no reliable access to Jesus' teaching. I argued in appendix 1 that his historical method can be improved on and that the gospel tradition is more, not less, reliable than Jeremias supposed. The gospels are portraits of Jesus' life and ministry which reflect the evangelists' viewpoints, but which are reliable portraits of Jesus, not self-portraits of the evangelists. To use a different analogy, they are lenses through which we can see and hear Jesus, lenses which focus our vision in various ways, but which reveal and do not conceal Jesus. If this is correct, then to interpret the present texts of the gospels is to explain the history of Jesus, and the gospels must be read and interpreted in the light of Jesus' own Palestinian context.

We conclude that modern literary and redactional approaches to the parables are useful if they are used in conjunction with, rather than as a substitute for, historical approaches.

## Conclusions

How then should we interpret Jesus' parables in the light of the history of their interpretation? In chapter 1 we suggested the following principles:

1. Pay close attention to the form and main emphases of each parable. Parables do often have one main point, but not always; we should not press every detail in parables, but seek to be sensitive to what is significant, given the form of the parable and the historical context of the first century.

2. Take account of the first-century Palestinian background of Jesus' ministry, including, notably, the Old Testament background.

3. Interpret the parable in the context of Jesus' ministry and in the context of his other teaching.

4. Be guided by the contextual and other interpretative hints given by the evangelists. These are, if nothing more, our earliest clues to the interpretation of the parables, and the common assumption that they are secondary is not well-founded. The broader context of other New Testament teaching should also not be neglected, since the teaching of Jesus, including his parables, was foundational to the thinking and teaching of the early church. So in the writings of

Paul, for example, we will often find illuminating parallels to the ideas expressed in and through Jesus' parables, and sometimes there is even reason to believe that he is using Jesus' parables consciously in the course of his argument (*e.g.* in 1 Thess 5).

5. Base reflection about the contemporary message of the parable on the historical meaning of the parable.

# APPENDIX 3
# THE PURPOSE OF THE PARABLES
# AND THE INTERPRETATION OF
# MARK 4:10–12

Why did Jesus characteristically speak in parables? The obvious answer is that he used parables in order to communicate effectively. The gospels confirm that this was Jesus' intention: for example, Mark's chapter of parables (Mk 4) is full of references to 'hearing' (Mk 4:9, 15–20, 23, 33); Jesus wants and invites people to 'hear', not, of course, just with the ears, but with understanding. And he uses pictorial language because of its power and effectiveness as a medium of communication.

That is not to say that the parables were always immediately or easily intelligible. The gospels make it clear that the disciples found various of Jesus' parables puzzling, and so had to ask for explanation (so Mt 13:36; Mk 7:17; Lk 8:9 *etc.*); indeed they had questions about the function of parables in general (*e.g.* Mt 13:10). But this does not contradict the conclusion that parables were meant to communicate. Broadly speaking, parables communicate by bringing parallel ideas together so that the one illuminates the other, but the effectiveness of such communication may actually be enhanced if the meaning of the parable is not obvious. One of the best-known parables in the Old Testament is the prophet Nathan's story of the poor man and his ewe-lamb (in 2 Sam 12), which engages the attention and interest of King David before the meaning is explained with devastating simplicity: 'You are the man!' That story is an example of brilliantly effective communication through a parabolic story the meaning of which was not apparent on the surface. Similarly, despite the influential contrary view of Jülicher and his successors, Jesus' parables were often teasing sayings that had to be figured out or explained, and which were all the more effective for that reason.

But how does this view of parables as designed to teach fit with the saying about the purpose of parables found in Matthew 13:11–17 and parallels? Mark's version of the saying is, on the surface at least, particularly problematic: in response to the disciples' questioning of him about 'the parables', Jesus says: 'To you the mystery of the kingdom of God has been given, but to those outside everything happens in parables, so that seeing they may see and not perceive and hearing they may hear and not understand, lest they turn and receive forgiveness' (Mk 4:11–12). In words that are a clear echo of Isaiah 6:9–10, this saying appears to suggest that the purpose of Jesus' parables was to prevent 'outsiders', i.e. non-disciples, coming to understanding and salvation.

Scholars have wrestled with the difficulty of the saying and offered numerous explanations of it. Some have 'solved' the problem of such an apparently negative view of parables being ascribed to Jesus by denying that the saying goes back to him at all. It is argued that the saying is a church formulation, designed to explain people's failure to believe the gospel. There is plenty of evidence to show that the early church found the Jews' failure to believe in Jesus the Messiah particularly perplexing, but explained that it was due to the judgement of God on the Jewish people (see Acts 28:25–27, where the same verses from Isa 6 are quoted, and Rom 9– 11). Jesus' parables were also seen as somewhat perplexing by the early church: what had been readily understood by Jesus' hearers in their context was not easily intelligible in the later church context. So putting two and two together, the church came up with the theory that Jesus never intended to help the Jews, but to harden them – hence his use of parables, hence their unbelief. Parables were an instrument of the divine judgement: this is the view held to be expressed in Mark 4:11–12 and the parallel passages in Matthew and Luke.

There are various problems with this explanation. In the first place, there is no good reason for denying that the saying goes back to Jesus, and there are some reasons for suspecting that it does so go back (*e.g.* the interesting pattern of verbal agreements between the Matthean, Markan and Lukan forms of the saying point to there having been a pre-synoptic form of the saying). There must be a suspicion that scholars have made this proposal about the saying's origin in order to 'save' Jesus from an offensive saying rather than because the evidence demands it; but it is not obvious that anything much is solved by ascribing the supposedly offensive view to the church rather than to Jesus! In the second place, the view that Jesus' parables were originally easily understood but that the early church forgot their meaning and came to find them difficult and mysterious is dubious. In the third place, the explanation does not do justice to the evidence that we noted before which points to the evangelists having a positive view of parables as something to be 'heard'.

A second popular method of dealing with the saying does not deny the saying to Jesus, but explains that the original words of Jesus were not as harsh as they appear in our Greek texts. There have been all sorts of proposals of this sort, many of them appealing to the presumed original Aramaic form of the saying. It has been suggested that originally the saying did not say that the parables were 'in order that' people might not see, but 'because' they do not see – the Matthean form of the saying has been said to support this view; the parables were therefore in fact meant to help people to see, not the opposite. Another suggestion is that the clause in Mark 4:12 'lest they turn and be forgiven' could be translated 'unless they turn . . .' or 'perhaps they will turn . . .', thus giving a final note of hope rather than of judgement. Yet another suggestion is that the saying was not originally about parables in particular, but about Jesus' whole ministry, which was a riddle ('in parables') to those outside the circle of the disciples.

Despite the ingenuity and learning of those who have

made these suggestions, none of the proposals is persuasive.)
The synoptic evangelists, who may well have had independent
access to a pre-synoptic form of the saying (hence, for
example the minor agreements of Matthew and Luke against
Mark – *e.g.* the verb 'to know' and the plural 'mysteries'),
are unanimous in understanding the saying to be about
parables (rather than about the whole ministry of Jesus) and
also in understanding it to say that parables have a judgemental purpose. And there is no good reason for ascribing
this idea to the church rather than Jesus, nor much obvious
advantage in doing so!

How then is the saying to be understood? There are two
points to note, which may be clues to its interpretation. The
first is the location of the saying in the synoptic narratives.
All three evangelists place the saying between the parable of
the sower and its interpretation, between a parable addressed
to the crowds and its interpretation which was addressed
specifically to the disciples. This positioning is significant.
There is some reason for thinking that in pre-synoptic
tradition the parable was followed immediately by the
interpretation, with no intervening saying; if that is so, then
the deliberate insertion of the saying between the parable
and its interpretation is particularly noteworthy. Its location
suggests that the saying is seen by the evangelists not so
much as a general statement about parables, but more as an
explanation of the distinction made in Jesus' parabolic
teaching between the crowds and the disciples. In other
words, the saying is addressing the question: Why do the
crowds get a parable like that of the sower without explanation but the disciples receive an explanation? The answer
given is that there are two categories of people: 'To you the
mystery is given ... To those outside everything is in
parables.' From this observation alone it becomes apparent
that what is being said in the saying is not that parables have
a purely negative function; but they have one function (an
educational function) for 'you' – *i.e.* the disciples, who
receive the interpretation – and a different function (a
judgemental function) for 'those outside', who get only the
parable.

The second clue to the meaning of the saying lies in a recognition of the probable Old Testament and Jewish background to the saying. The background to Jesus' teaching about the 'kingdom of God' and about himself as 'the Son of Man' was in Jewish apocalyptic writing and thinking, as expressed for example in the book of Daniel. The idea of a divine 'mystery' being given to some and hidden from others belong in the same Jewish world of thought (which is, incidentally, a confirmation of the authenticity of the saying as Jesus' teaching). For example, in Daniel 2 we read of a divine revelation given to King Nebuchadnezzar in a dream, and the word 'mystery' is used in this connection; in that story the dream is given to Nebuchadnezzar, who cannot understand it, but then the 'interpretation' is given to Daniel. There is obvious similarity between this and the synoptic idea of 'parables' being given to the crowds but the interpretation being given only to the disciples.

The same sort of ideas are found in the Habakkuk commentary of the Dead Sea Scrolls: here it is said that 'the mystery' was given to the Old Testament prophet, but he did not understand his own vision; the explanation of his vision was given centuries later to the Qumran community's 'Teacher of Righteousness'. The links between the Christian community and the Qumran community have often been noted by scholars, and it makes good sense to see the saying of Jesus about the parables in this context of thought: whereas everyone received the uninterpreted 'mystery' through the parables, only those in the community (of Jesus) have the divinely given explanation.

Given these two clues, it is possible to suggest the meaning of the controversial saying of Jesus about the purpose of parables. The explanation is that the parables have two functions. They are, like Nebuchadnezzar's dream in Daniel or the Old Testament prophetic messages (as these were understood by the Qumran community), revelations of divine truth and of God's plan, but it is only those who are granted divine insight who comprehend the revelation. To others things remain opaque, and they are left out. Parables thus have a dual function and purpose: to reveal and to conceal, to bring blessing and judgement. The whole of Jesus' ministry is seen in the New Testament as having this dual function (*cf.* Mt 11:25–26; 1 Cor 2, *etc.*), but parables such as that of the sower are seen to be doing this in a particularly clear way, because of the separation of the interpretation from the parable.

We may thus try to sum up the understanding of parables expressed in this saying as follows.

1. Parables are designed and intended to teach people about the kingdom of God, *i.e.* to be an effective medium of communication.

2. But parables are not so simple and unambiguous that no one could mistake their meaning: in fact only some 'get' the meaning of parables (their interpretation); others do not.

3. This is the pattern of Jesus' ministry as a whole: some see and respond to the mystery of the kingdom revealed in Jesus, some are blind and refuse to do so.

4. The disciples' understanding of the mystery is not their own achievement, but the gift of God.

5. The outsiders' failure to understand is a sign of God's judgement on people's hardness of heart, as it was in the prophetic ministry of people such as Isaiah.

6. Jesus' parabolic ministry therefore comes as God's gift to some and as his judgement to others. We might paraphrase the difficult saying: 'To you, the disciples, God has given understanding of the mysteries of the kingdom of God – the kingdom brought and taught by Jesus – and so you receive interpretation of the parables to expand your understanding; to those outside there are parables only, so that they fail to see or hear the mystery of the kingdom, receiving instead the divine judgement spoken of by Isaiah.'

This interpretation makes sense of the saying both in the context of Jesus' ministry and in the context of the gospels. It does not alleviate all the problems of the modern reader of the New Testament, who finds the idea of divine election and particularly of God 'hiding' things from some people difficult. But the way out of the difficulty is not to try and avoid the plain meaning of the text in question, but to recognise that in biblical thought, not least in the gospels, the idea of divine

predestination does not exclude the idea of human free will
and responsibility. In this passage it is significant that the
statement about the purpose of parables comes in the
context of the parable of the sower, with its description of
different responses to the 'word' of the gospel. The parable
speaks of human responsibility, and the gospels are quite
clear that Jesus' hearers are offered good news and a real
chance to respond to it; and judgement is not inevitable, but
is in Jesus' day (as in Isaiah's day) the just reward for
people's obstinacy and unbelief. In biblical thought the two
ideas (of election and free will) that seem to us to conflict are
seen to run in parallel and are both to be maintained.

# SELECT BIBLIOGRAPHY AND A NOTE ON FURTHER READING

E A Armstrong, *The Parables of Jesus* (Hodder, 1967)

K Bailey, *Poet and Peasant and Through Peasant Eyes* (Eerdmans, 1983)

C Blomberg, *Interpreting the Parables* (IVP, 1989)

M Boucher, *The Mysterious Parable* (Catholic Biblical Association, 1977)

—— *The Parables* (Glazier, 1981)

G B Caird, *The Language and Imagery of the Bible* (Duckworth, 1980)

J D Crossan, *Cliffs of Fall. Paradox and Polyvalence in the Parables of Jesus* (Seabury, 1980)

C H Dodd, *The Parables of the Kingdom* (Nisbet, 1935)

J Drury, *The Parables in the Gospels* (SPCK, 1985)

H Hendrickx, *The Parables of Jesus* (Chapman, 1986)

A M Hunter, *Interpreting the Parables* (SCM, 1969)

—— *The Parables Then and Now* (SCM, 1971)

J Jeremias, *The Parables of Jesus* (SCM, 1954)

G V Jones, *The Art and Truth of the Parables* (SPCK, 1964)

P R Jones, *The Teaching of the Parables* (Broadman, 1982)

J D Kingsbury, *The Parables of Jesus in Matthew 13* (SPCK, 1969)

W S Kissinger, *The Parables of Jesus: A History of Interpretation and Bibliography* (Scarecrow, 1979)

S J Kistemaker, *The Parables of Jesus* (Baker, 1980)

J Lambrecht, *Once More Astonished: The Parables of Jesus* (Crossroad, 1981)

E Linnemann, *The Parables of Jesus* (SPCK, 1966)

J Marcus, *The Mystery of the Kingdom of God* (Scholars, 1986)

I H Marshall, *Eschatology and the Parables* (Tyndale/TSF, 1963)

J R Michaels, *Servant and Son: Jesus in Parable and Gospel* (Knox, 1981)

K Snodgrass, *The Parable of the Wicked Husbandmen* (Mohr, 1983)

R H Stein, *An Introduction to the Parables of Jesus* (Westminster, 1981)

H Thielicke, *The Waiting Father: Sermons on the Parables of Jesus* (James Clarke, 1960)

M A Tolbert, *Perspectives on the Parables* (Fortress, 1979)

D O Via, *The Parables: Their Literary and Existential Dimension* (Fortress, 1967)

R S Wallace, *Many Things in Parables* (Oliver & Boyd, 1955)

## *A note on further reading*

Anyone studying Jesus' parables will find a wealth of material in the standard commentaries: for example, the recent and substantial commentaries by D A Carson on Matthew (Zondervan, 1984); by I H Marshall (Paternoster, 1977) and J Fitzmyer (Doubleday, 1985) on Luke; by R Brown (Doubleday, 1970) and R Schnackenburg (Chapman, 1982) on John; and by R A Guelich on the Sermon on the Mount (Word, 1982), to name but a few. There are also invaluable reference works such as the *Illustrated Bible Dictionary* (IVP, 1980), the *Theological Dictionary of the New Testament* (Eerdmans, 1964–76), J A Thompson's *Handbook of Life in Bible Times* (IVP, 1986), M Zohary's *Plants of the Bible* (CUP, 1982), and many others.

Those interested in following up the issues discussed in the appendices may like some more specific advice. On parables in general and on their interpretation J Jeremias' *The Parables of Jesus* is still a classic and worth reading. Kenneth Bailey's *Poet and Peasant and Through Peasant Eyes* has a wealth of insight into the social and cultural background to some of the parables in Luke's gospel. C Blomberg's *Interpreting the Parables* (which the author kindly let me see in typescript before publication) is an excellent and up-to-date guide to questions of method and interpretation. Other useful introductions to parable studies which also look at particular parables include those by R H Stein, M Boucher, P R Jones and H Hendrickx. Also of particular value is G B Caird's broad survey *The Language and Imagery of the Bible*.

The recent German works mentioned in the appendices were: D Flusser, *Die Rabbinischen Gleichnisse und der Gleichniserzähler Jesus* (Peter Lang, 1981); H-J Klauck, *Allegorie und Allegorese in Synoptischen Gleichnistexten* (Aschendorff, 1978); and H Weder, *Die Gleichnisse Jesu als Metaphern* (Vandenhoeck und Ruprecht, 1978).

On the question of the gospels and Jesus in history, there is an almost unlimited amount of literature. Useful introductory books include J Drane, *Introducing the New Testament* (Lion, 1986) and (somewhat more demanding) S Neill and N T Wright, *The Interpretation of the New Testament 1861–1986* (OUP, 1988). Other significant books include M Borg's *Conflict, Holiness and Politics in the Teaching of Jesus* (Edwin Mellen, 1984), A Harvey's *Jesus and the Constraints of History* (Duckworth, 1982), G Theissen's *The Shadow of the Galilean* (SCM, 1987), and (representing a more sceptical viewpoint) E P Sanders' *Jesus and Judaism* (SCM, 1985). My own approach to the gospels reflects and is reflected in my rather technical *The Rediscovery of Jesus' Eschatological Discourse* (JSOT, 1984). An accessible description of the thesis of the book and of the whole *Gospel Perspectives* series of which it was a part is to be found in Craig Blomberg's valuable *The Historical Reliability of the Gospels* (IVP, 1987).

# INDEX OF PARABLES

*The page numbers refer to the main discussion of each parable.*

# INDEX OF BIBLICAL REFERENCES

# SUBJECT AND NAME INDEX